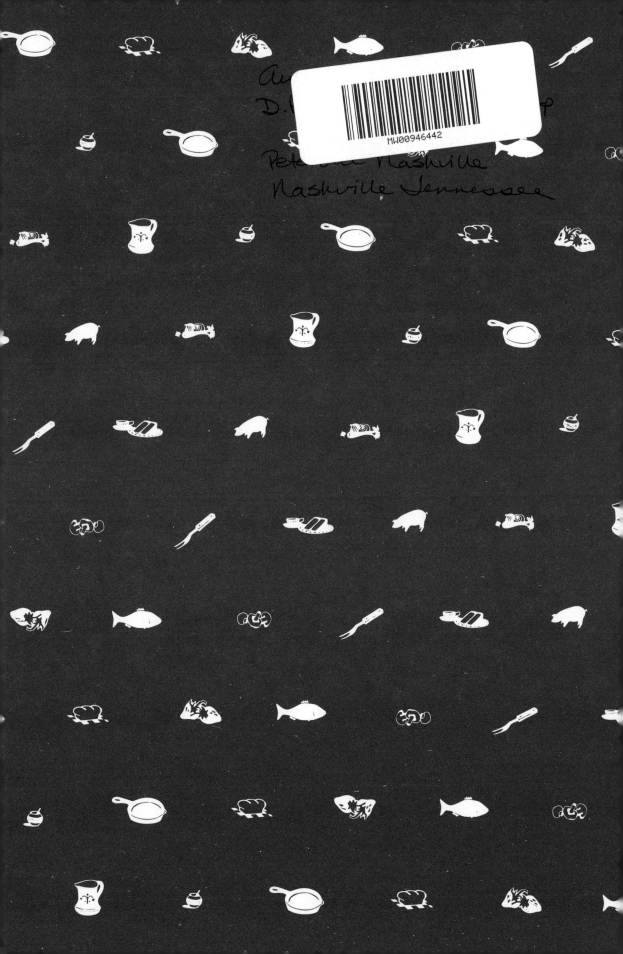

THE ORIGINAL
TENNESSEE HOMECOMING
COOKBOOK

*"Food is an ambassador of good will.
It is a link between our past and the present."*

MRS. CORDELL HULL

The Original
TENNESSEE HOMECOMING
COOKBOOK

EDITED BY *Daisy King*
INTRODUCTION BY *Helen McDonald Exum*

Rutledge Hill Press
Nashville, Tennessee

Published in Nashville, Tennessee, by Rutledge Hill Press, Inc., P.O. Box 140483, Nashville, Tennessee 37214.

Typography by ProtoType Graphics, Inc.
Printed by K & S Press
Designed by Harriette Bateman

Photographs on page 2 and 14 by Paul Weigle and reprinted by permission.

Photographs on pages 6, 33, 80, 97, 100, 105, 144, and 192 courtesy of State of Tennessee Photographic Services.

Photograph on page 11 courtesy of Anne Crawford.

Photographs on pages 40, 112, 136, and 213 by Robin Hood and reprinted by permission of Thomas Nelson Publishers from the book *The Tennesseans,* copyright © 1981 by The Alexander Committee.

Photograph on page 48 by Alex McMahan and reprinted courtesy of the *Chattanooga News-Free Press.*

Photograph on page 65 by Robin Hood and reprinted courtesy of the *Chattanooga News-Free Press.*

Photograph on page 73 by Bob Nichols and reprinted courtesy of the *Chattanooga News-Free Press.*

Photograph on pages 97 and 129 copyright © 1985 by Robin Hood and reprinted by permission.

Photograph on page 153 by State of Tennessee Photographic Services and courtesy of Homecoming '86.

Photographs on pages 160 and 177 copyright © 1985 by Bob Schatz/Photo Fair, Inc., and reprinted by permission.

Photograph on page 185 by Jean Nelson and reprinted by permission.

Photograph on page 192 by *Chattanooga News-Free Press* staff photographer and reprinted by permission.

Photograph on page 224 by John Egerton and reprinted by permission.

Library of Congress Cataloging-in-Publication Data
Main entry under title:

The Original Tennessee homecoming cookbook.

Includes index.
1. Cookery, American—Southern style.   2. Cookery—
Tennessee.   I. King, Daisy, 1945-
TX715.O725   1985   641.59768   85-22094
ISBN 0-934395-05-5

2 3 4 5 6 7 8 9 10 — 90 89 88 87 86 85
MANUFACTURED IN THE UNITED STATES OF AMERICA.

Contents

One thing I'm sure about: Not love, not money, not power, absolutely nothing on earth can make you feel as secure as knowing who you are and how you got to be that way.

I didn't learn that from being governor. I learned that from growing up in Maryville.

And that's what Tennessee's Homecoming '86 is all about. A giant statewide celebration of who we are and how we got to be that way— Tennesseans celebrating being Tennesseans. Part reunion, part history lesson and part good old-fashioned hoe-down.

We're going to take the time between now and 1986 to research our roots, community by community, and find out what each town has that we never want to lose—and take steps to see that we don't. Then in 1986 we're going to have a homecoming and invite everybody who has ever lived here to come home. And we'll welcome anybody else who wants to come.

If we make Homecoming '86 all that it can be, it'll go on far beyond a single year or an individual event. It will become a tradition. It will become a standing invitation. It will be a banner for who and what we are that will never fade. A preservation of Tennessee spirit and American values for generations to come.

And that's worth working for.

I can't wait.

Lamar Alexander

Foreword

My life has been blessed with homecomings. Growing up in a small town where the love of people and good food went hand in hand, I looked forward to Sunday visits by family and friends. Laughing and talking, making homemade ice cream, and feasting on a ripe watermelon was a way of life. Church homecoming celebrations featured Sunday dinner on the grounds. My high school celebrated its homecoming during the football season. College years brought more homecoming activities, and I always looked forward to going home during the holidays. Now, years later, I enjoy a homecoming with my husband and two sons at the end of a busy day as we settle down for our evening meal.

Whether you are a Tennessean by birth or have moved here recently, you probably know that like other southern states, Tennessee is rich in agriculture, producing corn, soybeans, and most fruits and vegetables. Poultry and livestock are grown in the state. Its deep, cool lakes provide us with an abundance of catfish, bass, and crappie. Native to Tennessee is spiced round, a beef product with rounds of pork fat intermingled with spices throughout the beef. I don't believe one could live in Tennessee without eating country ham. Tennesseans enjoy a rich variety of fine foods and friendly meals.

For that reason, when Governor Lamar Alexander, an eighth generation East Tennessean, proclaimed 1986 a year of Tennessee Homecoming, Rutledge Hill Press asked me to edit a cookbook celebrating the people of Tennessee and our food. Several thousand recipes were submitted, including a complete menu from Honey Alexander, the governor's wife.

The recipes chosen are a blend of the old and the new. Many are from treasured collections handed down from generation to generation and give a nostalgic glimpse of earlier days. In some instances, you will read notes about the contributors, how they acquired the recipe, and how many years the recipe has been in their families (some 100 to 200 years). No one invents a recipe. We have been using the same ingredients since the early settlers stirred their first pots of soup. But, you will enjoy reading about and using these older recipes reflected in their modern counterparts.

The photographs depict the different regions of Tennessee and many of its food festivals, from barbecuing beef in Memphis to cooking ramps in Cosby. These pictures beautifully reflect Tennessee life and the enjoyment of food.

I am so happy to be able to participate in Homecoming '86 by editing this cookbook. I know how good the recipes are, and I can't wait for you to try them. It was very difficult to select which would be in the book; I have never tasted such outstanding recipes. I hold those who contributed recipes responsible for my gaining ten pounds, as well as for making the task of selecting the right recipes so difficult . . . and fun.

Thirty-five years ago, another cookbook quoted Mrs. Cordell Hull, wife of the United States Secretary of State from 1933 to 1944 and winner of Nobel Peace Prize. She said, "Food is an ambassador of good will. It is a link between our past and the present." I hope you find this book your link between our present and the past. May the recipes and menus it contains be vehicles of sharing your heartfelt good will every day.

Have a joyful homecoming and happy eating!

DAISY KING
September, 1985

Introduction

Helen McDonald Exum

VICE PRESIDENT, *Chattanooga News-Free Press*

It was a Sunday morning in May.

The dinner tables were spread under the big trees at Oak Grove Cumberland Presbyterian Church in Tennessee's Sequatchie Valley, and women were unpacking baskets of fried chicken and potato salad, bowls of fresh green beans, and taking the pies and cakes from boxes. Chocolate cake. Coconut cake. Sour cream cake. Caramel cake.

"Alma, I was just hoping you'd bring that caramel cake. Someday I want to watch you make that icing. Mine always gets hard," said Kitty McDonald to her cousin Alma Ketner as they unpacked a yellow layer cake with rich caramel fudge icing.

It was homecoming in Sequatchie Valley, a long narrow valley between the mountains in East Tennessee where the fields are green, close to the big Tennessee River. And the same families that settled the valley in the early 1800s still keep in touch every year at Oak Grove's Homecoming. They're kin and connected by ties of blood and friendship, and as they've gathered over the years there has always been warm exchanging of news, greeting new brides or babies, and welcoming friends who come from distant parts to this event and to some of the great traditional food of Tennessee.

The tables are laden to the groaning point with six platters of fried chicken, the crisp kind, probably fried early that morning before church. This is not soggy or greasy. It is just right. Six or seven platters of everything else, too. How can this gracious plenty of meats, vegetables, and desserts always balance out right? No one knows. But as all these friends and family fill their plates once, sit under the trees and talk, go back for seconds, reminisce and exchange a few recipes before leaving for home, they have experienced an old-fashioned Tennessee happening in modern times. They've enjoyed Tennessee food. It is southern. It is traditional. It also includes some new. (Susan Overton's Seven Layer Salad at the homecoming.) It is simple. Straightforward. And based on all the foods that grow best here. It is always served with warmth and friendliness and hospitality. And it satisfies.

This is the kind of food that appears at Sunday dinners, funerals, picnics, Thanksgiving and Christmas. And the food of Tennessee is woven into our history. Tennessee is that horizontal slice of land between Georgia and Kentucky that was once included in the North Carolina Territory. It begins as a mountainous area in the east. The Appalachian chain of mountains that runs up the eastern seaboard starts just south of Chattanooga, and as it extends north, it shapes Maryville, Knoxville and Gatlinburg, all the way to Kingsport, Jonesboro—an early capital—and Bristol. Tennesseans who live in this magnificent scenery of East Tennessee have a tradition of independence.

The early settlers came over the mountains. First came the traders and the long hunters (so called because their hunting expeditions would last several months). Smoked bear grease and Indian corn were common fare. Davey Crockett tells of shooting a squirrel and then having to pull him out of a hole in a tree. "I relate such small matters," he said, "only to show what lengths a hungry man will go to to get something to eat." Wilderness living was hard. The settlers shared the land with the Cherokee Indians, the most civilized of all the Indian tribes. From these Indians the pioneers learned to make hoe cakes, small cakes of corn meal mush, fried in iron skillets over the fire. Not until 1832 in the "Great Removal"—when Andrew Jackson ordered the Indians moved to reservations in the West—did the last part of East Tennessee, the southeastern tip, become open for settlers.

Meanwhile, the middle part of the state was important for being at one end of the Natchez Trace, the Indian path that led from Natchez, Mississippi, all the way north to Nashville. The first settlers at Fort Nashborough crossed the frozen Cumberland River on Christmas Day, 1779, led by James Robertson. This small band was joined by John Donelson's flotilla on April 24, 1780. What a reunion that must have been! A rolling landscape and limestone outcroppings awaited this enterprising group that populated what would become the capital city of Tennessee. In one short generation, these Tennesseans established a tradition of gracious wilderness hospitality. Colonel John Overton built his famous home, Travellers' Rest. Andrew Jackson's Hermitage, a fine colonial home, soon graced his plantation. And when he was president at the White House, his meals were prepared by Boulanger, the superbly trained chef for Louis-Philippe, Duke of Orleans, King of France. The appreciation for fine living and fine eating that middle Tennesseans began then still holds today.

West Tennessee is different still. This is Mississippi Delta country, and the mighty river tied the settlement at Memphis with New Orleans, much farther south. Memphis became a port town whose interests were closely allied with the Mississippi cotton planters to the south, the rice planters of Arkansas to the west, and the cotton planters of Tennessee to the east. The rich land, with its crops and the bustling commerce up and down the Mississippi, made Memphis grow faster than the other cities in Tennessee. The large black population and the city's ties with the Delta land gave rise to food traditions completely different from those in the mountains to the East. It was easy to get oysters from New Orleans and fresh river catfish were plentiful. Memphis hostesses prided themselves on setting a fine table, one that was bounteous, with several meats, whatever vegetables that were in season, and the most fashionable new recipes from New Orleans.

Between the American Revolution and the War Between the States, Tennessee grew. We sent two presidents, Andrew Jackson and James Knox

After a preaching service at the Jones Chapel Methodist Church in 1923, everyone got together for "The Big Spread on the Benches." Dinner on the grounds has always been a favorite time for Tennesseans to get together. Jones Chapel was one of the churches on the Williston Charge, a preaching circuit in Fayette County.

Polk, to the White House; and following Abraham Lincoln's assassination, Vice-President Andrew Johnson, another Tennessean, became president. Railroads came in, connecting the various parts of our state and making transportation far easier. When the Western and Atlantic Railroad came to Chattanooga and a hotel, the Crutchfield House, was built across from the station, a new era began for east Tennesseans—that of railroads and hotels.

The Maxwell House in Nashville was built by Colonel John Overton, Jr. This was to be a center of activity for one hundred years, a mecca for politics, civic, business, and social affairs. Elaborate and sumptuous meals were served at the Maxwell House. And here were prepared famous Tennessee hams, as well as fine beef, spiced round for Christmas, wonderful pies and desserts. The fame of this Nashville hotel was spread far beyond our state when Joel Cheek formulated a special blend of coffees President Theodore Roosevelt called "Good to the Last Drop." Cheek went to New York and bought a $100,000 sign on Times Square advertising Maxwell House coffee. People said he would go broke, but instead he became rich and famous. Just before the Depression, he sold his Maxwell House Coffee business for $42 million and thus was able to be a benefactor to Nashville in many ways during the Depression.

In Memphis, the Peabody Hotel had a similar reputation for elegance and sophistication. Memphis families and cotton planters from the Delta met in the lobby of the Peabody, and then went to the dining room to stuff on oysters and seafood from the Gulf, as well as on Tennessee specialties: Tennessee ham, corn pudding, every manner of fresh vegetables and desserts.

There were well known and beloved inns in the smaller towns too. In Mc-

Minnville and in Manchester, in Franklin and in Murfreesboro, were small hotels usually run by a family and featuring fine and plenteous menus.

Wynnewood, at Castalian Springs near Gallatin, was built in 1828 to serve as a stagecoach inn and mineral springs resort. A row of cottages was added in the 1840s to accommodate visitors, the most famous being Andrew Jackson. Eagle Bluff, at Jacksboro, was best known for its wonderful cooking and nine mineral springs with seven different waters. The hospitality and delicious food at the Sedberry Inn in Warren County brought praise from the United States Congress in 1933. And in Bon Air Springs, grand balls given at the hotel would attract four or five thousand of the elite from all parts of the state.

Some of the most elegant dining took place not in hotels, but in private homes—the mansions that symbolized frontier elegance. Governor William Blount and his wife dispensed a gracious and lavish hospitality at the Blount Mansion in Knoxville. It was the first frame house west of the Alleghenies and has been called "the cradle of the state." Swan Pond, also in Knoxville, was built by Colonel Francis Alexander Ramsey and in 1800 was the most expensive and elegant mansion in Tennessee. Belmont was the palatial mansion in Nashville built for Adelicia Hayes Acklen; it included a private zoo, as well as wonderful feasts—both for the entertainment of her guests.

Imagine a beautiful old plantation house in Memphis, restored to antebellum grandeur, and inside its antique-filled rooms, dozens of tables seated with guests who are expecting a gourmet, southern experience. This is Justine's, the handsome, elegant restaurant that now occupies the 1843 French style mansion known for years as the old Coward Place.

Justine and Dayton Smith cook and serve the elegant sort of food one would expect in a dramatic and beautiful old mansion. They have made Justine's a mecca in Memphis for sophisticated diners.

The most famous frontier mansion, Nashville's Hermitage, was not only grand and gracious, but also had a reputation for fine entertaining before Andrew Jackson went to Washington. His wife, Rachel, had the ability to use the materials at hand. She knew what it was to seek food and warmth in the wilderness, and yet she also enjoyed the pleasures of a gentle, prosperous life. As the hospitality of the Hermitage became renowned, many famous visitors partook, such as Aaron Burr. Jackson was a good and successful farmer and was able to make his Hermitage completely self-sufficient, and Rachel was a wise administrator with great skill in training servants.

Of all the Tennessee specialties that have come down from the early days that are just as respected and loved today, Tennessee country ham is Number One. In rural Tennessee, usually in November after the first hard frost, there is the traditional hog killing.

In one account of hog killing at Fairview, the following directions are given. "Always kill in the dark of the moon! Hampshire hogs make the best hams and bacon. Let the meat air thoroughly, overnight is long enough." After trimming the meat comes the curing. "Put five pounds of salt for every 100 pounds of meat in a wash tub with molasses and home grown red peppers which have been ground. Rub this mixture into the skin on a sunny day. Let the hams stay in the sun until the pepper strikes in (melts), and put them into wooden boxes with more salt, molasses and pepper mixture. The hams stay in a box in the smokehouse for four to six weeks. Take them out, brush off the salt, and wipe them off with a cold, damp cloth. Then hang up in a smoke-house." The hams should hang in a smokehouse for three months, and then they are put into paper bags and may hang from two to three years more.

When cooked, a Tennessee country ham is tender, succulent, and deli-cious. One slice invariably calls for another. Sliced thin and placed between biscuits, this is the most satisfying breakfast, luncheon treat, hors d'oeuvre, or dinner specialty imaginable. Yet it must be cooked just right. A novice could end up with a very tough piece of pork.

After the War Between the States, Tennessee recovered slowly, as did the rest of the South. This affected what people ate. Almost all farm families kept a cow, some chickens and some hogs. They grew their own vegetables, such as greens, and thus evolved a diet featuring plenty of butter, cream and eggs, fresh vegetables, cornmeal and flour for bread and biscuits, with chicken, ham, and catfish from the river—foods that were easy to come by and local.

Many families, for instance, made their own hominy. During the cold win-ter months, the mother and children would shuck and shell corn. Then the shelled corn was washed and placed in an iron kettle with ashes from an open fireplace (later lye was used) to loosen the corn husk from the kernel. When the husk and kernel were loose, they could be separated by running cold water over the corn—the light husks would float to the top. The hominy would be placed in large earthen jars to be served later—fried, baked or boiled.

Some of the very best food in Tennessee is served at funerals. Once news of a death gets out, friends and neighbors bring food to the house for the griev-ing family to serve to those who call to pay their respects.

When Doc Ledbetter died in Murfreesboro in the 1960s, the funeral was held in the old house his father had built—red brick with wonderful Victorian gingerbread. That day the house had the sweet smell of flowers, and in the kitchen and dining room there was a reunion of relatives. There were several baked hams, along with congealed fruit salads and chicken salad. There were even chicken cutlets (chunks of chicken in a stiff cream sauce, formed into cro-quettes and fried). Added to that was pound cake, sour cream cake, and coco-nut cake; chess pies, pecan pies, and apricot pies.

Why do Tennesseans cook so for funerals? No one knows for sure. But it gives thoughtful friends something visible to do for a loved family. It is more personal than sending flowers because one has to deliver the food with a house call. Then there are the hugs and kisses and sympathy. The touching. The visit. As families care for one another in this way, over the years ties are cemented.

All across the state, Tennessee has little pockets of independent thinking people who have used what was there and made a good life. Take Lynchburg, a town with a population of 361 where Tennessee Blue Grass meets the Cum-berland Mountains. This is a farming community, and it has always had hogs, mules, chickens and hound dogs. On the town square is the White Rabbit Sa-loon, which offers a good lunch, and nearby, the Jack Daniels Distillery that sends its famous label all over the world. The county has been a "dry" county since 1922, but visitors come from around the country for tours of the old dis-tillery. They also come to learn about the Scottish-English pioneers who settled

Some of the best pies in Tennessee are baked for the Annual Fish Fry and Auction at College Grove United Methodist Church. The fanciest pies and cakes are not used for desserts, but are sold to the highest bidder.

here with their own music and dance, and to listen for traces of Elizabethan English that was kept alive until recently when the children began listening to television.

A center for good food in Lynchburg is Miss Mary Bobo's Boarding House. She died in 1983 at the age of 102, but her boarding house has now been turned into a restaurant. In the early days Miss Mary was up at dawn making breakfast. She then made yeast rolls for the noon meal, which was the main one, with about a dozen customers all the time. Supper was light. Some boarders stayed on for years at a time.

Life in Lynchburg was like life in many other small towns all across the state—towns such as South Pittsburg, Dyersburg, Dayton or Spring City. The ladies belonged to a bridge club, or sewing club, which usually met once a week at someone's home as an excuse to get together and enjoy food. In Lynchburg this might be tomato with chicken salad, or maybe a three-layer gelatin salad and open-faced sandwiches with tiny shrimp. Often a melted cheese sandwich on the side of the plate provided something hot, and for dessert, chocolate and vanilla ice cream with hot chocolate sauce, pecans and cherries topped off the lunch. Sometimes a tall angel food cake or a fresh coconut layer cake was included. This is fine eating. Yet you could have had this same menu in any part of the state in the 1900 to 1950 era, before so many women began to work outside the home.

Today a trip up Main Street in any city in Tennessee will tell you that we are in a new era. Fast food restaurants have made their way into every town.

And whether a Tennessean drives a truck or works at the bank, he often goes to the drive-in window to order ham and biscuits and coffee for breakfast, or a hamburger for lunch, or shrimp or pizza for dinner.

But look a little farther. For those who know how to find them, there is a wonderful little barbecue place or a catfish house or a neighborhood restaurant featuring fresh vegetables. In Chattanooga, it's Mr. Penney's on Brainerd Road for barbecued pork, succulently smoked and seasoned, cut up and packed, ready to pick up. Or it's the Whole Note Restaurant on 9th Street, a black restaurant featuring wonderful southern food such as country ham with red-eye gravy, a hen and dressing, chicken and dumplings, lemon meringue pie and strawberry-topped cheesecake. Just ask a native where to get a good meal, and you'll get a big smile, a description of the treat in store, and complete directions. Tennesseans love to eat!

All over Tennessee today there are food festivals. There is Memphis in May, a barbecue festival in Memphis where as many as 200 different groups barbecue pork, beef and chicken on the banks of the Mississippi to be judged as to who is the best. Memphis also has the Cotton Carnival, a time of festivities and parties when a queen is crowned and elegant feasts are held. In Chattanooga, it's the River Bend Festival. In Dayton, there is a Strawberry Festival. The elderly citizens of Atwood have an annual all-you-can-eat White Bean and Hamhock dinner in conjunction with the Carroll County Pork Festival. Nashville has its Swan Ball, an elegant gala that draws celebrities from all over the country, but it also has smaller festivals like the Germantown Festival, where for one Saturday in the fall Nashvillians go to buy pickles and breads from the German population of town. Knoxville's Dogwood Festival is held in the spring, with parties, dinners, and festive occasions.

Every summer are the family reunions, when families get together to picnic, usually over a covered-dish table with all of the old favorites. Some of the very best food is at the family reunions. Add to this the food celebrations in various churches which usually have cookbooks that are prized possessions. The Sale Creek Presbyterian Church possibly has more fine cooks for its size than any church in the world. Fried chicken that is exactly right. Potato salad, baked beans, pecan pie. And in May, it has fresh strawberry pie such as Mrs. List's, a pie that has gone all over the country. Given a choice of a beautiful strawberry pie from a French patisserie in Paris, and Mrs. List's Sale Creek Strawberry Pie, a layer of rich pastry topped with choice strawberries and a fresh glaze made from the smaller berries, I will choose Mrs. List's version any day. It has the fresh spring flavor of home-grown berries just out of Tennessee soil.

At New Emanuel Baptist Church in Chattanooga, the finest traditions of black southern cooking are upheld. To walk in to the church luncheon on Women's Days, when the project is to raise funds for the church, is to smell chicken frying. Women are arranging one tall cake after another on the dessert table and another line of women is filling plates with ham, chicken, sweet potatoes, green beans, pickled beets, new potatoes, cheese noodle casserole, tomato and lettuce salad, fresh cornbread and hot homemade rolls just from the oven. For dessert, there is sweet potato pie, apple pie, and pound cake. Friends of the church order plates ahead of time, come to the church, pay for them, and take away some of the finest Tennessee southern cooking in the world.

This is Tennessee. From the mountains in the East with huge gray rocks and ledges that have timeless quality and strength, across middle Tennessee, and all the way over to Memphis on the mighty Mississippi, we have cities, small towns and farm land. We are big people and little people. We come from many backgrounds and traditions. No one group of people is Tennessee. We are mountain people. We have Greek wedding feasts, Hungarian bakeries and German festivals. We have church suppers and family reunions. We have eaten everything from turnip greens and cornbread in the lean years, to country ham and oysters with important guests. We have had hoe cakes at home and fried chicken on the lakes and at picnics.

It is our people who make Tennessee cooking the very special thing that it is to those of us who love it and who live here. When a native Tennessean sits down to country ham and fried chicken, corn pudding, fresh green beans, new potatoes, lemon meringue pie, pecan pie, and angel food cake, we know we are eating a dinner that satisfies.

Or when we drive through a town on a summer afternoon and smell barbecue smoking and roasting, we stop to have some of the succulent roast pork on buns with plenty of slaw. This is soul food. And when at the end of the day a family gathers in to have smothered chicken, turnip greens, hoe cakes and boiled potatoes with a bowl of cold chopped oranges and grapefruit—which we call ambrosia—for dessert, then we know we are satisfied.

Tennessee food is different from Creole or Cajun food. It's different from the food of Maryland's Eastern Shore, and different from New England food. We are not like Texas. We are not like California. We are not famous for pizza, as is Chicago.

We're a little like Georgia or Kentucky or the Carolinas. What identifies our food must be its simplicity. It is genuine. And it is served with our special brand of friendly hospitality. Sometimes we put on airs, as when President Franklin Roosevelt came to the Hermitage or again when the Lyndon Johnsons came, or for fancy weddings. Or when the United Nations' delegates or all fifty state governors and their families came to Nashville. But mostly we are downhome people who take great pride in setting a fine table, enjoy cooking for our friends, are proud of the rich traditions behind us, and have faith in the future.

Chapter One

Menus

A Summer Supper
Tennessee's Executive Residence

Cold Cucumber Soup
Grilled Salmon Steaks, Hollandaise Sauce
Dill Fettucini
Asparagus in Yellow Squash Ring
Cantaloupe Alaska
Southern Rolls
Coffee

Cold Cucumber Soup

3 TABLESPOONS BUTTER	2 CUPS CHICKEN STOCK
1 MEDIUM ONION, FINELY CHOPPED	1 CUP HALF AND HALF
1 SMALL CLOVE GARLIC, MINCED	1 CUP PLAIN YOGURT
4 MEDIUM CUCUMBERS, PEELED, THINLY SLICED	SALT AND PEPPER
3 TABLESPOONS ALL-PURPOSE FLOUR	SLICED CUCUMBER (GARNISH)

Melt butter in large skillet over medium heat. Add onion and garlic and sauté until limp but not brown. Add sliced cucumbers and cook slowly until soft. Remove from heat. Stir in flour, then stock, blending well. Place over medium-high heat and bring to a boil. Reduce heat and simmer 5 minutes. Transfer to processor or blender in batches and puree. Pour into bowl. Cover and chill well. Just before serving, stir in half and half and yogurt and mix well. Taste and season with salt and pepper. Garnish each serving with cucumber slices. *Yield:* 4 to 6 servings.

Mrs. Lamar Alexander, *Nashville*

Grilled Salmon Steaks

Allow one-half the number of fish per person and grill 5 to 6 minutes on each side; keep moist by basting with equal parts melted butter, lemon juice and white wine.

Mrs. Lamar Alexander, *Nashville*

Hollandaise Sauce

¾ TO 1 CUP BUTTER, MELTED
3 EGG YOLKS
1 TABLESPOON COLD WATER
1 TABLESPOON LEMON JUICE

BIG PINCH SALT
1 TABLESPOON COLD BUTTER
PEPPER TO TASTE

Place egg yolks in stainless steel bowl and beat with wire whip for about 1 minute or until they become thick and sticky. Add lemon juice, water, salt and beat for ½ minute more. Place bowl over a saucepan with barely simmering water. Stir the egg yolks until they slowly thicken into a smooth cream (1 to 2 minutes). If mixture gets too thick add a couple of drops of cold water, then continue beating over simmering water. The egg yolks have thickened enough when you can begin to see the bottom of the pan between strokes and the mixture forms a light cream on the wires of the whip.

Immediately remove from heat and beat in the cold butter which will cool the egg yolks and stop their cooking. Then beating the egg yolks with a wire whip, pour on the melted butter by droplets until the sauce begins to thicken into a very heavy cream. Then pour the butter a little more rapidly. Omit the milky residue at the bottom of the butter pan. Season to taste with salt, pepper and lemon juice.

Mrs. Lamar Alexander, *Nashville*

Dill Pasta

1½ CUPS ALL-PURPOSE FLOUR
½ TEASPOON SALT
1 TABLESPOON DRY DILL OR 3 TABLESPOONS FRESH DILL

2 LARGE EGGS
1 TABLESPOON OIL
WATER
2 TABLESPOONS OLIVE OIL

Put metal blade into the food processor. Measure in the flour, salt and dill. Process briefly to blend them. Drop the eggs and oil through the feeding tube, and let the machine run until the dough begins to form a ball; around 15 seconds should be enough. If the dough seems too sticky, add a tablespoon or 2 of flour. If it is too dry, add a few drops of water. Process again briefly.

Turn dough onto floured surface. Dust your hands with flour and continue kneading. Work for 3 to 5 minutes, adding more if necessary until you have a smooth ball of dough. Set it to rest under a dish towel for at least 30 minutes.

After resting, roll out pasta by hand and cut fettucini to ¼ inch wide. If you have a pasta machine, just crank out the fettucini.

In a large saucepan, bring water to a boil with a teaspoon of salt and 2 tablespoons of olive oil; add fettucini. Bite the pasta to test that it is pliable with no hard core to it, then the pasta is done. Drain the pasta and toss it with olive oil or butter to keep it from sticking.

Mrs. Lamar Alexander, *Nashville*

Asparagus in Yellow Squash Ring

1 TO 2 POUNDS ASPARAGUS	BUTTER
2 TO 3 YELLOW SQUASH	

Trim asparagus spears. Slice yellow squash ³/₄ inch thick. Scoop out seeds, leaving enough of the outer pulp so ring won't break. Bring water to a boil in large saucepan. Add asparagus and blanch for 2 minutes. Drain and cool. Place 2 squash rings around 4 to 6 asparagus spears. Place the squash and asparagus in a casserole dish, add 1 cup of water, cover with foil. 5 to 10 minutes before dinner, place in a 350 degree oven until squash is tender. Remove from casserole dish and place on dinner plates. Place a pat of butter or dribble butter on the vegetables.

Mrs. Lamar Alexander, *Nashville*

Cantaloupe Alaska

Cut cantaloupe in half. Remove seeds. Fill cavity with ice cream. Top with meringue. Brown meringue and serve.

Meringue Topping:

4 EGG WHITES, ROOM TEMPERATURE	¼ TEASPOON SALT
6 TABLESPOONS SUGAR	½ TEASPOON VANILLA

Place all ingredients in mixing bowl. Beat until stiff and shiny. *Yield:* 2 to 3 servings.

Mrs. Lamar Alexander, *Nashville*

Homecoming Buffet Supper

Assorted Fruits with Honey Orange Dip
Crudités with Spinach Dip
Party Size Quiche Lorraine
Cheese and Ham Ball with Wheat Crackers
Shrimp Paté with Melba Rounds
Fillet of Beef with Port Butter*
Your Choice of Breads
Sliced Smoked Turkey Breast
Petite Pecan Tarts
Coffee served with Whipped Cream and Cinnamon

*The recipe for Fillet of Beef with Port Butter is on page 110.

Honey Orange Dip

2 TABLESPOONS HONEY
2 TABLESPOONS ORANGE JUICE
   CONCENTRATE

1 CUP SOUR CREAM
GRATED ORANGE RIND

Blend honey and orange juice. Fold into sour cream; add orange rind. Chill. Serve with fresh fruit.

Mrs. Jim (Dot) Holeman, Jr., *Old Hickory*

Spinach Dip

1 8-OUNCE PACKAGE CREAM CHEESE
1/3 PACKAGE FROZEN SPINACH, THAWED
2 TABLESPOONS CHIVES
2 TABLESPOONS CHOPPED ONION

1 TEASPOON ACCENT
1/2 TABLESPOON SALT
1/2 CUP WHIPPING CREAM
2 CUPS MAYONNAISE

Blend all ingredients together in blender and serve with raw vegetables. FANTASTIC!

Sherron De Vos, *Fairfield Glade*

Party Size Quiche Lorraine

1 2-CRUST PIE MIX
1 TABLESPOON BUTTER
1 SMALL ONION, DICED
1 POUND BACON SLICES
2 CUPS SWISS CHEESE, GRATED
4 EGGS

2 CUPS LIGHT CREAM
3/4 TEASPOON SALT
DASH SALT
DASH PEPPER
DASH NUTMEG
DASH GRANULATED SUGAR

Prepare pie crust in 15 x 10 x 1 inch pan. Refrigerate overnight. Fry onion in butter until tender. Fry bacon until crisp, drain, crumble. Sprinkle bottom of pie crust with onion mixture, bacon and grated cheese. Blend in blender or mixer eggs, milk and spices. Pour over bacon and cheese mixture. Bake in a 400 degree oven for 15 minutes, reduce heat to 350 degrees and bake 15 minutes longer. Cut into appetizer size pieces and serve immediately. May be reheated; may be frozen.

Carol C. Gibson, *Martin*

Cheese and Ham Ball

1 8-OUNCE PACKAGE CREAM CHEESE
2 CUPS (1/2-POUND) SHREDDED CHEDDAR CHEESE
1 TEASPOON DRY MUSTARD
1 21/2-OUNCE CAN DEVILED HAM

1 TEASPOON ONION, GRATED
1/2 TEASPOON PAPRIKA
1 TEASPOON PARSLEY FLAKES
1/2 CUP PECAN PIECES

Combine first 7 ingredients and mix well. Chill; shape into balls and coat with pecans. Chill until ready to serve.

Mrs. Wanda Powers, *Old Hickory*

Shrimp Paté

2 6-OUNCE CANS SMALL SHRIMP
2 8-OUNCE PACKAGES CREAM CHEESE
4 TABLESPOONS MAYONNAISE
4 TABLESPOONS LEMON JUICE

2 TABLESPOONS ONION, GRATED
1 TEASPOON SALT
CHOPPED OLIVES TO TASTE

Combine all ingredients except olives and shrimp in food processor until smooth. Crumble shrimp and add olives to mixture. Pour into mold and refrigerate overnight.

Sarah Boyce, *Nashville*

Petite Pecan Tarts

1 3-OUNCE PACKAGE CREAM CHEESE
1/4 CUP BUTTER OR MARGARINE

1 CUP ALL-PURPOSE FLOUR, SIFTED

Combine cream cheese and butter; blend in flour and chill for at least 1 hour. Shape into balls about 1 inch in diameter and press into tiny ungreased muffin tins.

Filling:

1 EGG
3/4 CUP BROWN SUGAR
1 TEASPOON VANILLA

1 TABLESPOON BUTTER OR MARGARINE, CHOPPED
2/3 CUP CHOPPED PECANS

Beat egg; add brown sugar, vanilla. Mix well and stir in pecans. Spoon into the already prepared tart shells and bake in a 325 degree oven for about 25 minutes. Cool before removing from pans. *Yield:* 24 petite pecan tarts.

Judy Jackson, *Blountville*

Homecoming Luncheon

Tomato-Orange Bouillon
Cheese Roll
Strawberry Congealed Salad
Broccoli and Chicken Casserole
Bran Pumpkin Muffins
Italian Cream Cake
Coffee and Tea Punch

Tomato-Orange Bouillon

12 OUNCE CAN FROZEN ORANGE JUICE, DILUTED AS INSTRUCTED	¾ CUP SUGAR
46 OUNCE CAN TOMATO JUICE	1 TEASPOON NUTMEG
⅓ CUP LEMON JUICE	½ TEASPOON SALT

Heat all ingredients together in large saucepan. Simmer 5 minutes. *Yield:* 12 servings.

Mrs. David G. Stone, *Hixson*

Cheese Roll

½ POUND AMERICAN CHEESE	½ CLOVE GARLIC
1 WHOLE PIMENTO	¼ CUP GRATED PECANS
1 3-OUNCE PACKAGE PHILADELPHIA CREAM CHEESE	PAPRIKA

Have cheese at room temperature and mix all ingredients thoroughly with hands. Make into a roll. Roll in paprika. Chill and slice.

Phyllis Hunt, *Clarksville*

Strawberry Congealed Salad

2 SMALL CANS CRUSHED PINEAPPLE	1 PINT WHIPPING CREAM, WHIPPED
1 LARGE PACKAGE STRAWBERRY JELLO	1 10-OUNCE PACKAGE FROZEN STRAWBERRIES
16 LARGE MARSHMALLOWS, QUARTERED	1 CUP PECANS, CHOPPED

Drain pineapple and heat the juice. Add Jello and stir. Melt marshmallows in heated juice. Add fruit and fold in cream that has been whipped. Add pecans to fruit and cream mixture. Refrigerate. *Yield:* 9 servings.

Judy York, *Nolensville*

Broccoli and Chicken Casserole

¼ CUP ONION, CHOPPED

¼ CUP BUTTER

2 CUPS CHICKEN, COOKED AND CUBED

2 BOXES CHOPPED BROCCOLI, COOKED

1 CUP RICE, COOKED IN 2 CUPS WATER

1 10¾-OUNCE CAN CREAM OF CHICKEN SOUP

½ CUP MILK

1 CUP SHARP CHEDDAR CHEESE, GRATED

2 TEASPOONS PEPPER

ADDITIONAL GRATED CHEESE

Sauté onion in butter. Combine all ingredients in a greased casserole dish. Sprinkle with additional grated cheese. Bake in a 300 degree oven for 30 minutes.

Variation: Leave out chicken for a delicious broccoli and rice side dish.

Carole Scott, *Memphis*

Bran Pumpkin Muffins

1½ CUPS ALL-PURPOSE FLOUR

2½ TEASPOONS BAKING POWDER

1 TEASPOON SALT

1 TEASPOON CINNAMON

1 TEASPOON NUTMEG

½ CUP SUGAR

1 CUP BRAN BUDS

⅔ CUP MILK

1 CUP SOLID PACK PUMPKIN

1 EGG

½ CUP SHORTENING

1½ TEASPOONS SUGAR

Sift together flour, baking powder, salt, cinnamon, nutmeg and sugar. Set aside. Measure Bran Buds, milk and pumpkin into large mixing bowl. Stir to combine. Let stand about 2 minutes or until cereal is softened. Add egg and shortening. Beat well. Add flour mixture, stirring until combined. Portion batter evenly into 12 greased 2½-inch muffin pan cups. Sprinkle with the 1½ teaspoon sugar. Bake in a 400 degree oven for about 35 minutes or until lightly browned.

Susan D. Gratz, *Morristown*

Tea Punch

6 SMALL TEA BAGS

4 CUPS BOILING WATER

1½ CUPS SUGAR

1 6-OUNCE CAN FROZEN ORANGE JUICE, THAWED AND UNDILUTED

1 6-OUNCE CAN FROZEN LEMONADE, THAWED AND UNDILUTED

10 CUPS COLD WATER

Steep tea bags in boiling water about 5 minutes. Discard tea bags. Add remaining ingredients. Serve over ice. Makes a gallon. This makes a delicious refreshing drink in the summertime.

Note: Any leftover fruit juice is delicious added to this mixture. This is the same recipe as served at Miss Daisy's.

Mrs. Bonnie Petty, *Jackson*

Italian Cream Cake

1/2 CUP MARGARINE	1 TEASPOON SODA
1/2 CUP SHORTENING	1 CUP BUTTERMILK
2 CUPS SUGAR	1 SMALL CAN FLAKED COCONUT
5 EGGS, SEPARATED	1 TEASPOON VANILLA
2 CUPS ALL-PURPOSE FLOUR, SIFTED	1 CUP PECANS

Cream margarine and shortening, add sugar and egg yolks, beat. Sift flour and soda, add to creamed mixture alternately with buttermilk. Stir in coconut, vanilla and nuts. Fold in stiffly beaten egg whites. Bake in 3 8-inch greased and floured pans in a 350 degree oven for 30 minutes.

Icing:

1 8-OUNCE PACKAGE CREAM CHEESE	1 TEASPOON VANILLA
1 BOX CONFECTIONERS' SUGAR	1/2 CUP PECANS

Mix all together. Frost each layer and top of cake. Sprinkle with nuts.

Norma Fraker, *Clinton*

Homecoming Dinner

Crab Paté with Wheat Thins
Strawberry Soup with a Dollop of Sour Cream
Spinach Salad with Dressing
Chicken Breast Continental or Simply Elegant Steak
Squash Casserole
Yeast Rolls
Chocolate Yummy

Crab Paté

1 10¾-OUNCE CAN CREAM OF MUSHROOM SOUP	1 16-OUNCE PACKAGE CRAB MEAT, DRAINED AND FLAKED
1 ENVELOPE UNFLAVORED GELATIN	1 SMALL ONION, FINELY CHOPPED
3 TABLESPOONS COLD WATER	1 CUP CELERY, FINELY CHOPPED
¾ CUP MAYONNAISE	PARSELY SPRIGS
1 8-OUNCE PACKAGE CREAM CHEESE, SOFTENED	

Heat soup in medium saucepan over low heat. Remove from heat. Dissolve gelatin in cold water, add to soup and stir well. Mix remaining ingredients with soup mixture. Spoon into an oiled 4 cup mold. Chill until firm.

Remove from mold and garnish with parsley. Serve with assorted crackers. *Yield:* 4 cups.

Amanda Borgognoni, *Memphis*

Strawberry Soup

1 CUP FRESH STRAWBERRIES	3/4 CUP COLD WATER
1/4 CUP HONEY	1/2 CUP DRY RED WINE
1/4 CUP SOUR CREAM	

Blend all ingredients. It is not necessary to strain. Chill. Stir well before serving. Serve in wine glasses or glass soup bowls. Garnish with dollop of sour cream and fresh strawberry. *Yield:* 3 to 4 servings.

Daisy King, *Nashville*

Chicken Breast Continental

6 WHOLE CHICKEN BREASTS, SPLIT AND DEBONED	1 10¾-OUNCE CAN CELERY SOUP
12 SLICES BACON	1 CUP SOUR CREAM
DRIED SLICED CHIPPED BEEF	1/4 CUP WHITE WINE

Line baking dish with dried beef. Wrap each piece of chicken with bacon (2 slices per each piece). Place on top of beef. Mix soup, sour cream and wine and pour over chicken. Bake uncovered in a 250 degree oven for a full 3 hours.

Virginia Weston, *Mt. Juliet*

Simply Elegant Steak

1½ POUND TENDERIZED BONELESS BEEF ROUND STEAK	1 10¾-OUNCE CAN CONDENSED CREAM OF MUSHROOM SOUP
1 ENVELOPE (4 SERVING SIZE) ONION SOUP MIX	1/2 CUP DRY SHERRY
1 4-OUNCE CAN SLICED MUSHROOMS, DRAINED, RESERVE LIQUID	3 CUPS HOT COOKED RICE

Cut steak into 6 pieces. Place in a buttered baking pan. Sprinkle with soup mix. Add mushrooms. Blend soup, sherry and liquid from mushrooms; pour over steak. Cover and bake in a 450 degree oven for 15 minutes; reduce the heat to 350 degrees and continue baking for 1 hour and 15 minutes or until steak is tender. Serve over rice. *Yield:* 6 servings.

Mrs. William Strasser, *Donelson*

Squash Casserole

6 SMALL SQUASH

1 MEDIUM ONION, SLICED

1 BELL PEPPER, CHOPPED

SALT AND PEPPER TO TASTE

¼ CUP BUTTER

½ CUP SHARP CHEESE, GRATED

1 TABLESPOON SUGAR

½ CUP MILK

2 EGGS, BEATEN

CRACKER CRUMBS

Cook squash, onions and bell peppers until tender and then mash; add salt and pepper, butter, cheese and sugar. Cool this mixture slightly and add milk and eggs which have been mixed together. (Cool mixture somewhat to avoid curdling of milk).

Put mixture in buttered baking dish and add cracker crumbs to top. Bake in a 325 degree oven for 1 hour or until brown and bubbly.

Virginia Coffman, *Livingston*

My Favorite Yeast Rolls

¾ CUP VEGETABLE OIL

1 CUP HOT WATER

2 EGGS, BEATEN

¾ CUP SUGAR

2 TEASPOONS SALT

1 CUP COLD WATER

2 CAKES OR PACKAGES YEAST

½ CUP LUKEWARM WATER

8½ CUPS ALL-PURPOSE FLOUR

Combine vegetable oil and hot water. Cool to lukewarm, stir in beaten eggs, sugar, salt and cold water. Stir well. Soften yeast in ½ cup lukewarm water, after dissolved add to other mixture, then stir in flour 1 cup at a time. Mix well and allow to rise in a warm place. When dough is light and double in size, place on floured board, roll and cut with round cookie cutter. Place a slice of butter in center and fold over, pinching edges closed. Place on greased pans and allow to rise until double in size. Bake in a 375 degree oven for 15 minutes. Ready for use or can be frozen up to 3 or 4 months. *Yield:* about 5 to 6 dozen.

Mrs. Robert (Myrtle) Hutcheson, *Columbia*

Chocolate Yummy

1 6 OUNCE PACKAGE CHOCOLATE CHIPS

4 TABLESPOONS WATER

2 EGGS, SEPARATED

PINCH SALT

1 LARGE CARTON COOL WHIP

½ CUP NUTS, CHOPPED

½ REGULAR ANGEL FOOD CAKE

GRATED SEMISWEET CHOCOLATE

Melt chocolate chips with water in top of double boiler (over hot, not boiling water). Beat egg yolks. Add chocolate mixture to eggs a little at a time, stirring constantly. Add salt. Cool. Beat egg whites until stiff. Fold into chocolate-egg mixture. Fold in about ¾ of the carton of Cool Whip. Fold in nuts. Break angel food cake into bite size pieces. Put a layer of cake in a large rectangular casserole, then a layer of the chocolate mixture over the cake. Repeat layers. Then spread remaining Cool Whip over all. Chill at least 2 hours. Cut into squares to serve. Sprinkle grated chocolate on top. *Yield:* 10 to 12 servings.

Mrs. Willie B. Gilliam, *Lenoir City*

Homecoming Brunch

Tomato Juice Appetizer or Tangy Bloody Marys
Stuffed Sausage Patties
Scrambled Egg Casserole
Garlic Cheese Grits
Hot Curried Fruit or Stuffed Cinnamon Apples
Southern Biscuits and Butter
Pumpkin Bread
Peanut Butter Brownies
Chess Cake Bars

Tomato Juice Appetizer

46 OUNCE CAN TOMATO JUICE
1/2 TEASPOON ONION SALT
1/2 TEASPOON CELERY SALT

1/2 TEASPOON BASIL, CRUMBLED
1/4 CUP SUGAR
2 TABLESPOONS WINE VINEGAR

Mix all ingredients together well and chill. *Yield:* 16 small juice glass servings.

Mrs. David G. Stone, *Hixson*

Stuffed Sausage Patties

1 1/2 POUNDS COUNTRY SAUSAGE
1 CUP PACKAGED HERB-SEASONED STUFFING MIX
1/4 CUP WATER
2 TABLESPOONS BUTTER OR MARGARINE
1 CUP TART APPLE, PEELED AND FINELY CHOPPED

1/2 CUP CELERY, FINELY CHOPPED
1/4 CUP ONION, FINELY CHOPPED
1/4 CUP PARSLEY, SNIPPED
2 TABLESPOONS CHILI SAUCE
1/4 TEASPOON DRY MUSTARD
6 SPICED CRAB APPLES

Shape sausage into 12 thin patties, 1/4-inch thick. Using water and butter or margarine, prepare stuffing mix following package directions. Add chopped apple, celery, onion, parsley, chili sauce, and dry mustard; toss together lightly to mix. Arrange 6 sausage patties in 13 x 9 x 2 inch pan. Top each patty with 1/2 cup stuffing mixture, then with another patty. Secure patties with wooden picks through center. Bake in a 375 degree oven for 45 minutes or until done. Top each with a spiced crab apple. *Yield:* 6 servings.

Mrs. Michael (Susan) Renshaw, *Old Hickory*

Scrambled Egg Casserole

1 CUP CANADIAN BACON

¼ CUP GREEN ONION, CHOPPED

3 TABLESPOONS MELTED BUTTER OR MARGARINE

1 DOZEN EGGS, BEATEN

1 4-OUNCE CAN SLICED MUSHROOMS, DRAINED

CHEESE SAUCE

¼ CUP MELTED BUTTER OR MARGARINE

2¼ CUPS SOFT BREAD CRUMBS

⅛ TEASPOON PAPRIKA

Sauté bacon and green onion in 3 tablespoons butter in a large skillet until onion is tender. Add eggs and cook over medium-high heat, stirring to form large, soft curds; when eggs are set, stir in mushrooms and cheese sauce. Spoon eggs into a greased 13 x 9 x 2 inch baking pan. Combine melted butter and crumbs, mixing well; spread evenly over egg mixture. Sprinkle with paprika. Cover and chill overnight. Uncover and bake in a 350 degree oven for 30 minutes or until heated thoroughly. *Yield:* 12 to 15 servings.

Cheese Sauce:

2 TABLESPOONS BUTTER OR MARGARINE

2½ TABLESPOONS ALL-PURPOSE FLOUR

2 CUPS MILK

⅛ TEASPOON PEPPER

½ TEASPOON SALT

1 CUP (4 OUNCES) SHREDDED PROCESSED AMERICAN CHEESE

Melt butter in a heavy saucepan over low heat; blend in flour and cook 1 minute. Gradually add milk; cook over medium heat until thickened, stirring constantly. Add salt, pepper and cheese, stirring until cheese melts and mixture is smooth. *Yield:* 2½ cups.

Mrs. Ruth Ramsey, *Piney Flats*

Garlic Cheese Grits

1 CUP QUICK GRITS

4 CUPS WATER

1 TUBE GARLIC CHEESE

½ CUP BUTTER

PINCH SALT

1 EGG

1 CUP SWEET MILK

Cook grits in water until well done. Remove from heat and add garlic cheese, butter and salt. Beat egg into sweet milk; add to grits mixture when cooled sufficiently not to cook egg mixture; stir well. Pour into baking dish and bake in a 350 degree oven for 1 hour. Serve hot. *Yield:* 6 to 8 servings.

Sarah Gammon Deck, *Blountville*

Hot Curried Fruit

1 16-OUNCE CAN PEACH HALVES

1 16-OUNCE CAN PEAR HALVES

2 TABLESPOONS BROWN SUGAR

1 TABLESPOON CURRY POWDER

1 15¼-OUNCE CAN PINEAPPLE CHUNKS
1 TABLESPOON CORNSTARCH

1 16-OUNCE JAR SPICED APPLE RINGS, DRAINED

Drain peaches, pears and pineapple and reserve juice. Pour juice into medium saucepan. Combine cornstarch, sugar and curry powder. Add to juice. Stir and cook over medium heat until it thickens. Stir fruit into hot mixture and cook until thoroughly heated. Prepare ahead and heat in oven or microwave later if desired.

Myrtle (Mrs. Charles D.) Taylor, *Johnson City*

Stuffed Cinnamon Apples

¾ CUP CINNAMON BEANS
2 CUPS HOT WATER

APPLES

Dissolve cinnamon beans in water in large pot. Put apples in cinnamon water and boil slowly until tender; lift out, put in bowl and pour syrup over and chill for several hours or until ready to fill.

Filling:

3 OUNCE PACKAGE CREAM CHEESE
1 TEASPOON LEMON JUICE
2 TABLESPOONS MILK

½ CUP DATES, CHOPPED
½ CUP CRUSHED PINEAPPLE
¼ CUP CHOPPED NUTS

Mix together, drain apples and stuff.

Barbara Brewster, *Clarksville*

Southern Homemade Biscuits

This recipe is special to me and my family because I have used it for more than 50 years. When I was a child my father ran a peddling wagon on the dirt roads in southern Madison and northern Hardeman counties. A Mr. Phelps from Model Mills in Jackson, Tennessee sold flour and meal to our house. He gave me the recipe for these biscuits. I have used them since that time. My father died in 1933.

2 CUPS ALL-PURPOSE FLOUR
2 TEASPOONS BAKING POWDER
½ TEASPOON SODA

½ TEASPOON SALT
¼ CUP SHORTENING
1 CUP BUTTERMILK

Sift flour, baking powder, soda and salt together. Cut in shortening, add milk, mix well. Turn out on floured board. Roll out and cut. Bake in a 450 degree oven until brown. *Yield:* 16 to 20 biscuits.

Leeaudry S. Hailey, *Jackson*

Pumpkin Bread

2/3 CUP OIL	1 TEASPOON SALT
1 1/2 CUPS MASHED PUMPKIN	2 TEASPOONS CINNAMON
2 2/3 CUPS SUGAR	1/2 TEASPOON GINGER
4 EGGS	1/2 TEASPOON NUTMEG
1 CUP WATER	1/2 TEASPOON CLOVES
3 1/3 CUPS ALL-PURPOSE FLOUR	2/3 CUP NUTS, COARSELY CHOPPED
2 TEASPOONS SODA	2/3 CUP RAISINS
1/2 TEASPOON BAKING POWDER	2/3 CUP CHOCOLATE CHIPS

Blend first 5 ingredients well. Add flour, soda, baking powder, salt, cinnamon, ginger, nutmeg and cloves; mix well. Stir in nuts, raisins and chocolate chips. Pour into 2 greased 9 x 5 inch loaf pans. Bake in a 350 degree oven for 70 minutes or until done when tested with a toothpick. Cool in pans for 1 hour before removing to wire racks. *Yield:* 2 loaves.

Margie Flynt, *Madison*

Peanut Butter Brownies

1 CUP PEANUT BUTTER	2 CUPS ALL-PURPOSE FLOUR
2/3 CUPS BUTTER	2 TEASPOONS BAKING POWDER
2 CUPS SUGAR	1/2 TEASPOON SALT
1 CUP PACKED BROWN SUGAR	2 6-OUNCE PACKAGES CHOCOLATE CHIPS
4 EGGS	1 TEASPOON VANILLA

Beat peanut butter and butter together until blended. Gradually add sugars and beat until fluffy. Add eggs, one at a time. Add dry ingredients and mix. Stir in chocolate chips and vanilla and spread in a buttered 13 x 9 x 2 inch square pan. Bake in a 350 degree oven for 30 to 35 minutes. Cool and cut into squares.

Holly Osborne Davison, *Watauga*

Chess Cake Bars

1 PACKAGE YELLOW CAKE MIX	1 PACKAGE CONFECTIONERS' SUGAR
2 EGGS	1 8-OUNCE PACKAGE CREAM CHEESE, SOFTENED
1/2 CUP MARGARINE, SOFTENED	1 TEASPOON VANILLA

Grease a 9 x 13 inch pan. Combine cake mix, eggs and margarine in mixing bowl; mix well. Press, using your hands, into greased baking pan. Combine confectioners' sugar, cream cheese and vanilla in mixing bowl. Beat until creamy and smooth. Spread over cake mixture. Bake in a 350 degree oven for 35 minutes. Cool and cut into squares.

Mrs. Wanda Powers, *Old Hickory*

Chapter Two

Appetizers and Beverages

Appetizers

Cheese Wafers

½ CUP BUTTER
½ POUND SHARP CHEDDAR CHEESE

1 CUP PECANS, FINELY CHOPPED
1½ CUPS ALL-PURPOSE FLOUR

Grate cheese or put through a grinder while it is cold. Let cheese soften in a bowl with butter. Mix all ingredients together. Roll mixture in three long rolls and wrap in waxed paper. Chill overnight. Slice into thin wafers and bake in a 425 degree oven for 10 minutes until light brown.

Margaret Hogshead, *Nashville*

Cheddar Cheese Sausage Biscuits

1 POUND SAUSAGE, COOKED AND DRAINED
1 SMALL ONION, CHOPPED
1 CAN CHEDDAR CHEESE SOUP

½ CUP WATER
3 CUPS BISCUIT MIX

Mix all together, drop by tablespoonfuls onto greased cookie sheet. Bake in a 425 degree oven for 12 to 15 minutes. Serve hot.

Marcella T. Epperson, *Johnson City*

Sausage Balls

1 POUND LEAN HOT SAUSAGE
1 8-OUNCE PACKAGE SHARP CHEESE, GRATED

2 CUPS BISQUICK
DASH TABASCO SAUCE

Mix together thoroughly, shape into small balls. Bake in a 350 degree oven for about 20 minutes.

Berniece Shamblin, *Etowah*

Vegetable Dip

2 CUPS COTTAGE CHEESE
2 CUPS MAYONNAISE
1 SMALL ONION
1/2 TEASPOON TABASCO SAUCE

1 1/2 TEASPOONS WORCESTERSHIRE SAUCE
1 1/4 TEASPOONS GARLIC SALT
1 1/4 TEASPOONS CELERY SALT

Mix all ingredients in blender.

Mrs. Elveta B. Croft, *Madisonville*

Shrimp Dip

1 8-OUNCE PACKAGE CREAM CHEESE,
   SOFTENED
1 8-OUNCE CONTAINER SOUR CREAM

1 POUND COOKED SHRIMP, MINCED
2 TABLESPOONS RAW ONION, MINCED
   DASH TABASCO SAUCE

Mix ingredients thoroughly. Serve chilled with chips. Also delicious as a vegetable dip. *Yield:* 2 cups.

Carole Scott, *Memphis*

Cucumber Dip

2 8-OUNCE PACKAGES CREAM CHEESE
2 TABLESPOONS ONION, GRATED
1 SMALL CUCUMBER, GRATED
   WHITE PEPPER TO TASTE

2 TEASPOONS CHIVES
2 TABLESPOONS RED PEPPER, CHOPPED
1 TEASPOON CHICKEN STOCK OR 1 BOUILLON
   CUBE
   MAYONNAISE

Mix well. Add enough mayonnaise to blend well. *Yield:* approximately 3/4 cup.
Note: Dip is better if made the day before it is used.

Dorothy E. Dorris, *Nashville*

Party Cheese Spread

1 CUP CHEDDAR CHEESE
1 CUP HOT PEPPER CHEESE
1 SMALL CAN TOMATO PASTE
3 TABLESPOONS ONION, GRATED

   PINCH GARLIC SALT
2/3 CUP MAYONNAISE
2 TEASPOONS OREGANO

Mix all ingredients together. Spread on small rye bread squares. Place them in a warm oven for a few minutes. Also good on crackers.

Mrs. Glenda Mays, *Goodlettsville*

Hot Pimento Cheese Spread

2 12-OUNCE PACKAGES MEDIUM CHEDDAR
   CHEESE
2 7-OUNCE JARS SLICED PIMENTOS
1 LARGE WHITE ONION
1 TEASPOON CRUSHED RED PEPPER

½ CUP SOUR CREAM
¼ CUP MAYONNAISE
1 TABLESPOON WORCESTERSHIRE SAUCE
1 TEASPOON FRESH LEMON JUICE

Grate cheese and onion on medium grater. Add all other ingredients and mix well. Store covered in quart jar in refrigerator. Keeps well for two weeks.

Note: To use as a dip, add more sour cream or buttermilk until of the desired consistency.

Mary D. Bell, *Chattanooga*

Chickens have their own beauty contest as part of the four-day Fayette County Egg Festival each October. The town square in Somerville is also the site of many other festivities and opportunities for good eating.

Photographic Services

Photographic Services

Tasty Black-Eyed Pea Dip

Southern custom says that you will have good luck if you eat black-eyed peas on New Year's Day. This is a little different way: as a flavorful dip.

1/2 POUND DRIED BLACK-EYED PEAS	1 CUP TOMATO JUICE
2 CUPS WATER	1/2 CUP ONION, CHOPPED
1 1/2 TEASPOONS SALT	1/8 TEASPOON GARLIC POWDER
1/3 CUP LEAN HAM, DICED	1/2 8-OUNCE JAR CHEESE SPREAD
1/2 TEASPOON RED FOOD COLORING	1/4 TEASPOON HOT PEPPER SAUCE
1 4-OUNCE CAN GREEN CHILIES	

Wash peas, cover with water and allow to soak overnight. Drain peas and cover with water in a heavy saucepan; bring to a boil. Lower temperature, cover pan, and simmer for 30 minutes. Add salt and ham and simmer 25 to 30 minutes longer; add red food coloring. Drain peas, reserving liquid.

Drain and chop chilies, reserving 2 tablespoons liquid. Place peas, chilies, reserved juice from chilies, tomato juice, onion and garlic powder in blender container; blend to make a puree. (If a blender is not available, put mixture through a food mill.) Add a small amount of liquid reserved from peas, if needed, to obtain desired consistency. Spoon mixture into top of double boiler; add cheese spread and pepper sauce. Cook over medium heat until cheese melts. Serve warm with crackers or corn chips. *Yield:* 10 to 12 servings.

Mrs. Henry N. Wilkinson, *Franklin*

Cheese Ball

1 4-OUNCE WEDGE BLUE CHEESE	1 3-OUNCE PACKAGE CREAM CHEESE
1 6-OUNCE PACKAGE SHARP CHEDDAR CHEESE	1 TABLESPOON PARSLEY
1 TABLESPOON ONION, GRATED	1/2 TEASPOON WORCESTERSHIRE SAUCE
1/2 CUP NUTS, CHOPPED	1/4 CUP NUTS, CHOPPED

Let cheese be room temperature. Combine cheeses and 1/2 cup nuts and parsley. Put on wax paper and shape into ball, then roll in 1/4 cup nuts and refrigerate. Serve with mixed crackers. Any leftovers may be frozen.

Mrs. Joe Sam Savage, *Hampshire*

Cheese Ball

10 OUNCES EXTRA SHARP CHEDDAR CHEESE, GRATED	2 TABLESPOONS GREEN PEPPER, MINCED
2 LARGE PACKAGES CREAM CHEESE	1 TABLESPOON GARLIC POWDER
1/4 CUP SLICED OLIVES, GREEN OR BLACK	2 TEASPOONS WORCESTERSHIRE SAUCE
2 TABLESPOONS GREEN ONION, MINCED	1 TEASPOON LEMON JUICE

Mix well and form into a large ball. Roll in chopped nuts.

Mrs. Dorothy Jacobs, *Elizabethton*

Beef Cheese Ball

1½ CUPS DRIED BEEF, FINELY CHOPPED
12 OUNCES CREAM CHEESE, SOFTENED
¾ CUP SOUR CREAM
3 TABLESPOONS INSTANT ONION FLAKES
3 TABLESPOONS PARSLEY FLAKES
3 TABLESPOONS GREEN PEPPER, FINELY CHOPPED
¼ TEASPOON SEASONED SALT
1 TEASPOON HORSERADISH

Combine dried beef, cream cheese, sour cream, onion flakes, parsley flakes, green pepper, seasoned salt and horseradish. Shape into 2 balls or logs and roll in chopped pecans or chopped fresh parsley. It will have a better flavor if prepared the day before using. *Yield:* 2 balls or logs.

Ann Cox, *Murfreesboro*

Cheese Roll

This is a very good cheese roll for parties or holidays.

1 8-OUNCE PACKAGE MILD CHEDDAR CHEESE
1 8-OUNCE PACKAGE SHARP CHEDDAR CHEESE
1 8-OUNCE PACKAGE PHILADELPHIA CREAM CHEESE
½ CUP MAYONNAISE
2 TABLESPOONS PIMENTOS, CHOPPED
1 TEASPOON ONION OR GARLIC POWDER
1 CUP NUTS, FINELY CHOPPED

Mix softened cheeses and all ingredients together. Form 2 rolls and roll in chopped nuts.

Brenda Kelley, *Lexington*

Shrimp Mold

This can be served as a main dish salad or with crackers as an hors d'oeuvre. Delicious!

1 POUND SHRIMP, COOKED
1 8-OUNCE PACKAGE CREAM CHEESE
1 CAN TOMATO SOUP
1 CUP MAYONNAISE
¾ CUP GREEN PEPPER, CHOPPED
1 SMALL ONION, CHOPPED
1¾ CUPS CELERY, CHOPPED
3 ENVELOPES KNOX GELATIN
1 TEASPOON SALT
1 TO 2 TEASPOONS HORSERADISH
CAYENNE PEPPER TO TASTE
1¼ CUPS COLD WATER

Boil soup with ¼ cup water. Soften gelatin in 1 cup water and dissolve in hot soup. Mix cream cheese and mayonnaise to a smooth paste and add to soup mixture. Mix with electric mixer until well blended. Cool slightly; combine all remaining ingredients and pour into a ring or fish mold and chill. This can be served as a main dish salad or with crackers as an hors d'oeuvre. Delicious!

Judy Jackson, *Blountville*

Crabmeat Delight

This is so quick to put together. I have used this as an appetizer many times before serving dinner to our guests, when it is our turn to host the "Dinners Eight" club to which my husband and I belong.

2 8-OUNCE PACKAGES CREAM CHEESE	½ BOTTLE CHILI SAUCE
2 TEASPOONS WORCESTERSHIRE SAUCE	1 CAN CRABMEAT
1 TEASPOON LIME JUICE	LETTUCE TO GARNISH
2 TEASPOONS MAYONNAISE	WHEAT CRACKERS OR MELBA ROUNDS
1 SMALL ONION, CHOPPED	

Mix cream cheese until smooth. Add Worcestershire sauce, lime juice, mayonnaise and onion. May be refrigerated until ready to serve. To assemble place lettuce on desired tray. Pile cream cheese mixture in mound or round about 1½ inches thick. Drizzle with chili sauce. Scatter crab meat over. Serve crackers on separate tray.

Carol C. Gibson, *Martin*

Party Franks

1 POUND WEINERS, HALVED	1 POUND BROWN SUGAR
1 POUND BACON	

Wrap bacon around each half of weiner; secure with toothpick. Put in crock pot. Pour brown sugar over. Cook until all of syrup is absorbed into franks.

Wanda Teague, *Knoxville*

Piquant Meatballs

Sauce:

1 12-OUNCE BOTTLE COCKTAIL SAUCE	1 CAN CRANBERRY SAUCE
2 TABLESPOONS PACKED BROWN SUGAR	1 TEASPOON REALEMON JUICE

Meatballs:

2 POUNDS GROUND CHUCK	2 TABLESPOONS DRIED ONION FLAKES
⅓ CUP CHOPPED DRY PARSLEY FLAKES	1 TEASPOON GARLIC SALT
1 CUP CORNFLAKE CRUMBS	¼ TEASPOON PEPPER
1 EGG	2 TABLESPOONS SOY SAUCE
½ CUP CATSUP	

Combine ingredients for sauce in saucepan and simmer for about 20 minutes, stirring to a smooth consistency. Mix ingredients for meatballs thoroughly. Form into small 1 inch meatballs and bake in a 375 degree oven for about 30 minutes. Serve warm. *Yield:* 24 meatballs.

Becky Makamson, *Lebanon*

Stuffed Mushrooms

1 PACKAGE STOVE TOP STUFFING   12 TO 24 LARGE FRESH MUSHROOMS

Prepare stuffing according to directions on package. Wash and remove the stems from mushrooms. Fill with the stuffing. Broil in pre-heated oven for 3 to 5 minutes.

Note: These can be prepared early, so that the flavors are well blended. Cover with waxed paper and refrigerate until time to broil. Serve hot.

Mrs. John Featherston, *Madison*

Stuffed Dates

A very simple, delicious, easy to fix addition for any party, or to take to work. Always gets great compliments.

Take dates and split them down the middle, but not all the way through. Insert 1/2 of a pecan.

Take pie crust dough and roll out very thin, cut in triangles. Roll dough around date and seal edges. Brush with butter; bake in a 350 degree oven until dough is light brown. Remove from oven and roll in confectioners' sugar.

Ms. Denise L. Dunlap, *Nashville*

Chicken Balls with Coconut

1 8-OUNCE PACKAGE CREAM CHEESE
1 CUP CHICKEN, GROUND
3/4 CUP ALMONDS, CHOPPED
2 TABLESPOONS MAYONNAISE
1/2 TEASPOON CURRY POWDER
SALT
WHITE PEPPER
4 TABLESPOONS CHUTNEY OR SWEET PICKLE RELISH
ANGEL FLAKE COCONUT

Mix well. Shape into small balls and roll in Angel Flake coconut.

Vivian Fults, *Antioch*

Beverages

Homecoming Punch

6 CUPS SUGAR

4 3-OUNCE PACKAGES LEMON JELLO

1 6-OUNCE CAN FROZEN ORANGE JUICE
   CONCENTRATE

1 6-OUNCE CAN FROZEN LEMON JUICE
   CONCENTRATE

2 LARGE CANS PINEAPPLE JUICE

1 OUNCE ALMOND EXTRACT

4 QUARTS GINGER ALE

2 GALLONS WATER

Combine sugar and 1 gallon water in pan. Heat until sugar is dissolved and mixture is syrupy. Add Jello and stir until dissolved. Add fruit juices, 1 gallon water and extract. Let stand until ready to serve. When ready to serve, pour 2 quarts mixture over crushed ice and add ½ quart ginger ale. *Yield:* 75 servings.

Jane Mee, *Cookeville*

Fruit Punch

This is an all-time favorite for fellowships at Gleason First Baptist Church. Children especially enjoy its delightful flavor.

1 3-OUNCE BOX CHERRY (OR FLAVOR
   DESIRED) JELLO

3 CUPS SUGAR

1 QUART BOILING WATER

3 QUARTS COOL WATER

1 46-OUNCE CAN PINEAPPLE JUICE

1 QUART BOTTLE 7-UP

Dissolve Jello and sugar in 1 quart boiling water. Add the cool water and pineapple juice. Store in refrigerator. When ready to serve, pour into punch bowl and add the 7-Up. Stir well. *Yield:* 50 4-ounce servings.

Note: Punch can be made a different color by using a different flavor Jello. Cherry makes red, lemon makes yellow, strawberry makes pink, orange makes a peach color and lime makes green.

Nelcene Dunning, *Gleason*

Ida Lou's Icy Punch

This recipe is nice because if you are running low on punch, you can add more Sprite and it does not alter the taste. Also, whatever color scheme you want, just use that color gelatin. We use lemon mostly, for bridal or baby showers. I used this at both my girls' weddings, and it was a big hit. We call this Ida Lou's Icy Punch because she is the lady who gave it to us.

2 SMALL PACKAGES JELLO (DESIRED COLOR)

2 CUPS WATER, HOT

2 CUPS SUGAR

2 CUPS WATER (NOT HOT)

2 QUARTS PINEAPPLE JUICE

2 CUPS REALEMON JUICE CONCENTRATE

1 OUNCE ALMOND EXTRACT

3 QUARTS GINGER ALE OR SPRITE

Mix together Jello and hot water. Add sugar and two more cups of water (not hot). Mix, adding pineapple juice, ReaLemon juice and almond extract. Mix and freeze in ½ gallon milk cartons. Take out of freezer about 2 hours before serving, depending on the weather. Add ginger ale or Sprite. *Yield:* 50 servings.

Mrs. Bonnie Petty, *Jackson*

Tea Punch

7 REGULAR TEA BAGS
2 CUPS SUGAR
1 12-OUNCE CAN FROZEN ORANGE JUICE CONCENTRATE
1 12-OUNCE CAN FROZEN LEMONADE CONCENTRATE
1 6-OUNCE CAN FROZEN LIMEADE CONCENTRATE

Brew tea. Pour into 1 gallon container. Add sugar and stir until dissolved. Add fruit juice concentrate and stir until dissolved. Add water to make 1 gallon. May be served hot or cold.

Mrs. James (Dot) Holeman, Jr., *Old Hickory*
Daisy King, *Nashville*

Wanda's Original Strawberry Punch

This is very refreshing and pretty. Also, it is inexpensive.

½ GALLON VANILLA ICE MILK (CUT IN 8 BLOCKS)
2 PINTS SLICED FRESH OR FROZEN STRAWBERRIES (SMALL BERRIES MAY BE LEFT WHOLE)
2 PACKAGES STRAWBERRY KOOL-AID, UNSWEETENED
2 QUART BOTTLES GINGER ALE, COLD

Mix ice milk and strawberries in a large punch bowl. Mix Kool-Aid according to directions on package, refrigerate. Pour over strawberries and ice cream. Add ginger ale to mixture. (If punch bowl is small, mix ½ of the above at a time.)

Wanda W. Richardson, *Gadsden*

Sparkling Cranberry Punch

1 6-OUNCE CAN FROZEN LEMONADE CONCENTRATE
1 QUART CRANBERRY JUICE
1 30-OUNCE CAN PINEAPPLE JUICE
1 6-OUNCE CAN FROZEN ORANGE JUICE CONCENTRATE
1 QUART GINGER ALE, CHILLED

Reconstitute lemonade and orange juice according to label directions. Pour into large container. Add cranberry juice and pineapple juice. Chill. Add ginger ale just before serving. Ice mold or ice cubes may be floated in punch bowl. Prepare mold or cubes with frozen cranberry juice and sliced pineapple, lemon and orange slices or wedges. *Yield:* 20 to 24 servings.

Ozie Lea Cox, *Bolivar*

Spiced Grape Punch

6 CUPS WATER

1 CUP SUGAR

1 QUART GRAPE JUICE

1 6-OUNCE CAN FROZEN LEMONADE
CONCENTRATE

1 6-OUNCE CAN FROZEN ORANGE JUICE
CONCENTRATE

4 STICKS CINNAMON, BROKEN

6 WHOLE CLOVES

In large saucepan combine water, grape juice, sugar and lemonade and orange juice concentrates. Tie cinnamon and cloves in cheesecloth bag or place in tea ball and add to punch. Simmer about 15 minutes. Remove spices before serving. Serve hot. *Yield:* 2 quarts. Good!

Mrs. Donald (Rolene) Pake, *Nashville*

Robin Hood

Home of John Rice Irwin in Norris

Quick and Easy Hawaiian Punch

Have two 1 gallon jugs in which to store the following mixture. In each jug pour:

1 12-OUNCE CAN FROZEN ORANGE JUICE PLUS 12 OUNCES WATER	1 6-OUNCE CAN FROZEN LIMEADE PLUS 6 OUNCES WATER
1 12-OUNCE CAN FROZEN LEMONADE PLUS 12 OUNCES WATER	1/2 CUP SUGAR
	1 46-OUNCE CAN UNSWEETENED PINEAPPLE JUICE

Shake to mix well. Fill jugs to 1 gallon with water. Refrigerate overnight to allow juices to blend. At serving time, pour 1 gallon mix in punch bowl. Slowly add 2 bottles chilled ginger ale or Sprite. *Yield:* 72 1/2 cups.

Note: Make frozen ring to use in the bowl decorating however you choose with orange slices, lime slices, cherries, etc.

Marie H. Hunter, *Kingsport*

Spiced Tea

This recipe is from a lady (now deceased) in our church who gave most young brides-to-be in the church a shower. She always served this delicious tea. It has become a family favorite and now Christmas wouldn't be the same without this tea.

1 QUART WEAK TEA	1 PINT WATER
2 3-OUNCE PACKAGES STRAWBERRY OR LEMON JELLO	1 CUP REALEMON JUICE
1/2 GALLON BOILING WATER	1 QUART WATER
6 CINNAMON STICKS	2 CUPS SUGAR
12 CLOVES	1 LARGE CAN PINEAPPLE JUICE

Dissolve Jello in boiling water. In separate pan, simmer cinnamon sticks and cloves in 1 pint water for 30 minutes. Combine all ingredients, and more water or juice if desired. Serve hot. Do not boil. *Yield:* 30 servings.

Carolyn Hileman Ruble (Mrs. J. H.), *Powell*

Instant Spice Tea

3/4 CUP SUGAR	1 TEASPOON CINNAMON
1/2 CUP INSTANT TEA	1/2 TEASPOON GROUND CLOVES
2 CUPS TANG INSTANT BREAKFAST DRINK	1/4 TEASPOON NUTMEG
1 2 QUART SIZE PACKAGE WYLER'S PRESWEETENED LEMONADE MIX	

Mix all ingredients well. Store in tightly closed container. Use 2 or more teaspoons per cup of hot water. If desired, garnish with lemon wedge, cinnamon stick or sprig of mint.

Carole Scott, *Memphis*

Front Porch Lemonade

1¼ CUPS GRANULATED SUGAR
½ CUP BOILING WATER
1½ CUPS FRESH LEMON JUICE

4½ CUPS COLD WATER
ICE CUBES
LEMON SLICES

To make lemonade base, place sugar, boiling water, and lemon juice in a 2-quart pitcher and stir vigorously with a spoon until sugar is dissolved. Cover and store in refrigerator until ready to use.

Add cold water, ice cubes and lemon slices and stir. Pour over ice cubes in a 10 or 12 ounce glass. *Yield:* 6 to 8 servings.

Mrs. Sherry Ligon Allison, *Cookeville*

Grapefruit Slush

A tangy, refreshing way to begin a special luncheon or dinner.

2 CUPS WATER
2 CUPS SUGAR
2 15-OUNCE CANS CRUSHED PINEAPPLE

2 16-OUNCE CANS GRAPEFRUIT SECTIONS
1 16-OUNCE JAR MARASCHINO CHERRIES, CHOPPED
GINGER ALE OR 7-UP

Mix water and sugar in saucepan. Heat until the sugar is dissolved. Cool.

In blender, combine crushed pineapple and grapefruit sections, blend until fine. Add maraschino cherries, sugar and water; freeze until firm. Pour 7-up or ginger ale over slush and serve.

Sherron De Vos, *Fairfield Glade*

Orange Julius

1 6-OUNCE CAN ORANGE JUICE CONCENTRATE, UNDILUTED
1 CUP MILK
1 CUP WATER

½ CUP SUGAR
1 TEASPOON VANILLA
12 ICE CUBES

Combine all ingredients in blender container, cover and blend until smooth, about 30 to 45 seconds. Serve immediately.

Carolyn Hileman Ruble (Mrs. J. H.), *Powell*
Meredith McDaniel, age 11, *Madisonville*

Chapter Three

Soups and Sauces

Soups

1886 Cheese Soup

¼ CUP BUTTER

½ CUP ONION, DICED

½ CUP CELERY, DICED

½ CUP CARROTS, DICED

¼ CUP ALL-PURPOSE FLOUR

1½ TABLESPOONS CORNSTARCH

4 CUPS CHICKEN BROTH, ROOM TEMPERATURE

4 CUPS MILK, ROOM TEMPERATURE

⅛ TEASPOON SODA

1 POUND PROCESSED CHEESE, CUBED

1 TEASPOON SALT

1 TEASPOON PEPPER

⅛ TEASPOON CAYENNE PEPPER

1 TABLESPOON DRIED PARSLEY

PAPRIKA

Melt butter in heavy saucepan. Sauté vegetables until tender. Stir in flour and cornstarch. Cook until bubbly. Add stock and milk gradually, blending into smooth sauce. Add soda and cheese cubes; stir until thickened. Season with salt and pepper, add parsley. Before serving heat thoroughly in double boiler. Do not let boil. Garnish with paprika.

Mrs. Artis W. Kemp, *Bradyville*

Broccoli Soup

2 TABLESPOONS MARGARINE

¾ CUP ONION, CHOPPED

6 CHICKEN BOUILLON CUBES

6 CUPS WATER

1 8-OUNCE PACKAGE EGG NOODLES

2 8-OUNCE PACKAGES BROCCOLI

6 CUPS MILK

½ TEASPOON GARLIC POWDER

1 POUND VELVEETA CHEESE

8 OUNCES SAUTEED MUSHROOMS

1½ CUPS CHUNKED CHICKEN

Sauté onions and mushrooms in butter; add water and bouillon cubes. Heat to boiling and dissolve cubes. Gradually add noodles. Boil uncovered 3 minutes. Stir in broccoli, garlic powder and chicken. Cook until cheese melts, but do not boil. Freezes well and may be reheated by adding a small amount of additional milk.

Charlene W. Collier, *Nashville*

Cream of Peanut Butter Soup

½ CUP BUTTER OR MARGARINE
1 TABLESPOON ONION, MINCED
1 TABLESPOON ALL-PURPOSE FLOUR
1 CUP PEANUT BUTTER

1 QUART CHICKEN STOCK
DASH PEPPER
1 TABLESPOON SALT
1 CUP CREAM

Melt butter or margarine, add onion and simmer until tender, but not brown. Add flour and peanut butter and stir to a smooth paste. Add stock gradually, season and cook 20 minutes in a double boiler, stirring constantly until thickened. Strain and add cream. *Yield:* 8 to 10 servings.

Kathleen M. Cummings, *Murfreesboro*

Country Chicken Soup

1 CARROT
¾ CUP CELERY
1 SWEET GREEN PEPPER
1 ONION
¾ CUP COOKED CHICKEN, CUBED
1 APPLE, PEELED AND CUBED
4 TABLESPOONS BUTTER

⅓ CUP ALL-PURPOSE FLOUR
2 WHOLE CLOVES
1 SPRIG PARSLEY
4 CUPS CHICKEN BROTH
1 CUP CANNED OR FRESH TOMATOES
SALT TO TASTE
2½ TO 3 CUPS MILK

Chop carrot, celery, green pepper and onion; sauté lightly in butter, stirring often. Add chicken and all ingredients, except milk. Simmer with cover on for 50 minutes. Add milk; bring to boil. *Yield:* 6 to 8 servings.

Mrs. Jim (Dot) Holeman, Jr., *Old Hickory*

Vegetable Cheese Chowder

1 QUART CHICKEN BROTH
1 10-OUNCE PACKAGE FROZEN WHOLE KERNEL CORN
1 10-OUNCE PACKAGE FROZEN CHOPPED BROCCOLI
1 CUP ONION, CHOPPED

2 TO 3 CUPS FRESH MUSHROOMS, SLICED (MAY USE CANNED)
4 TABLESPOONS MARGARINE
6 TABLESPOONS ALL-PURPOSE FLOUR
SALT AND PEPPER TO TASTE
2½ CUPS MILK
1 CUP CHEESE, GRATED

Bring broth, corn and broccoli to a boil in saucepan. Reduce heat and simmer for 5 minutes. Set aside. Cook onion and mushrooms in margarine until done but not brown. Blend in flour and salt and pepper to taste (if using bouillon cubes for broth omit salt). Slowly add milk; cook and stir until thick. Add broth, corn, broccoli and cheese. Heat thoroughly. Serve hot. *Yield:* 12 servings.

Nancy Conley Smith, *Murfreesboro*

Old-Fashioned Potato Noodle Soup

1 QUART WATER	MILK
1 TEASPOON SALT	1/2 CUP SALTED BUTTER
3 MEDIUM SIZED POTATOES, SLICED	1 CUP MILK
2 CUPS ALL-PURPOSE FLOUR	ONION, CHOPPED
2 EGGS, LIGHTLY BEATEN	

In a 6 quart pot bring water and 1/2 teaspoon salt to a boil. Add the potatoes; cook until potatoes are done. With a potato masher or fork mash these in the water.

While the potatoes are cooking sift the flour and 1/2 teaspoon salt together in a medium size mixing bowl. In a measuring cup, lightly beat the eggs and finish filling the cup with milk. Add the milk mixture to the flour mixture, making a real soft dough.

Have the potato water boiling. To this add 1/2 cup butter and 1 cup milk. Let this come to a simmering boil. Keep simmering. Dip a teaspoon into hot soup then dip up about 1/2 teaspoon of dough on tip of spoon, drop into the simmering soup; stir and keep up the process until all the dough has been used. Stir continuously. If it seems a little too thick, add milk. Cover and cook about 20 minutes. Serve with chopped onions sprinkled on top. *Yield:* 6 servings.

Eva J. Scott, *Watauga*

Multi-Vegetable Soup

2 TABLESPOONS BUTTER OR MARGARINE	2 BEEF BOUILLON CUBES
2 TABLESPOONS COOKING OIL	8 CUPS BOILING WATER
1 CUP CARROTS, THINLY SLICED	2 TEASPOONS SALT
1 CUP ZUCCHINI, THINLY SLICED	1 TEASPOON ACCENT
1 CUP CELERY, THINLY SLICED	1 16-OUNCE CAN STEWED TOMATOES
1 CUP CABBAGE, FINELY SHREDDED	1/2 CUP UNCOOKED SPAGHETTI, BROKEN
1 LARGE ONION, CHOPPED	1/2 TEASPOON THYME

Heat the butter or margarine and oil in a saucepan. Add the carrots, zucchini, celery, cabbage and onion. Cook uncovered about 10 minutes, stirring occasionally.

Add the bouillon cubes, water, salt and Accent to the vegetables. Bring to boiling, reduce heat and simmer uncovered 30 minutes.

Stir in the stewed tomatoes, spaghetti and thyme. Cook 20 minutes. Serve hot from a tureen. Accompany with a bowl of shredded Parmesan cheese. *Yield:* 2 quarts.

Carrie Treichel, *Johnson City*

Chili-Potato Soup

7 LARGE POTATOES	2 13-OUNCE CANS CHILI BEANS
1 13-OUNCE CAN CREAM OF MUSHROOM SOUP	1/2 TEASPOON GARLIC SALT
1 LARGE ONION	1/2 TEASPOON PEPPER
	1/2 CUP CHEDDAR CHEESE

Cook potatoes until tender. Drain potatoes, leaving 2 cups of liquid in the pot. Add cream of mushroom soup. Mix in chili beans and let simmer about 30 minutes. Add cheese and serve.

Audrey L. Hackler, *Norris*

Winter Soup

6 CUPS WATER	1 CUP CABBAGE, SHREDDED
6 CHICKEN BOUILLON CUBES OR	2 MEDIUM RIBS CELERY, CHOPPED
2 TABLESPOONS INSTANT POWDERED CHICKEN BOUILLON	1 MEDIUM ONION, CHOPPED
2 MEDIUM CARROTS, PARED AND DICED	1 SMALL WHITE TURNIP, CHOPPED
1 LARGE POTATO, PARED AND DICED	1/8 TEASPOON NUTMEG
	1/8 TEASPOON PEPPER

In a 3 quart saucepot, bring the water and bouillon cubes to a boil. Add carrot, potato, cabbage, celery, onion, turnip, nutmeg and pepper. Bring to boiling again; boil gently until vegetables are tender, about 25 minutes.

Gabriele Eisemann, *Clarksville*

Ham and Bean Soup

1 POUND DRIED GREAT NORTHERN BEANS	2 CUPS WATER
6 CUPS OF WATER	4 MEDIUM POTATOES, PEELED AND QUARTERED
1 1/2 POUNDS HAM OR HAMHOCK, COOKED AND CUBED	3 CARROTS, SCRAPED AND CUT INTO 1/2 INCH SLICES
2 TEASPOONS SALT	1 MEDIUM ONION, FINELY CHOPPED
3 CLOVES GARLIC, MINCED	

Sort and wash beans; place in a Dutch oven. Cover with water 2 inches above beans. Let soak overnight. Drain.

Combine beans, six cups of water, ham, salt and garlic in a large Dutch oven. Bring to a boil. Cover, reduce heat and simmer 1 1/2 hours. Add 2 cups water and vegetables to beans. Cover and simmer about 30 minutes or until vegetables are tender. *Yield:* About 1 gallon.

Gwendolyn P. Tant, *Dunlap*

Seven Bean Soup

½ CUP RED KIDNEY BEANS
½ CUP NORTHERN BEANS
½ CUP PINTO BEANS
½ CUP GREEN SPLIT PEAS

½ CUP LENTILS
½ CUP NAVY BEANS
2 QUARTS WATER

Wash beans, then soak overnight in water. The next day add to beans and water the following:

1 CUP ONION, CHOPPED
1 TABLESPOON PARSLEY, CHOPPED
1 GARLIC CLOVE, CHOPPED
4 CUBES BOUILLON

1 8-OUNCE CAN TOMATO SAUCE
½ CUP CELERY, CHOPPED
½ CUP CARROTS, SLICED

Cook covered until done, stirring occasionally. Top with grated Parmesan cheese when serving.

Norvelle Holloway, *Columbia*

Vegetable Soup

2 CUPS FRESH PEAS
4 CUPS FRESH OKRA
2 EARS CORN, CUT OFF THE COB
2 ONIONS, CHOPPED
4 CUPS POTATOES, PEELED AND DICED
2 CUPS FRESH CARROTS, THINLY SLICED

1 CUP CELERY, THINLY SLICED
2 CUPS DRIED BEANS, SHELLED
2 CUPS BEEF, CUBED
1 TO 2 CUPS WATER
4 FRESH TOMATOES, WHOLE
SALT AND PEPPER TO TASTE

Boil all vegetables in some water until done, except the tomatoes. Boil beef gently in some water until done. Drain the vegetables and the beef and combine them. Add the tomatoes, 1 to 2 cups water and seasonings. Bring to a boil; reduce heat and simmer 2 to 3 hours. Serve with homemade biscuits.

Diana Parks, *Madisonville*

Creamy Corn Chowder

¼ POUND BACON, DICED
1 CUP ONION, CHOPPED
1 GREEN PEPPER, CHOPPED
2 TABLESPOONS BACON DRIPPINGS
2½ CUPS CHICKEN BROTH
2 CUPS POTATOES, DICED

1 15-OUNCE CAN CREAMED CORN
1 TEASPOON PAPRIKA
½ TEASPOON PEPPER
¼ TEASPOON SAGE
2 CUPS MILK OR HALF AND HALF
SALT TO TASTE

Brown bacon in Dutch oven and drain, reserving 2 tablespoons of drippings. Sauté onion and green pepper in drippings until soft. Add chicken broth and diced potatoes. Bring to a boil and simmer until potatoes are cooked. Add creamed corn, seasonings, bacon and milk. Heat through.

Elaine L. Fronczek, *Hixson*

Alex McMahan

Jesse Lightfoot of Chattanooga, who has taught field cookery to Boy Scout leaders, browns his "Crazy Cobbler" over an open fire. "You can't really time a fire," he says. "You just check the foods every now and then. You use oak and hickory woods—no pine at all. Get the logs going good and add lumps of charcoal."

Sauces

Broccoli Sauce

1/4 CUP BUTTER OR MARGARINE, MELTED	1/2 TEASPOON TABASCO SAUCE
1 CUP MAYONNAISE	1/2 TEASPOON SALT
2 TABLESPOONS HORSERADISH	1 TEASPOON DRY MUSTARD
1/4 TEASPOON CAYENNE PEPPER	2 TABLESPOONS ONION, GRATED

Mix well. Arrange steamed broccoli on platter and pour mixture over the center. Do not heat sauce.

Mrs. Nathan Fox, *Columbia*

Tennessee Barbecue Sauce

1 CUP BROWN SUGAR, PACKED	2 CUPS VINEGAR
1 1/2 TEASPOONS ONION SALT	1 CUP BOTTLED BARBECUE SAUCE
1/2 TEASPOON SALT	1/2 CUP CATSUP
1/2 TEASPOON PAPRIKA	2 TABLESPOONS WORCESTERSHIRE SAUCE
1/2 TEASPOON PEPPER	1 TABLESPOON BOTTLED HOT PEPPER SAUCE
DASH GARLIC SALT	

In saucepan stir together brown sugar, onion salt, paprika, salt, pepper and garlic salt. Combine vinegar, barbecue sauce, catsup, Worcestershire sauce and bottled hot pepper sauce. Stir vinegar mixture into dry ingredients. Cook and stir over low heat until sugar dissolves. Remove from heat; cool. Store covered in refrigerator. *Yield:* about 4 cups.

Malinda Pafford, *Camden*

Tennessee Barbecue Sauce

1/2 CUP ONION, FINELY CHOPPED	1/8 TEASPOON CAYENNE PEPPER
4 TABLESPOONS DARK BROWN SUGAR	2 TABLESPOONS WORCESTERSHIRE SAUCE
1 TABLESPOON PAPRIKA	1/4 CUP VINEGAR
1/4 TEASPOON CHILI POWDER	1/4 CUP CATSUP
1 TEASPOON SALT	1 CUP TOMATO JUICE
1 TEASPOON DRY MUSTARD	1/2 CUP WATER

Mix together and simmer 15 minutes. This sauce is good on pork or poultry. *Yield:* 1 1/2 to 2 cups.

Mrs. Sue Reeves, *Murfreesboro*

Spaghetti Sauce

2 POUNDS GROUND BEEF, BROWNED AND CRUMBLED
1 LARGE ONION
3 CLOVES GARLIC
1 CUP CELERY, CHOPPED
2 CANS MUSHROOMS, OR 1 SMALL BOX FRESH MUSHROOMS

1 SMALL CAN TOMATO PASTE
2 CUPS WATER
3 CANS TOMATO SAUCE
1 QUART TOMATOES
4 TABLESPOONS ITALIAN SEASONING
SALT AND PEPPER TO TASTE
2 CUPS RED WINE

Mix together all ingredients but wine in large cooking pan. Cook for 1 hour, then add wine. Simmer 1 to 2 hours. This sauce can be frozen in small containers and used when needed.

Christine Littleton, *Newbern*

Spaghetti Sauce

1½ POUNDS GROUND CHUCK
½ GREEN PEPPER, CHOPPED
1 MEDIUM ONION, CHOPPED
4 8-OUNCE CANS TOMATO SAUCE
1 6-OUNCE CAN TOMATO PASTE
1 TEASPOON SEASONED SALT

1 TEASPOON OREGANO
1 TEASPOON CHILI POWDER
¼ TEASPOON GARLIC POWDER
⅛ TEASPOON PEPPER
1 TEASPOON SUGAR
1 WHOLE BAY LEAF

Brown the ground chuck with the green pepper and onion, breaking the meat up with a spoon. Add the remaining ingredients, stirring well. Cover and simmer 1 hour. Serve over cooked spaghetti.

Deborah Rinehart, *Talbott*

Italian Spaghetti Sauce

½ CUP COOKING OIL OR FAT
1½ POUNDS GROUND BEEF
1 SMALL CLOVE GARLIC
¼ CUP GREEN PEPPER, DICED
½ CUP MUSHROOM
1 6-OUNCE CAN TOMATO PASTE
1 NO. 2 CAN TOMATOES
2 TABLESPOONS CHILI POWDER

1 TEASPOON SUGAR
½ CUP CELERY
¼ TEASPOON OREGANO
½ ONION, DICED
1 BAY LEAF
SALT AND PEPPER TO TASTE
PARMESAN CHEESE

Sauté beef in oil. Add other ingredients, except Parmesan cheese, and simmer for one hour. Pour sauce over cooked spaghetti. Add Parmesan cheese to taste.

Ruth Eckel, *Knoxville*

Joseph's Marinating Sauce for Fondue Meat

¼ CUP WESSON OIL

¼ CUP VINEGAR

¼ CUP ONION, CHOPPED

1 TEASPOON SALT

JUICE OF 1 LEMON

DASH PEPPER

Combine ingredients, marinate cubed beef overnight. Use 1 cup margarine and 2 cups oil for cooking in fondue pot.

Joe Hamm, *Ramer*

White Cheese Sauce

2 TABLESPOONS BUTTER OR MARGARINE

2 TABLESPOONS ALL-PURPOSE FLOUR

¼ TEASPOON SALT

⅛ TEASPOON PEPPER

1 CUP MILK

½ TO 1 CUP CHEDDAR CHEESE, GRATED, OR

3 TO 4 SLICES AMERICAN CHEESE

Melt butter in saucepan over low heat. Blend in flour, salt and pepper. Cook over low heat, stirring constantly, until mixture is smooth and bubbly.

Remove from heat. Stir in milk. Heat to boiling, stirring constantly. Boil and stir 1 minute. Add cheese, reduce heat to low and stir until cheese melts and sauce is smooth.

Serve hot over broccoli, brussel sprouts, etc. *Yield:* approximately 1 to 1½ cups of sauce.

Amy Baragona, *Soddy Daisy*

Hot Fudge Sauce

The first hot fudge sundae was invented in Boston around 1900. Here's a Tennessee version of a real fudgy sauce that stiffens when it's poured on cold ice cream.

4 SQUARES UNSWEETENED CHOCOLATE

2 TABLESPOONS BUTTER OR MARGARINE

¾ CUP BOILING WATER

2 CUPS SUGAR

3 TABLESPOONS CORN SYRUP

2 TABLESPOONS VANILLA

Chop chocolate coarsely; heat with butter and boiling water in a large heavy saucepan over low heat, stirring constantly until chocolate is melted. Add sugar and corn syrup.

Bring mixture slowly to boiling; reduce heat; simmer gently 8 minutes. Watch carefully but do not stir. Add vanilla. Serve while warm. *Yield:* 2 cups.

Note: This sauce is great on ice cream, pound cake, ice cream filled meringue shells and over banana splits.

Mrs. Sam Durbin, *Jackson*

Seafood Cocktail Sauce

1 CUP TOMATO CATSUP

1/2 CUP CHILI SAUCE

JUICE OF 1 LEMON

1 TEASPOON WORCESTERSHIRE SAUCE

4 TABLESPOONS HORSERADISH

Mix all ingredients; chill. Use as a sauce for shrimp, oysters, lobster, crab or seafood cocktail. *Yield:* 1 1/2 cups.

Mrs. Brandon Key, *Clarksville*

Tangy Lemon Sauce

1 CUP SUGAR

2 1/2 TABLESPOONS CORNSTARCH

2 CUPS WATER

2 EGG YOLKS, SLIGHTLY BEATEN

2 TEASPOONS GRATED LEMON RIND

1/3 TO 1/2 CUP LEMON JUICE

2 TABLESPOONS BUTTER

Combine sugar and cornstarch in saucepan. Gradually add water, blending until smooth. Cook over medium heat, stirring constantly, until mixture is thick and clear. Remove from heat. Blend about 1/2 cup of hot mixture into egg yolks. Add to hot mixture in pan and cook 2 minutes. Add lemon juice, rind and butter. Serve warm or cold. Sauce may be refrigerated and re-heated. *Yield:* 2 3/4 cups.

Mrs. E. L. Rawlings, Jr., *Oak Ridge*

Caramel Pecan Sauce

1 TABLESPOON ALL-PURPOSE FLOUR

1/2 CUP WHITE SUGAR

1/2 CUP BROWN SUGAR

1 TABLESPOON WHITE CORN SYRUP

DASH SALT

1 TABLESPOON BUTTER

3/4 CUP WATER

1 CUP PECANS

Combine flour and sugar and blend. Add remaining ingredients except pecans and heat to a rolling boil. Add the pecans and continue cooking until mixture forms a very soft ball. Serve on ice cream hot or cold. (If sauce is too thick, add a little water and cook until blended.)

Sherron De Vos, *Fairfield Glade*

Chapter Four

Salads and Dressings

Salads

Chicken Salad

3 CUPS CHICKEN, COOKED AND DICED
1½ CUPS CELERY, DICED
3 TEASPOONS LEMON JUICE

1½ CUPS SEEDLESS GREEN GRAPES
¾ CUP TOASTED SLIVERED ALMONDS

Combine chicken, celery, and lemon juice; chill 1 hour. Add grapes and almonds.

Dressing:

1 CUP MAYONNAISE
¼ CUP LIGHT CREAM
1½ TEASPOONS SALT

WHITE PEPPER
1 TEASPOON DRY MUSTARD

Mix dressing ingredients and combine with chicken mixture. *Yield:* 6 servings.

Mrs. McKinnie Weaver (Peggy), *Hickory Valley*

Lettuce Salad

1 HEAD LETTUCE, TORN INTO BITE SIZE PIECES
1 CUP CELERY, DICED
6 EGGS, HARD BOILED AND SLICED
1 10-OUNCE PACKAGE FROZEN PEAS, UNCOOKED

½ CUP GREEN PEPPERS, DICED
1 MEDIUM ONION, CHOPPED
1 CAN SLICED WATER CHESTNUTS
8 SLICES BACON, COOKED AND CRUMBLED

Layer each item as listed above in a 9 x 12 inch casserole dish. Spread dressing on top of all.

Dressing:

2 CUPS SALAD DRESSING
1½ TABLESPOONS SUGAR

Mix well. Sprinkle grated cheese over top if desired.

Betty Johnson, *Antioch*
Becky Makamson, *Lebanon*

Three Green Melody

1 PACKAGE FROZEN FRENCH STYLE GREEN
   BEANS

1 PACKAGE FROZEN BABY LIMA BEANS
1 PACKAGE FROZEN PEAS

Cook and salt frozen vegetables according to the package directions. When cooled, mix with the following sauce.

Sauce:

1 SMALL ONION, FINELY MINCED
2 EGGS, HARD BOILED AND GRATED
1 TEASPOON MUSTARD

1½ TEASPOONS WORCESTERSHIRE SAUCE
1½ TEASPOONS LEMON JUICE
   DASH TABASCO
1 CUP MAYONNAISE

Make sauce the day before and refrigerate. Take from refrigerator and let set to room temperature while the vegetables cook. Blend and add to cooked vegetables. Place in casserole dish sprayed with Pam, top with Pepperidge Farms cornbread stuffing crumbs. Heat in a 325 degree oven for 20 minutes or until bubbly. This can also be served cold as a salad, omitting crumb topping.

Judy Jackson, *Blountville*

Sauerkraut Salad

1 NO. 3 CAN SHREDDED SAUERKRAUT
½ CUP CELERY, CHOPPED
½ CUP GREEN PEPPER, CHOPPED
½ CUP ONION, CHOPPED

2 TABLESPOONS CHOPPED PIMENTO
½ CUP SUGAR
¼ CUP ALL-PURPOSE OIL
¼ CUP VINEGAR

Combine sauerkraut, celery, green pepper, onion, and pimento in a separate bowl. Mix together sugar, oil, vinegar. Pour over sauerkraut mixture. Cover and refrigerate at least 12 hours, stirring once or twice.

Mildred A. Booher, *Bristol*

Marinated Cole Slaw

4 CUPS CABBAGE, SHREDDED
1 ONION, THINLY SLICED
1 CARROT, SHREDDED
1 GREEN PEPPER, THINLY SLICED
½ CUP SUGAR

¾ CUP VINEGAR
¼ CUP WATER
¼ CUP WESSON OIL
½ TEASPOON SALT

Combine all vegetables and toss. Mix together the dressing and pour over vegetables. Cover and refrigerate at least 4 hours before serving.

Susan Lee Wilson, *Johnson City*

Bean Salad

1 NO. 2 CAN FRENCH CUT GREEN BEANS
1 NO. 2 CAN WAX BEANS (LIBBY BLUE LAKE)
1 NO. 2 CAN KIDNEY BEANS

1 LARGE ONION, CHOPPED
1/2 TO 1 CUP GREEN AND RED SWEET PEPPER, CHOPPED

Drain beans well; combine in large bowl. Add onion and pepper.

Sauce:

1½ CUPS SUGAR
2/3 CUP VINEGAR
2/3 CUP WESSON OIL

2 TEASPOONS SALT
2 TEASPOONS BLACK PEPPER
1 TABLESPOON CELERY SEED

Mix and pour over vegetables to season at least overnight. When ready to serve, strain off sauce and save to return to leftover salad or save for next time. It keeps well.

Mrs. Pauline Watkins, *Clarksville*

Pretzel Salad

2 CUPS PRETZELS, CRUSHED
1/2 CUP SUGAR

3/4 CUP MARGARINE, MELTED

Mix above ingredients together and spread in a 9 x 13 inch pan. Bake in a 350 degree oven for 10 minutes. Let cool.

1 8-OUNCE PACKAGE CREAM CHEESE, SOFTENED

1 CUP SUGAR
1 10-OUNCE CARTON WHIPPED TOPPING

Mix cream cheese, sugar and topping together. Spread on top of cooled pretzel layer.

1 6-OUNCE PACKAGE STRAWBERRY JELLO
2 CUPS BOILING WATER

2 10-OUNCE PACKAGES FROZEN STRAWBERRIES WITH JUICE

Dissolve Jello in boiling water; add strawberries. Let partially set. When Jello mixture is partially firm, spread on top of cheese layer and chill thoroughly.

Variations: You may use 3 tablespoons sugar instead of 1 cup. If desired, use unsalted pretzels and unsweetened Jello.

Helen F. Murphy, *Lenoir City*
Betty J. Anglin, *Jonesborough*
Mrs. Sena Smith, *Bristol*

Sour Cream Potato Salad

⅓ CUP ITALIAN SALAD DRESSING	5 EGGS, HARD BOILED
6 CUPS HOT POTATOES, COOKED AND CUBED	1 CUP MAYONNAISE
1 CUP CELERY, SLICED	½ CUP SOUR CREAM
⅓ CUP ONION, CHOPPED	2 TABLESPOONS HORSERADISH MUSTARD

Pour Italian dressing over hot cubed potatoes. Chill about 2 hours. Mix chopped celery, onions, eggs, mayonnaise, sour cream and mustard. Pour over potatoes and mix well. Chill at least 2 hours before serving.

Mrs. Willie B. Gilliam, *Lenoir City*

Baked Potato Salad

1 MEDIUM ONION, FINELY CHOPPED	½ CUP WATER
¼ CUP SALAD OIL OR SHORTENING	¼ CUP VINEGAR
1 TABLESPOON ALL-PURPOSE FLOUR	6 CUPS POTATOES, COOKED AND CUBED
1 TEASPOON SUGAR	1 CUP CELERY, DICED
¼ TEASPOON PAPRIKA	¼ CUP GREEN PEPPER, DICED
1 TABLESPOON DRY MUSTARD	½ POUND SLICED CHEESE
1 TEASPOON SEASONED SALT	1 PIMENTO, CUT IN STRIPS

Sauté onion in oil until soft. Stir in flour, sugar, paprika, mustard, and salt. Slowly add water and vinegar. Cook over medium heat, stirring constantly until thickened and bubbly. Combine potatoes, celery, green pepper, and sauce. Spoon half of mixture into buttered 1½-quart casserole. Reserve 2 or 3 cheese slices for garnish, arrange remainder over potato layer. Top with rest of potato mixture. Cut reserve cheese slices into triangles. Arrange around edge of casserole, and garnish with pimento strips. Bake in a 350 degree oven 15 to 20 minutes or until cheese is nicely melted and salad is hot. Serve at once.

Glendith Brady, *Crossville*

Pea Salad

2 CUPS GREEN PEAS, DRAINED	1 TABLESPOON SALAD DRESSING
½ CUP PICKLES AND JUICE, CHOPPED	4 EGGS, HARD BOILED AND CHOPPED
¼ CUP ONIONS, CHOPPED	1 TEASPOON SALT
1 CUP VELVEETA CHEESE, CUBED	1 CUP TOMATOES, CHOPPED
1 TABLESPOON MUSTARD	

Mix all ingredients together. Chill and serve.

Jane Mee, *Cookeville*

Garden Rice Salad

1 6-OUNCE PACKAGE LONG GRAIN AND WILD RICE MIX	1 CUP TOMATO, CUBED
1/2 CUP MAYONNAISE	1/2 CUP CUCUMBER, DICED
1/3 CUP PLAIN YOGURT	2 TABLESPOONS PARSLEY, CHOPPED
1 CUP CELERY, SLICED	1/8 TEASPOON SEASONED SALT
	1/8 TEASPOON PEPPER

Cook rice as directed on package; omit butter or margarine, cool. Toss lightly with next 8 ingredients. Cover, chill. *Yield:* 4½ cups.

Gabriele Eisemann, *Clarksville*

Hot Fruit Casserole

1 PACKAGE DRIED PITTED PRUNES GROUND CINNAMON	2 SMALL CANS MANDARIN ORANGES, DRAINED
1 PACKAGE DRIED APRICOTS	1 25-OUNCE JAR MUSSELMAN'S CHERRY PIE FILLING
1 LARGE CAN PINEAPPLE CHUNKS, DRAINED	

Place prunes in Pyrex casserole and sprinkle with cinnamon. Layer, and sprinkle with cinnamon, apricots, pineapple chunks, mandarin oranges and cherry pie filling. Bake in pre-heated oven at 325 degrees for 30 or 40 minutes. Keeps well.

Mrs. Peggy Mowrey, *Nashville*

Orange Jello Salad

2 3-OUNCE BOXES ORANGE JELLO	1 CUP OR MORE APPLES, DICED
1 NO. 303 CAN CRUSHED PINEAPPLE, DRAINED (SAVE JUICE FOR TOPPING)	1 CUP OR MORE BANANAS, DICED
	1 SMALL CAN ORANGES, DRAINED

Make Jello following instructions, using only 3½ cups boiling water. Stir pineapple, apples, bananas and oranges into Jello, chill.

Topping:

1 EGG	1½ TABLESPOONS CORN STARCH
1/2 CUP PINEAPPLE OR ORANGE JUICE	1 8-OUNCE PACKAGE WHIPPED TOPPING
2 TABLESPOONS SUGAR	

Beat egg into juice. Add sugar, then corn starch. Mix well; no lumps. Cook until thick like a pudding, stirring constantly. Cover and cool, so it doesn't get a hard crust on top. Then add the whipped topping. Place topping on top of Jello. Chill, or serve and enjoy!

Kathy Dowda, *Kingsport*

Tomato Aspic

2½ CUPS TOMATO JUICE	1 TABLESPOON LEMON JUICE
1 TEASPOON INSTANT MINCED ONION	1 TABLESPOON WORCESTERSHIRE SAUCE
1 BAY LEAF	1 TABLESPOON PREPARED HORSERADISH
1 3-OUNCE PACKAGE LEMON GELATIN	1 CUP CELERY, CHOPPED

Combine tomato juice, onion and bay leaf. Heat to boiling. Remove bay leaf. Pour hot tomato juice over lemon gelatin, and stir until dissolved. Stir in lemon juice, Worcestershire sauce, and horseradish. Chill until slightly thickened. Fold in celery. Pour into 1-quart ring mold or an 8-inch square dish. Garnish with sliced stuffed olives. *Yield:* 8 servings.

Glendith Brady, *Crossville*

Five Cup Salad

1 CUP MANDARIN ORANGE SECTIONS	1 CUP MINIATURE MARSHMALLOWS
1 CUP PINEAPPLE CHUNKS	1 CUP COCONUT
1 CUP SOUR CREAM	

Mix all ingredients together and let stand overnight. *Yield:* 8 servings.
Variations: For *Six Cup Salad* add 1 cup chopped nuts. For *Seven Cup Salad* add 1 cup chopped nuts and 1 small package orange Jello.

Mrs. Sue Gray Walker, *Knoxville*
Mrs. Pauline Watkins, *Clarksville*
Mrs. Wanda Powers, *Old Hickory*
Mrs. Jean Pierce, *Manchester*

Blueberry Salad

2 3-OUNCE PACKAGES BLACKBERRY GELATIN	1 15-OUNCE CAN BLUEBERRIES
2 CUPS BOILING WATER	1 8¼-OUNCE CAN CRUSHED PINEAPPLE

Dissolve gelatin in boiling water, drain blueberries and pineapple. Use juices and add enough water to make 1 cup. Add this liquid to the gelatin mixture. When cool, add the drained blueberries and pineapple. Refrigerate and allow to jell.

Topping:

1 8-OUNCE PACKAGE CREAM CHEESE	½ TEASPOON VANILLA
½ CUP SUGAR	½ CUP NUTS (PECANS), CHOPPED
½ PINT SOUR CREAM	

Let cream cheese soften at room temperature. Add sour cream and other ingredients. Beat until smooth. Spread over jelled gelatin mixture.

Mrs Robert (Myrtle) Hutcheson, *Columbia*
Lynn Toy, *Huntingdon*

Molded Ambrosia

I like this because it can be used as a dessert also. It is very pretty at Thanksgiving or for the fall months. It is very good, and I always have many compliments when I serve it.

1 CUP GRAHAM CRACKER CRUMBS	⅓ CUP SUGAR
¼ CUP BUTTER OR MARGARINE, MELTED	1 CUP HOT WATER
1 9-OUNCE CAN CRUSHED PINEAPPLE	1 CUP DAIRY SOUR CREAM
1 3-OUNCE PACKAGE ORANGE FLAVORED GELATIN	¼ TEASPOON VANILLA
	1 CUP MANDARIN ORANGES, DICED
	½ CUP FLAKED COCONUT

Combine crumbs and butter, reserve ⅓ cup for topping. Press remaining crumbs into an 8 x 8 x 2 inch baking dish. Drain pineapple, reserving liquid. Dissolve gelatin and sugar in hot water. Stir in reserved syrup. Chill until partially set. Add sour cream and vanilla, whip until fluffy. Fold in the pineapple, oranges and coconut. Pour into crumb dish. Sprinkle with reserved crumbs. Chill until firm. Cut into squares, trim with cherries if desired. *Yield:* 9 servings.

Bonnye W. Allen, *Decaturville*

Pistachio Salad

1 PACKAKGE INSTANT PISTACHIO PUDDING AND PIE FILLING MIX	½ CUP MINIATURE MARSHMALLOWS
1 20-OUNCE CAN CRUSHED PINEAPPLE, UNDRAINED	½ CUP PECANS, CHOPPED
	1 8-OUNCE CARTON COOL WHIP

Pour dry pudding mix over undrained pineapple and mix. Add marshmallows and nuts. Slowly fold in Cool Whip. Refrigerate 3 to 4 hours. *Yield:* 6 to 8 servings.

Barbara Vawter DeFur, *Jackson*

Arley's Apple Salad

6 APPLES	2 TABLESPOONS ORANGE JUICE
1 BANANA, DICED	1 TABLESPOON SUGAR OR HONEY
½ CUP RAISINS, SOAKED UNTIL PLUMP	1 TEASPOON DRIED ORANGE PEEL
½ CUP WALNUTS, CHOPPED (OPTIONAL)	½ TEASPOON GROUND CELERY SEED
¾ CUP MIRACLE WHIP SALAD DRESSING	½ TEASPOON CINNAMON

Peel and dice apples. Add banana, raisins and nuts. Mix remaining ingredients and pour over fruit, stirring until coated.

William A. Dupuy, *Clarksville*

Frozen Fruit Salad

1 LARGE PACKAGE CREAM CHEESE
1/2 CUP ORANGE JUICE
1/2 CUP CONFECTIONERS' SUGAR

1 TEASPOON VANILLA
1 CUP CRUSHED PINEAPPLE, DRAINED
1/2 CUP PECANS, FINELY CHOPPED

Soften cheese with orange juice. Add sugar and vanilla, pineapple and nuts. Freeze in casserole dish sprayed with Pam. *Yield:* 8 servings.
Note: Chopped maraschino cherries may be added for color.

Sue Brummel Harris, *Humboldt*

Yum Yum Jello Salad

1 SMALL CAN CRUSHED PINEAPPLE
WATER
1 PACKAGE ORANGE JELLO
1 PINT VANILLA ICE CREAM

1 1/2 CUPS SHARP CHEDDAR CHEESE, GRATED
1 TABLESPOON LEMON JUICE
1 TABLESPOON MAYONNAISE
PINCH OF SALT

Drain juice off pineapple and add water to make 1 cup liquid. Boil juice, remove from heat, add Jello and dissolve. Add ice cream and stir well. Add other ingredients and pinch of salt. Let set for at least 2 hours to congeal before serving. Will keep for some time in refrigerator.

Mrs. Beth Ghormley Spurling, *Madisonville*

Cranberry Salad

2 SMALL PACKAGES RED RASPBERRY JELLO
1 CUP BOILING WATER
1/4 CUP COLD WATER
1 CUP FRESH CRANBERRIES, GROUND
1 ORANGE, SEEDED AND GROUND

1 APPLE, CORED AND FINELY CHOPPED
1 SMALL CAN CRUSHED PINEAPPLE, DRAINED
1 CUP PECANS, CHOPPED
1 1/4 CUPS SUGAR

Dissolve the Jello with the boiling water and add cold water and chill. Mix remaining ingredients and fold into chilled Jello. Chill until set. *Yield:* 10 to 12 servings.

Pat Tyler, *Alamo*

Apricot Salad

2 3-OUNCE PACKAGES ORANGE JELLO
2 CUPS BOILING WATER

1 MEDIUM CAN APRICOTS, DRAINED (SAVE THE JUICE)
1 MEDIUM CAN CRUSHED PINEAPPLE, DRAINED (SAVE THE JUICE)
1 CUP SMALL MARSHMALLOWS

Add 2 cups boiling water to the 2 packages of Jello. Stir well and add 1 cup of mixed juices that were drained from fruit, mix well. Refrigerate until partially set. Remove from refrigerator, cut up the apricots in pieces and add to mixture. Also add crushed pineapple and the marshmallows. Mix well and pour into large pan. Return to refrigerator to set completely.

Topping:

- 1 EGG, BEATEN
- 1 CUP MIXED JUICES
- 2 TABLESPOONS BUTTER
- 1/2 CUP SUGAR
- 3 TABLESPOONS ALL-PURPOSE FLOUR
- 2 TEASPOONS VINEGAR
- 1 MEDIUM CONTAINER COOL WHIP
  SHARP CHEDDAR CHEESE, SHREDDED

Combine ingredients, except Cool Whip and cheese, and cook on medium heat until thick, stirring constantly. Cool and cover Jello mixture with topping. Cover topping with Cool Whip and cheese. Refrigerate until ready to serve.

Susan Lee Wilson, *Johnson City*

Pink Party Salad

- 1 SMALL PACKAGE STRAWBERRY JELLO
- 2/3 CUP BOILING WATER
- 1 3-OUNCE PACKAGE CREAM CHEESE
- 1/2 CUP MAYONNAISE
- 1 SMALL CAN CRUSHED PINEAPPLE, DRAINED
- 1 CUP WHIPPED TOPPING
- 1/2 CUP NUTS, CHOPPED (OPTIONAL)

Dissolve Jello in boiling water and cool in refrigerator until it begins to thicken. Mix cream cheese, mayonnaise and pineapple. Add whipped cream or topping. Fold this mixture into chilled Jello. Add nuts. Pour into a 1-quart mold and chill until firm. Garnish with fresh strawberries. *Yield:* 6 servings.

Mrs. Jay E. Ellis, *Joelton*

George Washington Salad

- 2 SMALL BOXES CHERRY JELLO
- 2 CUPS BOILING WATER
- 1 NO. 2 CAN CRUSHED PINEAPPLE
- 1 CAN CHERRY PIE FILLING

Mix Jello in water, add undrained pineapple and pie filling. Let set, then add topping.

- 1 8-OUNCE PACKAGE CREAM CHEESE
- 1 CARTON SOUR CREAM
- 1/2 CUP CONFECTIONERS' SUGAR
- 1 TEASPOON VANILLA
- 1/2 CUP NUTS, CHOPPED

Combine all ingredients except nuts, mix well. Cover with chopped nuts. Keep refrigerated.

Norma Fraker, *Clinton*

Dressings
Russian Salad Dressing

1 SMALL ONION
1½ CUPS SUGAR
1 CAN TOMATO SOUP
1 CUP WHITE VINEGAR
1½ CUPS SALAD OIL
2 SMALL CLOVES GARLIC

1½ TABLESPOONS DRY MUSTARD
1½ TABLESPOONS WORCESTERSHIRE SAUCE
1½ TABLESPOONS SALT
½ TEASPOON PEPPER
1 TEASPOON PAPRIKA

Mix all ingredients in blender until smooth. *Yield:* 1 quart.

Julia Cooper, *Oak Ridge*

Uncle John's French Dressing

1 CUP WESSON OIL
¼ CUP VINEGAR
⅓ CUP SUGAR
1 TEASPOON SALT
1 TABLESPOON TOMATO CATSUP

2 HEAPING TEASPOONS PAPRIKA
1 TEASPOON CHILI POWDER
½ TEASPOON GARLIC
DASH CAYENNE PEPPER
1 ONION, SCRAPED

Mix all ingredients. Slowly stir in Wesson oil. Refrigerate.

Mrs. Campbell M. Sowell, *Columbia*

Honey Dressing

½ CUP SUGAR
1 TEASPOON DRY MUSTARD
1 TEASPOON PAPRIKA
1 TEASPOON CELERY SEEDS
⅓ CUP HONEY

⅓ CUP VINEGAR
1 TABLESPOON GRATED ONION
1 TABLESPOON LEMON JUICE
1 CUP VEGETABLE OIL
¼ TEASPOON SALT

Mix ingredients in blender. This is delicious over fresh fruit.

Carolyn Barnett, *Humboldt*

Roquefort Dressing

1 CUP ROQUEFORT CHEESE, CHOPPED
1 CUP FRENCH DRESSING

1 CUP MAYONNAISE

Mix ingredients and keep in refrigerator.

Belle B. Broadbent, *Clarksville*

Chapter Five

Breads

Oyster Stuffing

1 CUP BUTTER, MELTED	1/4 TEASPOON PEPPER
1/2 CUP ONIONS, FINELY CHOPPED	2 TEASPOONS SAGE
1/2 CUP CELERY, CHOPPED	2 1/2 TO 3 1/2 QUARTS BREAD (2/3 BISCUITS TO 1/3 CORNBREAD)
1 QUART OYSTERS AND THEIR LIQUID	MILK (IF NEEDED)
1/2 TEASPOON SALT	

Heat butter. Add onions, celery and chopped oysters. Add seasonings and bread; mix together. Add some milk if needed to moisten. Divide contents into 2 9-inch pie pans. Bake in a 375 degree oven for 45 to 60 minutes.

Doris Melton, *Sweetwater*

Hush Puppies

1 CUP MEAL	1 PINCH SUGAR
1/2 CUP ALL-PURPOSE FLOUR	1 TEASPOON SALT
1 EGG	1 CUP ONION, GRATED
1 HEAPING TABLESPOON BAKING POWDER	SWEET MILK AS NEEDED
1/2 CUP CRACKER MEAL	

Mix ingredients and add enough sweet milk to make a soft ball. Drop by spoonsful into deep fat.

Lucille Pitt, *Newbern*

Velvet Waffles

3 EGGS, SEPARATED	4 TEASPOONS BAKING POWDER
1 3/4 CUPS MILK	1 TEASPOON SALT
1/2 CUP WESSON OIL	2 CUPS ALL-PURPOSE FLOUR

Separate eggs and beat yolks until light. Stir milk into beaten yolks and add Wesson oil. Stir this mixture gradually into dry ingredients. Beat whites well and then fold them into mixture. Bake on hot waffle iron until browned.

Julia Cooper, *Oak Ridge*

Best Tasting Dressing (for Chicken and Turkey)

1/4 CUP ONION, FINELY CHOPPED
1/2 TEASPOON BLACK PEPPER
3/4 CUP BUTTER, MELTED
4 CUPS CRUMBLED BISCUITS

3 CUPS CRUMBLED CORN BREAD
2 TEASPOONS SALT
1 CUP CELERY, CHOPPED
1 TEASPOON POULTRY SEASONING
2 CUPS BROTH FROM GIBLETS (COOKED)

Brown the onion and celery in butter in a heavy skillet. Combine with bread cubes and seasonings. Pour on the broth and stir lightly to blend. Stuff fowl and roast according to weight of bird. This amount of dressing is for a 4 to 5 pound bird; for larger fowl, double the amount.

Note: If you would rather bake the dressing in a dish than roast in bird, put ingredients in a casserole dish and cover. Bake in a 345 degree oven for 20 minutes. Uncover and bake for 10 more minutes.

Willie Mae Carter, *Lexington*

Jalapeno Cornbread

3 CUPS CORN MEAL
2 1/2 CUPS COLD MILK
1/2 CUP VEGETABLE OIL
3 EGGS, BEATEN
1 LARGE ONION, GRATED
3 TABLESPOONS SUGAR

3 STRIPS BACON, CRISPED AND CRUMBLED
1 SMALL JAR PIMENTOS
1 CAN CREAMED CORN
1 TEASPOON JALAPENO PEPPERS, FINELY CHOPPED
1 1/2 CUPS AMERICAN CHEESE, GRATED

Mix in order as given above. Bake in large, greased baking dish in a 400 degree oven for 25 to 30 minutes until golden brown. Do not overcook, or the cornbread will be soggy.

Pam Savage, *Sparta*

Cornbread

1 CUP BUTTERMILK
1 CUP WATER
1 EGG
1 TEASPOON HONEY

1/2 TEASPOON SODA
1/2 TEASPOON BAKING POWDER
SELF-RISING FLOUR
PLAIN MEAL

Mix buttermilk, water, egg, honey, baking soda and baking powder in mixing bowl. Add equal amounts of flour and meal to make batter just right. Place mixture in flat cake pan and bake in a 450 to 500 degree oven until bread is browned on top, usually about 15 minutes.

Note: Fresh ground meal is much better than factory bolted meal. When I can get home ground meal in the Fall, I sift it, place it in glass jars, seal it, and keep in deep freeze for freshness.

Mrs. John L. Seawell, *Crossville*

Annie Lewis, her two sons and two daughters, and their children gather in Chattanooga for a three-day family reunion.

Robin Hood

Crackling Bread

2¾ CUPS CORN MEAL	2 EGGS, BEATEN
1 TEASPOON SALT	1 TEASPOON BAKING POWDER
1 TEASPOON SODA	¼ CUP BACON DRIPPING GREASE
1½ CUPS BUTTERMILK	1½ CUPS CRACKLINGS, DICED

Combine and sift together dry ingredients. Add well beaten eggs, buttermilk and bacon grease; stir until well blended, adding diced cracklings. Bake in a 400 degree oven for 35 minutes. Serve *hot*.

Ruby Lucille Plant, *Memphis*

Mexican Cornbread

1½ CUPS SELF-RISING CORN MEAL	2 EGGS
1 CUP CHEDDAR CHEESE, GRATED	1 CUP ONION, CHOPPED
1 CUP BUTTERMILK	2 OR 3 HOT PEPPERS, CHOPPED
⅔ CUP COOKING OIL	1 SMALL CAN CREAM STYLE CORN

Mix all ingredients lightly and bake in an 8 or 9-inch baking dish or iron skillet in a 350 degree oven for 45 minutes or until done.

Mrs. Tom Bullifin, *Brownsville*

East Tennessee Cornbread

1 EGG	½ TEASPOON SALT
1 TABLESPOON OIL	1 CUP BUTTERMILK
¾ CUP PLAIN MEAL	½ TEASPOON SODA
1 TEASPOON BAKING POWDER	1 TEASPOON WATER

Put oil in mixing bowl; stir in the egg. Add the meal, baking powder, salt and buttermilk. Mix, then add the soda, dissolved in the water, and mix. Batter will be thin. Pour into a very hot and well-greased 8½-inch cast-iron skillet and bake in a 500 degree oven for 15 minutes.

Mrs. R. P. Thomas, *Oak Ridge*

Johnny Cake

1 CUP SELF-RISING FLOUR
3/4 CUP CORNMEAL
1/4 CUP SUGAR
1 EGG, BEATEN

2 TABLESPOONS SHORTENING OR MARGARINE
1 CUP MILK

Mix dry ingredients. Melt shortening in pan, then add to egg and milk. Add this to dry ingredients, mix and pour into pan. (An iron skillet may be used instead of a pan.) Bake in a 400 degree oven for 30 minutes. Cut and spread with butter like cornbread.

Mary Crowell Walker, *Maryville*

Southern Spoon Bread

This was my aunt's favorite. It is a very old recipe.

2 CUPS WHITE CORN MEAL
2 1/2 CUPS WATER, BOILING
1 1/2 TABLESPOONS BUTTER, MELTED
1 1/2 TEASPOONS SALT

2 EGG YOLKS, LIGHTLY BEATEN
1 TEASPOON SODA
1/2 CUP BUTTERMILK
2 EGG WHITES, BEATEN STIFF

Add corn meal gradually to boiling water and let stand a few minutes. Add butter, salt and egg yolks; dissolve baking soda in buttermilk and add. Fold in egg whites. Turn into a buttered casserole. Bake in a 375 degree oven for 40 minutes.

Mrs. Nathan Fox, *Columbia*

Tennessee Cornlight Bread

2 TABLESPOONS CRISCO SHORTENING
2 CUPS SELF-RISING CORNMEAL
1/2 CUP SELF-RISING FLOUR

3/4 CUP WHITE SUGAR
1 PACKAGE DRY YEAST
2 CUPS BUTTERMILK

Melt shortening in loaf pan. In a separate bowl, add cornmeal, flour, sugar. Sift together and add yeast. Add buttermilk; mix well. Add melted shortening to mixture; stir. Pour mixture into loaf pan. Bake in a 375 degree oven for 45 minutes.

Vickie Ghee Stinson (Mrs. Ron), *Chapel Hill*

Pop Up Rolls

1 CUP SELF-RISING FLOUR

1 TABLESPOON MAYONNAISE

1/2 CUP MILK

2 TABLESPOONS SUGAR

Mix all ingredients well. Melt a pat of butter in each muffin tin (or grease with oil). Pour mixture into muffin tins and bake in a 350 degree oven until golden brown. *Yield:* 9 rolls.

Malinda Pafford, *Camden*

Gran's Sweet Potato Rolls

One of those absolutely guaranteed no-fail recipes.

1 PACKAGE ACTIVE DRY YEAST

1½ CUPS WARM WATER (105 TO 115 DEGREES)

1/3 CUP SUGAR

1¼ TEASPOONS SALT

2/3 CUP SHORTENING

2 EGGS

1 CUP LUKEWARM MASHED SWEET POTATOES

7 TO 7½ CUPS ALL-PURPOSE FLOUR

SOFT MARGARINE OR BUTTER

In mixing bowl, dissolve yeast in warm water. Stir in sugar, salt, shortening, eggs, sweet potatoes and half the flour. Mix in remaining flour until dough is easy to handle.

Turn dough onto lightly floured board and knead until smooth and elastic, about 5 minutes. Put into greased bowl; turn dough so a greased side is up; cover with plastic wrap. Refrigerate.

Two hours before baking, divide dough into 2 halves. Roll each half into a 16-inch circle, about ¼ inch thick. Spread with soft margarine. Cut each circle into 16 wedges.

Beginning at rounded edge, roll each triangle up. Place point underneath on baking sheet. Let rise until light, about 1 hour.

Bake in a 400 degree oven for 15 to 20 minutes.

Mrs. Andrew P. Davis, *Nashville*

Quick Batter Yeast Rolls

1 PACKAGE ACTIVE DRY YEAST

3/4 CUP MILK, SCALDED

3/4 CUP VERY WARM WATER

2 TABLESPOONS SUGAR

4 TABLESPOONS VEGETABLE OIL

1/4 TEASPOON SALT

3 CUPS SELF-RISING FLOUR

In large mixing bowl, dissolve yeast in warm milk and water mixture. Stir in sugar, oil and salt. Add flour and mix well. Spoon into greased muffin pans. Bake in a 425 degree oven about 15 minutes or until brown. Tops may be brushed with butter before baking if desired. *Yield:* 12 to 18 rolls.

Mrs. Sanford Downs, *Martin*

Friendship Yeast Rolls

When I moved to Friendship, Tennessee, my neighbors had a pan of these rolls rising on my cabinet for me to bake for supper. This recipe was used all over the area for school and church suppers and family meals. Since it kept so well in the refrigerator, we were seldom without some roll dough.

11 CUPS ALL-PURPOSE FLOUR, SIFTED	6 TABLESPOONS WARM WATER
1 CUP SHORTENING, MELTED	4 CUPS MILK
1 CUP SUGAR	2 TABLESPOONS BAKING POWDER
1 PACKAGE ACTIVE DRY YEAST (OR 1 CAKE COMPRESSED YEAST)	1 TABLESPOON SODA
	1 TABLESPOON SALT

Scald together the milk, shortening and sugar. Cool to lukewarm (about 85 degrees). Dissolve yeast in 3 tablespoons of slightly warm water and add to milk mixture along with 4 cups flour. Stir until all the flour is moistened. Let this sponge rise in a warm place for about 2 hours, until doubled. Dissolve the baking powder, soda, and salt in 3 tablespoons warm water. Add this to the risen sponge and enough flour for a soft dough (approximately 6 to 7 cups). Knead about 200 times. Shape rolls and place in a greased muffin tin. Set in a warm place and let rise until double. Bake in a 400 degree oven for 18 to 20 minutes. *Yield:* approximately 100 Parker House or Cloverleaf rolls.

Note: The dough will keep in the refrigerator for 5 days. Grease the top and cover to store. Pinch off the amount needed for each batch and return the rest to the refrigerator. Shape rolls and let rise and cook as above.

To freeze dough, after kneading and rising, punch down and make packets of unshaped dough. Wrap in foil and freeze. To use, let thaw 2 hours, shape rolls, let rise and cook. This is a basic roll recipe and can be used for cinnamon rolls.

Zora Shofner Brasher, *Martin*

Des' Rolls

½ CUP SHORTENING	2 EGGS
2 CUPS WARM MILK	½ TEASPOON SODA
½ CUP SUGAR	2 TEASPOONS BAKING POWDER
½ CUP MASHED POTATOES	2 TEASPOONS SALT
¼ CUP WARM WATER	6 CUPS ALL-PURPOSE FLOUR
3 PACKAGES YEAST	

Warm together first 4 ingredients; set aside. Dissolve yeast in ¼ cup warm water, then add other warm ingredients. Sift flour with soda, baking powder, and salt. Add eggs to warm ingredients. Add flour as you stir. Let rise in refrigerator; keep covered. Punch down, knead, roll out and shape into rolls. May keep part of the dough in the refrigerator if desired, will keep a week. Bake in a 350 degree oven until brown as desired.

Bonnie Henderson, *Clinton*

Apple Butter Nut Bread

2 CUPS ALL-PURPOSE FLOUR
1 TEASPOON BAKING POWDER
1/4 TEASPOON SODA
1 TEASPOON CINNAMON
1 1/4 TEASPOONS NUTMEG
1 CUP CRISCO OIL

3 EGGS
1 CUP SUGAR
3/4 CUP SMUCKER'S APPLE BUTTER
1/2 CUP RAISINS, BOILED AND DRAINED
1/2 CUP PECANS, CHOPPED

Sift flour, baking powder, soda and spices together. Cream oil, eggs and sugar. Add apple butter, raisins and nuts to the oil, eggs and sugar. Then add the sifted dry ingredients; mix well. Pour into a 9 x 5 inch loaf pan. Bake in a 375 degree oven for about 1 1/2 hours. *Yield:* 1 loaf.

Mrs. Ruby Plant, *Memphis*

Apricot Bread

1 PACKAGE DRIED APRICOTS
WARM WATER
2 CUPS SIFTED ALL-PURPOSE FLOUR
1 TEASPOON SALT
1/2 TEASPOON SODA
2 TABLESPOONS BUTTER

1 CUP SUGAR
1 EGG
1/2 CUP ORANGE JUICE
1/4 CUP MILK
1/2 CUP NUTS

Wash apricots, cover with warm water. Let stand 20 minutes, drain and cut into small pieces.

Sift flour, salt and soda together; set aside. Blend butter and sugar together; mix well. Add egg, beat until light and fluffy. Add orange juice and milk; mix well. Stir in dry ingredients, blend until smooth. Add nuts and apricots. Pour into greased loaf pan. Bake in a 350 degree oven for about 1 hour.

When bread is cool, wrap in aluminum foil. Store in refrigerator overnight to ripen. Slice thinly and spread with softened cream cheese for a snack or party sandwiches. *Yield:* 1 loaf.

Reba A. Jones, *Clinton*

Banana Nut Bread

1/2 CUP VEGETABLE OIL
1 CUP SUGAR
2 EGGS, BEATEN
3 BANANAS, MASHED TO A PULP
2 CUPS SIFTED FLOUR
1 TEASPOON SODA

1/2 TEASPOON BAKING POWDER
1/2 TEASPOON SALT
3 TABLESPOONS MILK
1/2 TEASPOON VANILLA
1/2 CUP CHOPPED NUTS

Beat oil and sugar together. Add eggs and bananas; beat well. Sift flour, soda, baking powder and salt. Add to first mixture with milk and vanilla. Beat well and stir in nuts. Pour into a 9 x 5 inch greased and floured pan or two 7½ x 4 inch pans. Bake in a 350 degree oven about 45 minutes or until done.

Moiselle Newsom, *Newbern*

Carrot Bread

2 CUPS ALL-PURPOSE FLOUR	1 TEASPOON VANILLA
2 TEASPOONS BAKING POWDER	2 CUPS GRATED CARROTS
2 TEASPOONS CINNAMON	3 EGGS, BEATEN
½ TEASPOON SALT	½ CUP RAISINS
1½ CUPS SUGAR	½ CUP FLAKED COCONUT
1 CUP SALAD OIL	½ CUP NUTS, CHOPPED

Sift together dry ingredients, add oil, vanilla, carrots and eggs and blend thoroughly. Fold in raisins, coconut and nuts. Bake in 2 small pans or 1 large pan in a 350 degree oven for 1 hour and 15 minutes.

Lola McWhirter, *Newbern*

Jule Kaga

A Norwegian Christmas bread passed down to me from my mother and from her mother. My mother used to bake Jule Kaga at Christmas for family and friends. Now I am carrying on the tradition.

¾ CUP MILK	1 EGG, ROOM TEMPERATURE
3 TABLESPOONS SUGAR	3½ TO 4½ CUPS UNSIFTED FLOUR, DIVIDED
2 TABLESPOONS SALT	1 CUP SNIPPED PITTED DATES
½ CUP BUTTER	½ CUP CANDIED RED CHERRIES, CHOPPED
½ CUP WARM WATER (105 TO 115 DEGREES)	½ CUP PECANS, CHOPPED
2 PACKAGES ACTIVE DRY YEAST	¼ CUP CHOPPED CANDIED CITRON OR RAISINS

Scald milk, stir in sugar, salt, and butter. Cool to lukewarm. Measure warm water into large warm bowl. Sprinkle in yeast; stir until dissolved. Add lukewarm milk mixture, egg and 2 cups flour; beat until smooth. Stir in enough additional flour to make a stiff batter. Cover bowl tightly with aluminum foil. Refrigerate at least 2 hours or overnight. Punch dough down, turn out onto floured board. Knead in dates, cherries, pecans and citron. Divide dough in half. Roll each half into an 8 x 12 inch rectangle. Roll up, jelly roll fashion, from short end; seal edges. Place in 2 greased 8½ x 4½ x 2½ inch loaf pans. Cover; let rise in warm place, free from draft, until doubled in bulk, about 1½ hours. Bake in a 375 degree oven for 35 minutes or until done. Lightly cover loaves with aluminum foil during last 15 minutes of baking. Remove from pans and cool on wire racks.

Lynda Kunz Harper, *Mt. Juliet*

Old-Fashioned Gingerbread

From first edition of cookbook dated 1796.

2¾ CUPS ALL-PURPOSE FLOUR, SIFTED	½ CUP BUTTER, SOFTENED
1 TEASPOON SALT	½ CUP SUGAR
1 TEASPOON SODA	2 EGGS
2 TEASPOONS GINGER	1 CUP MOLASSES
1 TEASPOON CINNAMON	1 CUP BUTTERMILK

Sift together into mixing bowl flour, salt, soda, ginger and cinnamon. Cream butter until light and fluffy. Gradually add sugar to butter, beating well after each addition. Add eggs to creamed mixture one at a time. Stir in molasses; add dry ingredients alternately with buttermilk, and mix until smooth after each addition. Pour into buttered and floured 13 x 9 x 2 inch baking pan. Bake in a 350 degree oven 35 minutes or until tested done. Cool. Serve topped with slightly sweetened whipped cream and sliced bananas. *Yield:* 16 to 20 servings. May also be served with lemon sauce.

Mrs. E. L. Rawlings, Jr., *Oak Ridge*

Lemon Bread

¾ CUP BUTTER	¼ TEASPOON BAKING SODA
1½ CUPS SUGAR	¾ CUP BUTTERMILK
3 EGGS	GRATED RIND OF 1 LEMON
2¼ CUPS ALL-PURPOSE FLOUR	¾ CUP PECANS
¼ TEASPOON SALT	JUICE OF 2 LEMONS
	¾ CUP CONFECTIONERS' SUGAR

Cream butter and sugar, beat in eggs one at a time. Combine dry ingredients and add to the creamed mixture alternately with buttermilk. Stir in grated lemon rind and nuts.

Spoon into greased and floured 9 x 5 x 3 inch loaf pan. Bake in a 325 degree oven for 1 hour 20 minutes. Cool 15 minutes in pan, then remove to wire rack to cool completely. While loaf is baking, prepare glaze by combining powdered sugar and lemon juice. Let stand to allow sugar to dissolve. After removing loaf from pan, pierce top with tooth pick in a number of places and spoon glaze over loaf. This freezes well and is delicious.

Mrs. Robert (Myrtle) Hutcheson, *Columbia*

Monkey Bread

1 CUP MILK	1 TEASPOON SALT
1 CUP BUTTER OR MARGARINE, MELTED AND DIVIDED	1 PACKAGE DRY YEAST
4 TABLESPOONS SUGAR	3½ CUPS ALL-PURPOSE FLOUR

Combine milk, ½ cup butter, sugar and salt in a saucepan; heat until butter is melted. Cool to lukewarm; stir in yeast until dissolved. Place flour in a large bowl, make a well in flour and pour in liquid mixture. Stir until blended.

Cover and let rise until doubled in bulk, about 1 hour and 20 minutes. Turn dough out on a floured surface. Roll ¼ inch thick. Cut into 3-inch squares. Dip each square in remaining butter. Layer squares in a 10-inch tube or Bundt pan. Let rise until doubled in bulk, about 30 to 40 minutes. Bake in a 375 degree oven for 30 to 40 minutes.

Variation: Pour remaining melted butter over the squares before the last rising.

Carolyn Hileman Ruble (Mrs. J. H.), *Powell*
Margie Flynt, *Madison*

Edward Houston, owner of Old Time Bar-B-Q in Chattanooga, says the secret of his success is his sauce, "and I'm going to keep it that way—a secret." Houston smokes his meat six to eight hours over an open pit of smoldering hickory chips and bastes the meat ten times during the smoking process.

Bob Nichols

Oatmeal Bread

2 CUPS QUAKER OATS	2 CUPS COLD WATER
1 CUP BROWN SUGAR	4 PACKAGES YEAST
2 TABLESPOONS SALT	1/2 CUP WARM WATER
6 OUNCES VEGETABLE OIL	3 CUPS WHOLE WHEAT FLOUR
1/3 CUP SORGHUM MOLASSES	1/2 CUP WHEAT GERM
2 CUPS BOILING WATER	5 TO 8 CUPS ALL-PURPOSE FLOUR

Mix oats, brown sugar, salt, vegetable oil and molasses with 2 cups boiling water. Stir well. Add 2 cups cold water and set aside until just warm. Dissolve yeast in warm water. Add yeast, whole wheat flour and wheat germ to the first mixture. Mix thoroughly. Add white flour and knead until smooth. Place in large greased bowl, turning to grease sides of dough. Let rise for 1 1/2 hours. Punch down and divide into 4 greased loaf pans. Let rise again until doubled in bulk. Bake in a 350 degree oven for 40 to 45 minutes. *Yield:* 4 loaves.

Lucy L. Graves, *Humboldt*

Orange Slice Nut Bread

1 CUP CANDIED ORANGE SLICES, FINELY CHOPPED	2 1/2 CUPS SIFTED ALL-PURPOSE FLOUR
1 TABLESPOON SUGAR	2 TEASPOONS BAKING POWDER
1/4 CUP BUTTER	1/2 TEASPOON SODA
1/2 CUP SUGAR	1/2 TEASPOON SALT
1 EGG	1/2 CUP NUTS, CHOPPED
1/2 CUP (1) BANANA, MASHED	1 CUP MILK

Sprinkle chopped orange slices with 1 tablespoon sugar to prevent pieces from sticking together. Cream butter with sugar; add egg and banana and mix well. Sift dry ingredients together; add nuts and orange slices; add alternately with milk to creamed mixture. Pour into greased, floured 8 1/2 x 4 x 3 inch loaf pan. Bake in a 350 degree oven for 65 minutes or until done. Let stand overnight before slicing. *Yield:* 1 loaf.

Sarah B. Loggins, *Clarksville*

Pumpkin Bread

1 CUP GRANULATED SUGAR	1/2 TEASPOON CINNAMON
1/2 CUP BROWN SUGAR	1/2 TEASPOON SALT
1 CUP PUMPKIN	1/2 TEASPOON NUTMEG
1/2 CUP VEGETABLE OIL	1/4 TEASPOON GINGER
2 EGGS	1 CUP RAISINS
2 CUPS ALL-PURPOSE FLOUR, SIFTED	1/2 CUP NUTS, CHOPPED
1 TEASPOON SODA	1/4 CUP WATER

Combine sugar, pumpkin, oil and eggs; beat well. Sift together flour, salt, soda and spices; add to sugar mixture and mix well. Stir in raisins, nuts and water. Spoon into well greased 9 x 5 x 3 inch loaf pan. Bake in a 350 degree oven for 65 to 70 minutes. Cool.

Jane Goodman, *Clarksville*

Zucchini Bread

2 CUPS SUGAR	1 TEASPOON SODA
3 EGGS	1/4 TEASPOON BAKING POWDER
1 CUP OIL	3 CUPS ALL-PURPOSE FLOUR
1 TEASPOON SALT	1 TO 3 TEASPOONS CINNAMON
2 CUPS ZUCCHINI, GRATED	3/4 CUP NUTS
3 TEASPOONS VANILLA	1 8-OUNCE CAN CRUSHED PINEAPPLE, DRAINED

Mix all ingredients together and bake in a 325 degree oven for 1 hour. Grease loaf pan well.

Mrs. Gary E. Gross, *Bluff City*

Angel Biscuits

1 PACKAGE YEAST	4 TABLESPOONS SUGAR
2 TABLESPOONS WARM WATER	1 TEASPOON SALT
5 CUPS ALL-PURPOSE FLOUR	1 CUP SHORTENING
1 TEASPOON SODA	2 CUPS BUTTERMILK
3 TEASPOONS BAKING POWDER	

Dissolve yeast in lukewarm water. Sift flour, soda, baking powder, sugar and salt into bowl. Cut in shortening. Add buttermilk, then yeast mixture. Stir until all flour is dampened. Knead on floured board for 1 or 2 minutes. Roll out to desired thickness, cut with biscuit cutter. Bake in a 400 degree oven about 12 to 15 minutes. Brush with melted butter before or after baking. This recipe can be made up several days in advance and used from as needed. Store in airtight container in refrigerator.

Mrs. Claude Hope, *Spring City*

Lucy's Biscuits

In 1977 my husband was in the military, and we were stationed overseas. He wrote home to Lucy Fitzhugh at Lucy's Cafe on the square in Dover, Tennessee, and requested her recipe for biscuits. He thought they were the best in the world, and he wanted to give the recipe to the cook on his ship. In return my husband sent her a color aerial photo of the submarine squadron at Polaris Point, Guam. She displayed the photo and his letter requesting her biscuit recipe in the cafe until it closed. They are the best biscuits in the world. I have included my own version.

5 CUPS SELF-RISING FLOUR	2 CUPS BUTTERMILK
1/2 TEASPOON SODA	1 PACKAGE YEAST
1 CUP LARD	1/4 CUP WARM WATER

Dissolve yeast in warm water and set aside. In large bowl, sift together 4 cups flour and baking soda. Cut in lard until it looks like coarse crumbs. Mix together remaining 1 cup flour with the buttermilk; add yeast mixture. Add buttermilk and yeast mixture to the flour and mix well. Turn out onto lightly floured surface and knead. Place in greased bowl, covered, in refrigerator. Biscuits are ready to bake at any time. When ready to bake, roll and cut as many as needed. Bake in a 425 degree oven for about 15 minutes. *Yield:* approximately 3 dozen biscuits.

Susan Gould, *Tennessee Ridge*

Marmalade Biscuits

2 CUPS ALL-PURPOSE FLOUR	1/4 CUP PLUS 1 TABLESPOON SHORTENING
1 1/3 TABLESPOONS BAKING POWDER	1 EGG, SLIGHTLY BEATEN
1/2 TEASPOON SALT	1/3 CUP MILK
	1/3 CUP ORANGE MARMALADE

Combine flour, baking powder and salt, mixing well; cut in shortening with pastry blender until mixture resembles coarse meal. Combine egg, milk and marmalade; mix well. Add to flour mixture, stirring until moistened. Turn dough onto a lightly floured surface. Knead lightly 8 or 10 times. Roll dough 1/2 inch thick; cut with 2-inch biscuit cutter. Place biscuits on ungreased baking sheet. Bake in a 450 degree oven for 8 to 10 minutes or until golden brown. Serve piping hot with butter and additional marmalade, if desired. *Yield:* 1 1/2 dozen biscuits.

Nola Mae Needham, *Livingston*

Sweet Potato Biscuits

3/4 CUP MILK	4 TABLESPOONS BUTTER OR MARGARINE, MELTED
3/4 CUP SWEET POTATOES, BOILED AND MASHED (CAN USE CANNED)	1 1/2 CUPS ALL-PURPOSE FLOUR

| 2 TABLESPOONS SUGAR | 1/2 TEASPOON SALT |
| 4 TABLESPOONS BAKING POWDER | PINCH SODA |

Mix milk, potatoes and shortening. Mix together flour, sugar, baking powder, salt and soda. Mix all together and turn onto a floured board and knead 30 seconds. Roll 1/2-inch thick and cut with biscuit cutter. Bake in a 425 degree oven for 12 to 15 minutes. Can use heart-shaped cookie cutter for fancy biscuits for tea or luncheon.

Variation: Add plumped raisins to mixture for additional flavor.

Fanchion Wells, *Columbia*

Peanut Butter Biscuits

2 CUPS ALL-PURPOSE FLOUR, SIFTED	2 TABLESPOONS SHORTENING
3/4 TEASPOON SALT	1/4 CUP PEANUT BUTTER
2 1/2 TEASPOONS BAKING POWDER	3/4 CUP MILK, APPROXIMATELY

Sift dry ingredients together and work in the shortening and peanut butter. Add the milk slowly, stirring until a soft dough is formed. Knead a few times on a lightly floured board, roll or pat to the desired thickness and cut into biscuits. Bake on an ungreased baking sheet in a 450 degree oven for 15 minutes. *Yield:* 16 2-inch biscuits.

Variation: To make drop biscuits, increase milk to 1 cup; drop from spoon to greased baking sheet and bake as above.

Mrs. C. C. (Pearl) Kelly, *Chattanooga*

Dad's Favorite Blueberry Muffins

2 CUPS ALL-PURPOSE FLOUR, SIFTED	1 CUP FRESH BLUEBERRIES (WASHED AND WELL DRAINED) OR 1 CUP FROZEN BLUEBERRIES
1/2 CUP SUGAR	1 CUP MILK
3 TEASPOONS BAKING POWDER	1 EGG, SLIGHTLY BEATEN
1/2 TEASPOON SALT	1/3 CUP SHORTENING, MELTED

Grease 18 to 20 2 1/2-inch muffin pan cups (paper liners can be used). Sift flour with sugar, baking powder and salt into a large bowl. Stir in blueberries. Measure milk in a 2-cup measure. Add egg and melted shortening; beat with a fork to mix well. Make a well in the center of the flour mixture. Pour in milk mixture all at once; stir quickly with fork, just until dry ingredients are moistened. Do not beat; batter will be lumpy. Using a 1/4-cup measuring cup, quickly dip batter into muffin cups, filling each slightly more than half full. Bake in a 350 to 400 degree oven 20 to 25 minutes, or until golden. Loosen edge of each muffin with a spatula; turn out. Serve hot.

Christine P. Caldwell, *Bristol*

Best Ever Oatmeal Muffins

1 CUP QUICK COOKING OATS, UNCOOKED
1 CUP BUTTERMILK
1 EGG, BEATEN
½ CUP BROWN SUGAR
½ CUP COOKING OIL

1 CUP ALL-PURPOSE FLOUR
1 TEASPOON BAKING POWDER
½ TEASPOON SODA
½ TEASPOON SALT
½ CUP RAISINS

Mix oats and buttermilk. Let stand 1 hour. Then add egg, sugar and oil, mixing well. Combine flour, baking powder, soda and salt. Then mix well with the oat mixture. Add the raisins. Spoon the mixture into greased muffin pans, filling ¾ full. Bake in a 400 degree oven for 18 minutes. *Yield:* 1 dozen muffins.

Mrs. Riley Broadwell, *Columbia*

Orange Pecan Muffins

1 3-OUNCE PACKAGE CREAM CHEESE, SOFTENED
3 CUPS BISCUIT MIX
½ CUP SUGAR

1 EGG, BEATEN
1¼ CUPS ORANGE JUICE
½ CUP PECANS, CHOPPED

Beat cream cheese with electric mixer until light and fluffy. Add biscuit mix and sugar; mix well. Add remaining ingredients, stirring just until moistened. Spoon into greased muffin pans, filling ⅔ full. Bake in a 375 degree oven for 20 to 25 minutes. *Yield:* 1½ dozen.

Carol C. Gibson, *Martin*

Peanut Butter Muffins

2 CUPS ALL-PURPOSE FLOUR, SIFTED
3 TABLESPOONS SUGAR
1 TABLESPOON BAKING POWDER
1 TEASPOON SALT

1 EGG
1 CUP MILK
⅓ CUP CRUNCHY PEANUT BUTTER

Sift flour, sugar, baking powder and salt into a medium bowl. Beat egg with milk in a small bowl; beat in peanut butter. Add all at once to flour mixture; stir until mixture is evenly moist. Spoon into greased muffin pan cups, filling each about ⅔ full. Bake 20 minutes or until puffed and golden. Remove from cups to wire racks. Serve warm with margarine and honey.

Margie Flynt, *Madison*

Chapter Six

Entrees

Pork

Country Ham

Boiling Country Ham. Cut off hock, clean whole ham thoroughly with a brush and rough cloth. Trim off any dark, dry edges and discolored fat. Since the hams have a dry cure, soaking in water around 8 hours before cooking is often desirable. Use fresh water for cooking. Fill large roaster with rack about $1/2$ full of water. Put ham in skin side up. Start ham cooking at high heat, when water boils reduce heat to simmer and continue cooking until ham is tender. Cook approximately 30 minutes per pound or until meat thermometer registers 160 degrees. One tablespoon of brown sugar or molasses per quart of water may be added; $1/4$ cup vinegar or red wine may be added to the water if desired. Allow ham to cool in the juice 4 or 5 hours; this will bring the internal temperature to 170 degrees. Remove from broth and skin ham. Use your favorite glaze.

Baking Country Ham. Prepare as for boiling. Place ham, skin side up, on a rack in an open pan. Start ham covered or in aluminum foil in a 375 degree oven for 1 hour. Reduce heat to 200 to 225 degrees and cook until the center of the ham registers 160 degrees on a meat thermometer. This will take about 45 to 50 minutes per pound for whole hams. Hams continue to cook after removal from oven. For well done meat, internal temperature should reach 170 degrees. Remove skin and allow ham to cool slightly. Either serve as is or glaze. *To glaze baked or boiled ham:* after ham is cooked remove skin with sharp knife, score, cover with glaze, stick cloves about every inch and bake at 350 to 400 degrees for about 30 minutes or until lightly browned. Glaze may be made of combinations of brown sugar and fruit juice, crushed pineapple or baste ham with honey. Serve hot or cold.

Note: Baked hams are much easier to slice when chilled. Cut slices thin and perpendicular to the bone.

Fried Country Ham. Skin should only be removed from the area from which the slices will be taken. Cut ham slices $1/4$ to $3/8$ inch thick. Do not trim any excess fat from the slices until after frying. Use heavy skillet that will distribute heat evenly. Place slices in skillet with fat edges toward the center. Fat edges should be scored to prevent buckling. Do not cover; fry slowly at medium heat. Turn frequently. Do not over-fry or cook on high heat; grease should not splatter. Cook until both sides of ham are very lightly browned. Best served hot.

Mrs. Wm. H. (Mary) Colley, *Donelson*

The International Barbecue Cooking Contest is part of Memphis in May—a month-long extravaganza of carnivals and events. In 1985, the Swine Lake Ballet, Hillbilly Hogs, Porter Piglets, and more than 200 other groups from 21 states and 2 foreign countries competed for $6,000 in cash prizes while 100,000 people watched in Tom Lee Park.

Pork Barbecue

Cook a large pork roast until tender (20 minutes to the pound). Cut off all fat, discard bone, tear into shreds, cover with sauce and reheat.

Sauce:

1 TEASPOON SALT
1 TEASPOON BLACK PEPPER
1 TEASPOON PAPRIKA
4 TABLESPOONS SUGAR
2 TABLESPOONS WORCESTERSHIRE SAUCE
1 ONION, CHOPPED
3 STALKS CELERY, CHOPPED
1 GREEN PEPPER

2 LARGE PODS RED HOT PEPPER (OR 2 TABLESPOONS CRUSHED)
2 CUPS VINEGAR
2 CUPS WATER
1 CUP TOMATO CATSUP
½ CUP BUTTER
ANYTHING ELSE YOU HAVE IN THE KITCHEN AND WANT TO THROW IN

Cook all together about ten minutes. Strain and pour over meat. Cook about 30 minutes.

Mrs. Roy (La Rue) Hughes, *Nolensville*

Barbecue

This is a delicious and easy crock pot recipe.

1 POUND STEW BEEF, CUBED
1 POUND PORK, CUBED
¼ CUP CHILI POWDER
1 LARGE GREEN PEPPER, CHOPPED
1 LARGE ONION, CHOPPED
1 CAN TOMATO PASTE

½ CUP PACKED BROWN SUGAR (LESS, IF DESIRED)
¼ CUP VINEGAR
1 TEASPOON MUSTARD
1 TEASPOON WORCESTERSHIRE SAUCE
SALT
PEPPER

Mix well and cook about 10 hours on low in a crock pot. Stir and serve.

Gail N. Steele, *Knoxville*

Sausage and Celery Casserole

4 CUPS CELERY, CUT IN 1-INCH PIECES
¼ CUP ONIONS, CHOPPED
1 CAN CREAM OF CHICKEN SOUP
1 5-OUNCE CAN WATER CHESTNUTS, THINLY SLICED
¼ CUP PIMENTO, CHOPPED

¾ POUND SAUSAGE, COOKED AND DRAINED
⅓ CUP SOUR CREAM
½ CUP SLIVERED ALMONDS
¼ CUP SESAME SEED
2 TABLESPOONS BUTTER

Cook celery and onion for 8 minutes and drain. Add soup, water chestnuts, pimento and sausage. Fold in sour cream. Put in casserole dish. Toast almonds and sesame seeds in butter; place on casserole. Bake in a 350 degree oven for 35 minutes. *Yield:* 8 to 9 servings.

Mrs. Robert L. Scofield, *Clarksville*

Honey Ham Kabobs

This is a favorite that I serve at my Christmas parties. This recipe of mine was published in the 1980 edition of Southern Living's Annual Recipes.

1 CUP BROWN SUGAR, FIRMLY PACKED	1 1½-POUND HAM STEAK, COOKED, CUT INTO 1 INCH CUBES
½ CUP HONEY	1 SMALL PINEAPPLE, PEELED, CORED, CUT INTO 1 INCH CHUNKS
½ CUP ORANGE JUICE	16 LARGE PIMENTO-STUFFED OLIVES

Combine brown sugar, honey, and orange juice; mix well and set aside. Alternate ham, pineapple, and olives on skewers. Grill over medium heat 10 to 12 minutes, turning often. Baste liberally with honey mixture after each turn. *Yield:* 4 servings.

Carol C. Gibson, *Martin*

Country Ham Casserole

¾ CUP BUTTERED CRACKER CRUMBS	2 CUPS GROUND COUNTRY HAM
4 EGGS, HARD BOILED AND CHOPPED	2 CUPS WHITE SAUCE

Sprinkle cracker crumbs in buttered casserole. On top of cracker crumbs, layer half of chopped eggs, ¼ of sauce, half of ham, ¼ of sauce, then repeat, topping with crumbs. Bake in a 350 degree oven for 30 minutes.

White Sauce:

3 TABLESPOONS BUTTER	3 TABLESPOONS ALL-PURPOSE FLOUR
2 CUPS MILK, DIVIDED	

Over medium heat, melt butter. Slowly add 1 cup milk. In jar, shake flour with 1 cup milk until flour is dissolved. Add to warm milk and cook, stirring constantly, until thickened.

Mrs. Jim (Dot) Holeman, Jr., *Old Hickory*

Pork Chops with Sage and Apricots

These pork chops are delightfully different and are delicious cold when taken to a picnic.

6 LOIN PORK CHOPS, 1 INCH THICK, BONE REMOVED, SALTED TO TASTE	4 TEASPOONS SAGE
6 TABLESPOONS BUTTER	1 CUP SOUR CREAM
½ CUP ALL-PURPOSE FLOUR	1½ CUPS SWEET MILK
2 CLOVES GARLIC, MINCED	1 16-OUNCE CAN APRICOT HALVES, DRAINED

In a stainless steel skillet heat the butter over medium heat until bubbling. Add well floured pork chops, the garlic and sage sprinkled on top. Cook the pork chops until light brown on both sides. Transfer them to a casserole dish. Mix the remaining flour, sour cream and milk until smooth, pour it into the skillet and simmer, scraping up any brown bits. Pour the mixture over the pork chops, cover and bake in a 300 degree oven for 30 minutes. Remove from the oven and lay the apricots on top of the pork chops, cut side up, put a maraschino cherry in each apricot, return to the oven for 15 minutes more. Garnish the top with parsley sprigs. *Yield:* 6 servings.

Mrs. Carrie B. Bartlett, *Gallatin*

Pork Chop Casserole

6 PORK CHOPS	IRISH POTATOES, SLICED
SALT	1 SMALL ONION
PEPPER	1 CAN GOLDEN MUSHROOM SOUP
SHORTENING OR CRISCO	1/2 CUP MILK

Take pork chops and season with salt and pepper; dip lightly in flour. Place in skillet, using shortening or Crisco, and fry until golden brown. Drain on paper towel and set aside. Then layer potatoes in long Pyrex dish and dice onion; salt and pepper the potatoes. To this layer add the pork chops and pour mushroom soup over potatoes and meat. Then add milk over all ingredients. Cover with aluminum foil and bake in a 325 degree oven for approximately 45 minutes. Delicious! Serve with green salad, French bread and iced tea!

Mrs. John Stanford, *Murfreesboro*

Baked Tennessee Pork Chops

PORK CHOPS, 1 TO 1 1/2-INCHES THICK	BROWN SUGAR
SALT	ALL-PURPOSE FLOUR
BLACK PEPPER	BUTTER OR MARGARINE
GRANULATED SUGAR	PINEAPPLE SLICES

Sprinkle both sides of chops with salt and pepper, dredge with granulated sugar, then dip both sides in flour. Heat a heavy iron skillet until hot, using just enough vegetable oil to keep chops from burning. Brown chops quickly on both sides. Cover skillet tightly, place in a 325 degree oven and bake chops 2 to 2 1/2 hours, basting now and then. Add a little water if necessary. When tender, remove chops, pour in a little water for gravy and thicken. Sauté pineapple slices. Glaze chops lightly with brown sugar and melted butter. Serve chops, encircled by pineapple slices, on platter.

Morris B. Baker, *Memphis*

Meal in a Skillet

4 TABLESPOONS BUTTER OR MARGARINE	1 SMALL CAN MUSHROOMS
4 ½ TO ¾-INCH PORK CHOPS	1 PACKAGE FROZEN GREEN PEAS
1 CUP RICE	1 SMALL BELL PEPPER, CHOPPED
2 CUPS WATER	4 TO 5 PIMENTOS, CHOPPED (OPTIONAL)
1 SMALL ONION, CHOPPED	SALT AND PEPPER TO TASTE

In a large 10-inch skillet with lid, melt 2 tablespoons of butter. Place pork chops in skillet and brown on both sides. Remove and keep in warm place. Add 1 cup of rice to 2 more tablespoons of butter, stirring until it begins to brown. Slowly stir in 2 cups of water and add chopped onion and mushrooms. Bring to a boil. Stir one more time, cover and cut temperature to simmer. Simmer covered for 15 minutes.

Remove lid, add green peas, bell pepper, pimento, salt and pepper and stir until well mixed. Place pork chops on top of mixture, cover with lid and simmer additional 25 minutes. *Yield:* 4 servings.

John McCoy, *Ooltewah*

Honey Glazed Pork Roast with Sweet Potatoes

6 POUND PORK ROAST	3 TEASPOONS GRATED ORANGE RIND
SALT AND PEPPER TO TASTE	6 SWEET POTATOES
½ CUP HONEY	

Rub roast well with salt and pepper. Cut slits in fat with a sharp knife. Roast fat side up in shallow pan at 350 degrees for 2 hours. Quarter and cook potatoes in water until almost tender; place around roast and drizzle with honey and orange peel. Increase heat to 400 degrees and cook 20 minutes longer until meat and potatoes are golden brown.

Mary F. Cunnyngham, *Cleveland*

Fried Mush with Sausage

SALT AND PEPPER	1½ CUPS SAUSAGE, FRIED AND CRUMBLED
3 CUPS CORNMEAL	2 EGGS, BEATEN
WATER	2 CUPS BREAD CRUMBS

Mix salt, pepper and cornmeal together. Add enough water to make a medium textured batter. Add sausage to this mixture. Pour into a plastic loaf pan (or Tupperware cheese keeper). Refrigerate overnight. Take out and slice mush. Dip each slice into the beaten egg, then roll in the bread crumbs. Deep fry these until golden brown. Can be eaten plain or with syrup.

Priscilla Oxendine, *Jonesborough*

Mom's Barbecued Ribs

4 POUNDS PORK SPARE RIBS, CUT INTO 4 RIB SIDES
1 LEMON, SLICED
1 ONION, SLICED
1 CUP CATSUP
1/3 CUP WORCESTERSHIRE SAUCE
1 CLOVE GARLIC, CHOPPED
1 TEASPOON CHILI POWDER
1 TEASPOON SALT
2 CUPS WATER
JUICE OF 1 LEMON
3 DASHES TABASCO SAUCE (OR TO TASTE)

Place ribs in roasting pan and place slices of lemon and onion on each section. Bake in a 450 degree oven for 30 minutes.

Combine remaining ingredients in saucepan and bring to boil. Drain excess fat from ribs. Pour sauce over ribs, cover and lower oven heat to 350 degrees. Bake 45 minutes, then uncover and bake 15 more minutes.

MaryAnn Rohm, *Tennessee Ridge*

Impossible Ham'n Swiss Pie

2 CUPS SMOKED HAM, FULLY COOKED AND CUT UP
1 CUP SHREDDED NATURAL SWISS CHEESE (ABOUT 4 OUNCES)
1/3 CUP GREEN ONION OR ONION, CHOPPED
4 EGGS
2 CUPS MILK
1 CUP BISQUICK BAKING MIX
1/4 TEASPOON SALT, IF DESIRED
1/8 TEASPOON PEPPER

Grease 10-inch pie plate 1 1/2-inches deep. Sprinkle ham, cheese and onions in plate. Beat remaining ingredients until smooth, 15 seconds in blender on high or 1 minute with hand beater. Pour into pie plate. Bake in a 400 degree oven until golden brown and knife inserted in center comes out clean, 35 to 40 minutes. Cool 5 minutes. *Yield:* 2 servings.

Mrs. Jimmy Freeman, *Cookeville*

Oriental Pork Roast

1 TABLESPOON ALL-PURPOSE FLOUR
1/4 TEASPOON SALT
1 TABLESPOON SUGAR
1/2 TEASPOON GINGER
1 CLOVE GARLIC, MINCED
1/2 CUP ORANGE JUICE
1/4 CUP LEMON JUICE
1/4 CUP SOY SAUCE
2 TABLESPOONS CATSUP
PORK ROAST

Mix ingredients together and pour over roast. Marinate several hours in refrigerator. Place in cooking bag and bake in a 325 degree oven for 2 to 3 hours, depending on size of roast.

Sue Bucy, *Paris*

German Pizza

1½ TABLESPOONS OIL

3 MEDIUM POTATOES, PARED AND THINLY SLICED

SALT AND PEPPER

½ CUP ONION, CHOPPED

½ CUP GREEN PEPPER, CHOPPED

2 CUPS (1 12-OUNCE CAN) JULIENNE STRIPS CANNED LUNCHEON MEAT OR HAM

3 EGGS

½ CUP SHARP PROCESS AMERICAN CHEESE, SHREDDED (CHEDDAR IS EVEN BETTER)

Put oil in 10-inch skillet. Spread half of the potato slices over bottom; sprinkle with salt and pepper. Top with a layer of half of the green peppers, seasoning with salt and pepper. Arrange half of the meat on top. Repeat layers of vegetables, reserving the remaining meat for garnish. Cover; cook over low heat until potatoes are tender, about 20 minutes. Break eggs into bowl and beat with fork; pour eggs evenly over potatoes. Add meat, spoke-fashion. Cover and cook until eggs are set, about 10 minutes. Top with cheese; cover until cheese starts to melt, about 2 minutes. Put parsley into center. Cut in wedges to serve. *Yield:* 5 to 6 servings.

Carolyn A. Wilhite, *Millington*

Poultry

Chicken-Rice Pilaf

1 LARGE FRYER OR 8 CHICKEN BREASTS, SPLIT, STEWED AND SALTED

RESERVE 2 CUPS BROTH

1 POUND GROUND BEEF

½ CUP LONG GRAIN RICE

1 TEASPOON SALT

½ TEASPOON CINNAMON

¼ TEASPOON BLACK PEPPER

3 TABLESPOONS PINE NUTS

2 TABLESPOONS BUTTER, MELTED

½ CLOVE GARLIC, MASHED

½ LEMON, JUICED

1 TEASPOON OREGANO

Brown beef in 1 tablespoon shortening. Add rice, salt, cinnamon, pepper and pine nuts. Cook 5 minutes over low heat. Stir often. Stir in hot broth (2 cups) and bring to a boil. Turn heat low, cover and simmer 20 minutes or until rice is done.

Place boned chicken in foil-lined pan. Mix melted butter, garlic, lemon and oregano and brush on chicken. Seal foil. Bake in a 350 degree oven for 30 minutes. Uncover last 10 minutes. Serve hot rice mixture on large platter topped with chicken pieces. Garnish with parsley.

Mrs. Paul Fox, *Chattanooga*

Hot Brown

6 ENGLISH MUFFINS, LIGHTLY BROWNED

3 TOMATOES, SLICED

TURKEY OR CHICKEN BREAST, SLICED

12 SLICES BACON, COOKED

CHEESE SAUCE

Arrange tomato slices on muffin halves, then turkey slices; criss-cross bacon slices on top and pour on cheese sauce.

Cheese Sauce:

½ CUP BUTTER	4 CUPS MILK
½ CUP ALL-PURPOSE FLOUR	3 CUPS SHARP CHEESE, GRATED

Melt butter over low to medium heat; stir in flour, add milk slowly. When it is almost thickened, blend in cheese. Blend well and pour over sandwiches and serve. *Yield:* 6 servings.

Regina Albright, *Clarksville*

Sautéed Chicken Livers

1 POUND CHICKEN LIVERS	½ TEASPOON GARLIC SALT
½ CUP WATER	¼ TEASPOON MARJORAM
2 PACKETS INSTANT CHICKEN BROTH AND SEASONING MIX	¼ TEASPOON NUTMEG
1 TEASPOON ONION POWDER	¼ TEASPOON PEPPER
½ TEASPOON PAPRIKA	¼ TEASPOON THYME
	2 CUPS ENRICHED RICE, COOKED

Place chicken livers in a colander, pour boiling water over them and allow to drain; cut in half. Combine remaining ingredients (except rice) in non-stick skillet; add livers and cook, turning constantly, until browned on all sides and cooked through, about 5 minutes. Serve over hot rice. *Yield:* 4 servings.

Katherine C. Rives, *Clarksville*

Cambridge Chicken with Ham

1 LARGE FRYER, CUT IN PIECES	1 4-OUNCE CAN MUSHROOMS, DRAINED
FLOUR	1 SLICE HAM, DICED
SALT	1 CLOVE GARLIC, MINCED
PEPPER	PINCH OF THYME
¼ POUND BUTTER OR MARGARINE	SALT AND PEPPER TO TASTE
¼ CUP GREEN ONIONS, CHOPPED	1 CUP RED WINE

Shake chicken piece by piece in a paper bag containing flour, mixed with salt and pepper. Brown chicken in butter and place in a casserole dish. Mix together all remaining ingredients and pour over chicken. Spoon the juice over the chicken so it is well saturated. Bake in a 350 degree oven for 1 hour. Remove and cool for a short time before placing in refrigerator overnight. The next day, when ready to bake again, spoon liquid over the chicken and place covered in a 300 degree oven for 1 hour.

Margaret Hogshead, *Nashville*

Chicken Loaf

1 HEN ABOUT 6 POUNDS, OR 2 BROILERS	SALT AND PEPPER TO TASTE
1 CARROT	1 CUP RICE, COOKED
1 SMALL ONION	2 CUPS FRESH BREAD CRUMBS (MAY USE SOME CORNBREAD)
3 STALKS CELERY	1 CUP PIMENTO, CHOPPED
1 CARROT, SLICED	3 CUPS CHICKEN BROTH
1 CUP ONION, CHOPPED	5 EGGS, WELL-BEATEN
1 CUP CELERY, CHOPPED	

Cover chicken with water and add carrot, onion, celery and salt and pepper to taste. Let simmer until done and cool in broth. Bone chicken and combine with sliced carrot, chopped onion and celery to other ingredients. Put into greased 13 x 9 x 2 inch baking dish and bake in a 350 degree oven for 1 hour. Let set for several minutes, then cut into squares and serve with the following sauce.

Sauce:

¼ CUP ALL-PURPOSE FLOUR	2 CUPS CHICKEN BROTH
½ CUP MARGARINE	DASH OF LEMON
1 CAN CREAM OF MUSHROOM SOUP	

Combine flour, margarine, soup and broth; cook until thick. Add lemon and serve over chicken squares.

Mrs. Sue Reeves, *Murfreesboro*

Chicken Curry

1 LARGE STEWING HEN	1 CUP CELERY, CHOPPED
1 MEDIUM ONION	1 CUP ONION, CHOPPED
TOPS FROM BUNCH CELERY	½ CUP BUTTER
RED PEPPER TO TASTE	½ CUP FLOUR
1 TABLESPOON SALT	1 LARGE CAN MUSHROOMS
⅛ TEASPOON BLACK PEPPER	3 TABLESPOONS CURRY POWDER
7½ CUPS WATER	

Stuff hen with onion and celery tops. Add red pepper, salt and black pepper to the water and bring to the boiling point. Simmer until meat is tender. When cool remove meat from bone and cut meat into large bite-size pieces. Sauté chopped celery and onions in a small amount of chicken fat. Melt butter and add flour, stirring constantly. Cook until thickened; add chicken pieces, celery, onions, mushrooms and curry powder. Serve over rice with: grated egg white, grated egg yolk, coconut and ground nuts. *Yield:* 15 servings.

Barbara Brewster, *Clarksville*

Fried Chicken

2½ TO 3 POUND FRYING CHICKEN, CUT IN
   SERVING PIECES
1 CUP ALL-PURPOSE FLOUR
1 TEASPOON SALT
⅛ TEASPOON GROUND PEPPER

¼ TEASPOON GARLIC POWDER
1 TEASPOON PAPRIKA
1 TEASPOON SAGE OR OREGANO
  BUTTER OR VEGETABLE OIL

Rinse chicken and pat dry. Combine flour with remaining dry ingredients. Toss chicken with flour mixture to coat. In skillet, heat butter or oil to ¼ inch depth. Cook chicken until golden brown. Place browned chicken in crock pot, adding wings first. Add no liquid. Cover and cook on low setting for 4 to 8 hours.

Judy J. Tippit, *Jefferson City*

Country Fricassee

1 3½-POUND CHICKEN, EITHER WHOLE OF
  CUT UP
1 LARGE ONION, PEELED AND DICED
1 CUP CELERY AND LEAVES, DICED
3 CUPS WATER

1 TABLESPOON SALT
¼ TEASPOON PEPPER
½ CUP WATER
¼ CUP ALL-PURPOSE FLOUR

Place chicken, onion, celery, leaves, salt, pepper and 3 cups water in Dutch oven. Cover. Heat to boiling, then simmer 1 hour, or until chicken is tender. Remove chicken from broth. Cool until easy to handle; slip off skin and take meat off bones, either leaving meat in large pieces or cutting into as small pieces as you wish. Discard bones. Set meat aside. Strain broth into a 4-cup measure; add water if needed to make 4 cups. Press vegetables through strainer into broth; return to kettle. (Vegetables can be left whole and not put through strainer if you wish.)

Stir ½ cup cold water into flour in cup to make a smooth paste, stir into hot broth. Cook stirring constantly, until gravy thickens and boils 1 minute. Return chicken to kettle, heat slowly to boiling while stirring up Fluffy Paprika Dumplings.

Fluffy Paprika Dumplings:

2 CUPS ALL-PURPOSE FLOUR, SIFTED
3 TEASPOONS BAKING POWDER
1 TEASPOON SALT
¼ TEASPOON PAPRIKA

2 TABLESPOONS SHORTENING
1 CUP MILK
  PARSLEY FOR GARNISH

Sift flour, baking powder, salt and paprika into bowl; cut in shortening until mixture is crumbly. Stir in milk until mixture is moist. Dough will be soft. Drop batter in 6 to 8 mounds on top of chicken. Cook covered for 20 minutes. No peeking, or they will not steam puffy-light! Arrange chicken and dumplings on a platter. Pass gravy separately. Sprinkle dumplings with paprika and garnish with parsley.

Mrs. Jon McDearman, *Cookeville*

Barbecued Chicken

2 MEDIUM FRYING CHICKENS	1/2 CUP WORCESTERSHIRE SAUCE
1/2 TEASPOON SALT	1 1/2 TABLESPOONS CELERY FLAKES
1 TABLESPOON PEPPER	1 1/2 TABLESPOONS PARSLEY FLAKES
1/4 CUP LEMON JUICE	2 TABLESPOONS CHILI SAUCE
1/2 CUP BUTTER	LEMON SLICES
1/2 CUP SOY SAUCE	

Mix all ingredients together and completely cover chicken. Let stand overnight. Approximately 3 hours before dinner preheat oven to 350 degrees and bake chicken and sauce mixture in shallow pan, uncovered, for about 2½ hours. Place lemon slices over top of mixture while baking.

Note: It works well to make up the dish the night before baking it.

Georgia Thomas, *Lenoir City*

French Country Chicken

4 CHICKEN BREASTS	1 TEASPOON TARRAGON LEAVES
1/2 CUP CELERY, CHOPPED	1 1/3 CUPS UNCOOKED RICE
1/2 CUP CARROT, CHOPPED	2 1/2 TEASPOONS BUTTER
1/2 CUP ONION, CHOPPED	3 TEASPOONS ALL-PURPOSE FLOUR
1 1/2 CUPS DRY WHITE WINE	1 CUP HOT MILK
2 CUPS CHICKEN BROTH	1/3 TO 1/2 CUP WHIPPING CREAM
SALT AND PEPPER TO TASTE	2 1/2 OUNCES SWISS CHEESE

In a large saucepan, layer chicken and vegetables. Pour on wine and chicken broth, adding water if necessary to cover chicken. Bring to a simmer until it bubbles. Salt lightly to taste and add tarragon. Cover and simmer 15 minutes. Uncover, add rice until it is in the juice. Add pepper as needed, cover and simmer 15 to 20 minutes until rice comes to the top.

Melt butter in a small sauce pan, add flour and stir over medium heat until the flour and butter mix, usually 2 minutes. Remove from heat and add hot milk. Whip well. Return to heat and stir until the mixture thickens and comes to a boil. Thin out with cream, 1/3 then to 1/2 cup if needed. Add salt and pepper to taste. Remove from heat, beat in 1/2 cup cheese. Pour sauce over chicken and layer with remaining cheese. Place in a 400 degree oven until brown on top. *Yield:* 4 servings.

Amanda Borgognoni, *Memphis*

Old-Fashioned Chicken and Dumplings

1 2 1/2 TO 3-POUND FRYER	1/2 TEASPOON SODA
2 QUARTS WATER	1/2 TEASPOON SALT
2 TEASPOONS SALT	3 TABLESPOONS SHORTENING
1/2 TEASPOON PEPPER	3/4 CUP BUTTERMILK
2 CUPS ALL-PURPOSE FLOUR	

Place chicken in a Dutch oven; add water and 2 teaspoons salt. Bring to a boil; cover, reduce heat, and simmer 1 hour or until tender. Remove chicken from broth and cool. Bone chicken and cut meat into bite-size pieces; set aside. Bring broth to a boil; add pepper.

Combine flour, soda, and 1/2 teaspoon salt; cut in shortening until mixture resembles coarse meal. Add buttermilk, stirring with a fork until dry ingredients are moistened. Turn dough out onto a well-floured surface, and knead lightly 4 or 5 times. Pat dough to 1/2-inch thickness. Pinch off dough in 1 1/2-inch pieces, and drop into boiling broth. Reduce heat to medium-low, and cook about 8 to 10 minutes, or until desired consistency, stirring occasionally. Stir in chicken. *Yield:* 4 to 6 servings.

Cheryl Fransioli, *Somerville*

Sherried Parmesan Chicken

3 CHICKEN BREASTS, SPLIT, BONED AND SKINNED	1 TABLESPOON SHERRY
	PAPRIKA
1 10-OUNCE CAN GOLDEN MUSHROOM SOUP	HOT COOKED RICE
1 4-OUNCE CAN MUSHROOMS, DRAINED	1/4 CUP SOUR CREAM
1/3 CUP (1 1/2 OUNCES) KRAFT GRATED PARMESAN CHEESE	

Place chicken in a 12 x 8 inch baking dish. Combine soup, mushrooms, cheese and sherry and top the breasts with mixture. Sprinkle with paprika. Bake in a 350 degree oven for 1 hour or until tender. Remove chicken to rice covered serving platter, keep warm. Stir sour cream in pan drippings; serve over chicken and rice. *Yield:* 4 to 6 servings.

Moiselle Newsom, *Newbern*

Calico Chicken

2 CHICKEN BREASTS, BONED AND CUBED	1/4 TEASPOON McCORMICK ITALIAN SEASONING
2 TABLESPOONS SHORTENING	
1 CAN CREAMY CHICKEN MUSHROOM SOUP	1 8-OUNCE CAN VEG-ALL MIXED VEGETABLES
1/3 CUP MILK	1 TABLESPOON PARSLEY, CHOPPED

In skillet brown chicken in shortening, drain off fat. Stir in soup, milk and seasoning. Cover, simmer 30 minutes or until done. Stir occasionally, add vegetables and parsley. Heat thoroughly. Serve over cooked rice or noodles. *Yield:* 4 servings.

Elaine Geren, *Calhoun*

Chicken Tetrazzini

This recipe is a delicious dish, easily prepared, and has become a legend at my company's annual Christmas Dinner.

3 CUPS BOILED CHICKEN, CHOPPED (BROTH RETAINED)
1 10¾-OUNCE CAN CREAM OF CHICKEN SOUP
1 16-OUNCE CAN ENGLISH PEAS
1 CAN CREAM OF MUSHROOM SOUP
2 OUNCE PACKAGE SLICED ALMONDS
2 TABLESPOONS INSTANT ONIONS
4 OUNCES GRATED CHEDDAR CHEESE
1 8-OUNCE PACKAGE EGG NOODLES, CRUSHED
SALT AND PEPPER TO TASTE

Boil one large fryer chicken in 4 cups of water. Bone and chop chicken. Retain two cups of broth. In a 9 x 13 inch dish, spread chopped chicken. On top of the chicken, add in layers cream of chicken soup, can of English peas, dried onions, can of mushroom soup, first cup of broth, almonds, crushed noodles and second cup of broth. Top with cheese. Bake in a 350 degree oven for 25 to 30 minutes until bubbly and the cheese melts. *Yield:* 8 to 10 servings.

Variations: Top with chopped bell peppers and/or mushrooms.

Add to two cups of broth: 1 medium onion, chopped, 1 medium bell pepper, chopped, and ½ cup mushrooms. Cook until vegetables are tender and add broth as described in above recipe. (If this option is used, omit dried onions.)

Duell Coleman, *Smyrna*

Stir Fry Chicken

1 CUP CHICKEN BROTH
2 TABLESPOONS SOY SAUCE
¼ TEASPOON GARLIC POWDER
1 TEASPOON SALT
½ CUP ONION, CHOPPED
1 CUP CELERY, DICED
2 CUPS COOKED CHICKEN
1 CAN BEAN SPROUTS
1 CAN BAMBOO SHOOTS
1 CAN SLICED WATER CHESTNUTS
1 SMALL CAN SLICED MUSHROOMS
1 6-OUNCE PACKAGE FROZEN SNOW PEAS (OR EQUAL AMOUNT FRESH SNOW PEAS)

Heat broth in pan until simmering. Add soy sauce, garlic powder, salt, onion and celery. Cook about 5 or 6 minutes. Add the rest of the ingredients and cook 10 minutes. If using fresh snow peas add the last 5 minutes. Serve over hot rice and top with LaChoy rice noodles or Chow Mein noodles. *Yield:* 4 servings.

Peggy Rich, *Nashville*

Chicken Pot Pie

1 STEWING CHICKEN
1½ QUARTS WATER
3½ CUPS CHICKEN BROTH
½ CUP ALL-PURPOSE FLOUR

2 TEASPOONS SALT	½ TEASPOON ONION SALT
1 SMALL ONION	½ TEASPOON CELERY SALT
1 CARROT	PEPPER TO TASTE
1 STALK CELERY	

Place chicken in kettle with next 5 ingredients, using 1 teaspoon of the salt. Cook until tender. Strip meat from chicken. Combine flour, salts and pepper with ½ cup of broth and mix until smooth. Heat 3 cups of broth to boiling, add flour mixture and cook until thick. Add chicken. Pour into casserole and cover with pastry; seal well. Make slits in top. Bake in a 400 degree oven for 45 minutes or until brown.

Emilie Maynard, *Sparta*

Smoked Turkey

Extraordinarily good.

12 TO 14 POUND TURKEY	1 CUP ICE CREAM SALT
2 GALLONS WATER	8 TABLESPOONS LIQUID SMOKE
2 CUPS MORTON'S TENDER QUICK MEAT CURE	

Place turkey in plastic tub. Mix remaining ingredients and pour over turkey. Weight with a heavy plate. Soak 24 hours or more in a cool place.
Remove turkey and dry. Place on rack in roasting pan, uncovered, breast side down. Roast at 250 degrees, 1 hour per pound.
Turkey will appear dark brown and dry but meat will be moist and tender.

Mrs. James (Dorothy) Holeman, *Old Hickory*

Turkey Divan

2 11-OUNCE PACKAGES FROZEN RICE PILAF	1 10¾-OUNCE CAN CREAM OF MUSHROOM SOUP
2 10-OUNCE PACKAGES FROZEN CUT BROCCOLI WITH CHEESE SAUCE	1 2½-OUNCE JAR SLICED MUSHROOMS, DRAINED
2 CUPS TURKEY, COOKED AND CUT UP	½ CUP MAYONNAISE OR SALAD DRESSING
1 8-OUNCE CAN WATER CHESTNUTS, DRAINED AND SLICED	1 3-OUNCE CAN FRENCH FRIED ONIONS

Cook rice and broccoli according to package directions. Spread rice in bottom of 7½ x 11¾ inch baking dish. Cover with turkey, then broccoli in cheese sauce. Mix together water chestnuts, soup, mushrooms and mayonnaise. Pour over broccoli mixture. Bake in a preheated 350 degree oven for 30 to 40 minutes. Remove from oven, cover with onions and bake an additional 10 minutes.

Carolyn Barnett, *Humboldt*

Turkey Casserole

2 CUPS TURKEY, COOKED AND CHOPPED
1 CAN CREAM OF CHICKEN SOUP
2 TEASPOONS ONION, FINELY CHOPPED
1 CUP CELERY, FINELY CHOPPED
1/2 TEASPOON BLACK PEPPER
1/2 TEASPOON SALT
1 CUP SLIVERED ALMONDS
1 TEASPOON LEMON JUICE
1/4 CUP MAYONNAISE
1/2 CUP CRACKER CRUMBS

Combine all ingredients except cracker crumbs and mix well. Pour into baking dish. Sprinkle cracker crumbs over top (or potato chips may be used). Bake in a 375 degree oven for 25 minutes.

Mrs. Jessie Harris, *Clarksville*

Chicken Crunch Casserole

3 CUPS COOKED CHICKEN, DICED
2 1/2 CUPS COOKED RICE
4 HARD COOKED EGGS, CHOPPED
1 1/2 CUPS CELERY, CHOPPED
1 SMALL ONION
1 CUP MAYONNAISE
1 2 1/2-OUNCE CAN SLICED ALMONDS
2 CANS MUSHROOM SOUP
1 TEASPOON SALT
2 TEASPOONS LEMON JUICE
2 CUPS BREAD CRUMBS
4 TABLESPOONS MARGARINE

Mix all ingredients except bread crumbs and margarine. Place in 9 x 12 inch buttered baking dish. Brown bread crumbs lightly in margarine. Sprinkle over casserole. Put in refrigerator overnight. Remove 1 hour before cooking. Bake in a 350 degree oven for 40 minutes. Freezes well.

Eula Catlett, *Sevierville*

Baked Chicken Casserole

1 CHICKEN, COOKED AND DICED
1 ONION, CHOPPED
1 CUP CELERY, DICED
1/3 CUP BUTTER
7 CUPS SOFT BREAD CRUMBS
1/2 TEASPOON BAKING POWDER
1/2 TEASPOON SALT
1/4 TEASPOON PEPPER
2 TEASPOONS SAGE
2 EGGS
1 1/2 CUPS MILK
1 CAN CREAM OF MUSHROOM SOUP
2 TABLESPOONS BUTTER

Place diced chicken in buttered rectangular baking dish. Sauté onion and celery in 1/3 cup butter. Mix bread crumbs, baking powder, salt, pepper, and sage. Beat eggs slightly, add milk, and mix all together with sautéed onion and celery. Pour over chicken. Top with mushroom soup. Cover with bread crumbs tossed with 2 tablespoons melted butter. Bake in a 350 degree oven for 50 minutes. *Yield:* 12 to 15 servings.

Mrs. Thelma Hammon, *Gallatin*

Five Can Casserole

1 SMALL CAN BONED CHICKEN OR TURKEY
1 SMALL CAN EVAPORATED MILK
1 CAN CREAM OF CHICKEN SOUP
1 CAN CREAM OF MUSHROOM SOUP
1 5-OUNCE CAN CHINESE NOODLES

Mix all ingredients together. Bake in buttered casserole 25 minutes in a 350 degree oven or heat and serve from chafing dish. It may be served plain or in patty shells.

Mrs. Bertie C. Lyon, *Lenoir City*

Creamed Chicken Casserole

6 OUNCES NOODLES, COOKED
2 CUPS CHICKEN, COOKED AND DICED
1/2 CUP CELERY, CHOPPED
1/2 CUP CHOPPED ONION
1/2 CUP PIMENTO, CHOPPED
1/4 CUP BUTTER, MELTED
1/2 TEASPOON SALT
1/4 TEASPOON PEPPER
1 CAN CONDENSED CREAM OF CELERY SOUP
1/2 CUP MILK
1 CUP AMERICAN CHEESE, GRATED

Prepare noodles and mix with diced chicken, celery, onion, pimento, butter, salt and pepper. In separate pan, heat cream of celery soup, milk and cheese, slowly until cheese has melted. Mix all ingredients together and pour into a 2-quart greased rectangular baking dish. Top with buttered bread crumbs. Bake in a 425 degree oven for 25 minutes. *Yield:* 8 servings.

Mrs. Debra Wilson, *Spring City*

Crisp Noodle Chicken

1 BROILER FRYER CHICKEN, CUT UP
1 10 1/2-OUNCE CREAM OF MUSHROOM SOUP
1 CUP DAIRY SOUR CREAM
3 TABLESPOONS (1/2 PACKAGE) DRY ONION SOUP MIX
1/8 TEASPOON PEPPER
1 3-OUNCE CAN CHOW MEIN NOODLES

Place chicken in single layer casserole dish; in a bowl combine soup, sour cream, soup mix and pepper; blend thoroughly. Spread over chicken; sprinkle with noodles. Bake in a 375 degree for 1 hour or until chicken is tender.

Doris Melton, *Sweetwater*

Chicken and Broccoli Casserole

8 CHICKEN BREASTS

2 10-OUNCE PACKAGES FROZEN CHOPPED
  BROCCOLI

1 CAN CREAM OF MUSHROOM SOUP

1 8-OUNCE CARTON FRENCH ONION PARTY
  DIP

2 CUPS PRE-COOKED RICE

Cook chicken until tender, remove from bone and cut into small pieces. Cook broccoli according to package directions and season with salt and pepper. Add remaining ingredients to chicken and broccoli. Cook in a glass casserole dish in a 350 degree oven for 15 minutes, or microwave on high for 5 minutes. *Yield:* 8 servings.

Jan Moore, *Sweetwater*

Chicken Spinach Noodle Casserole

1 CUP CELERY, CHOPPED

1 CUP ONION, CHOPPED

1 CUP GREEN PEPPER, CHOPPED

2 TABLESPOONS BUTTER

2 CANS CREAM OF MUSHROOM SOUP

4 OUNCES VELVEETA CHEESE

1/2 CUP GREEN STUFFED OLIVES

1 8-OUNCE CAN OF MUSHROOMS, DRAINED

2½ CUPS COOKED CHOPPED CHICKEN

8 OUNCES SPINACH NOODLES

Sauté celery, onion and green pepper in butter. In separate bowl, combine cream of mushroom soup, cheese, olives and mushrooms, add chicken. Cook spinach noodles and drain; mix with sautéed vegetables, cream mixture and chicken. Put in a lightly buttered casserole dish. Bake in a 350 degree oven for 30 to 35 minutes or until bubbly.

Note: According to individual taste you may add slivered almonds to top of casserole, or sprinkle with Parmesan cheese. To make a richer taste, cook spinach noodles in leftover broth.

Mrs. Wayne Gilchrist, *Martin*

Taco Casserole

1 CAN CREAM OF CHICKEN SOUP

1 CAN CREAM OF MUSHROOM SOUP

1 LARGE CAN PET MILK

1 CAN BONED CHICKEN

1 SMALL CAN CHOPPED GREEN CHILLIES

1 BAG TACO FLAVORED DORITOES

1 SMALL ONION, CHOPPED

1 CUP CHEDDAR CHEESE, GRATED

Mix canned ingredients and onion in pan and simmer for 15 minutes. In a buttered casserole dish, crumble Doritoes and layer with creamed ingredients. Top with grated cheese. Bake in a 350 degree oven until bubbly in center.

Mrs. Richard Cobble, *Shelbyville*

Photographic Services

Robin Hood

Photographic Services

Grandmother Wirwa's Brunswick Stew

Grandaddy was a great hunter, as was his father before him. In fact, he was a gunsmith by trade. This, combined with the abundance of squirrel and rabbit in West Tenneseee and his strong German heritage, meant that a favorite fare at the Wirwa table was Brunswick stew. It still is, over one hundred years later!

2 MEDIUM FRYERS (CAN SUBSTITUTE SQUIRREL OR RABBIT, OR A COMBINATION OF THE THREE)

2 LARGE CANS TOMATOES

1 SMALL CAN WHOLE GRAIN CORN (OR ABOUT 2 EARS)

2 MEDIUM POTATOES, BOILED AND MASHED

1 LARGE ONION, CHOPPED

SALT AND PEPPER TO TASTE

TABASCO SAUCE TO TASTE

Boil chickens until meat falls from bone (about 1 hour). Remove bones and skin. Place meat back in broth. Continue cooking at slow boil. Add tomatoes and onion. Cook potatoes separately and cream when done. Add to stew. Add salt and pepper to taste. (We like a lot of pepper.) Let cook until liquid has nearly disappeared. Wait until 20 minutes before serving to add corn. Add Tabasco to taste. *Yield:* 6 generous servings.

Amy Blake Wirwa Hearn, *Milan*

Beef

Green Bean Chili (or Chili Tomorrow)

1 POUND LEAN GROUND BEEF, BROWNED AND DRAINED	1 CUP ONION, CHOPPED
1 QUART TOMATO JUICE	1 CUP CELERY, CHOPPED
1 QUART WATER	1 TABLESPOON CHILI POWDER
2 BEEF BOUILLON CUBES	1 QUART GREEN BEANS
1 CUP GREEN PEPPER, CHOPPED	SALT, PEPPER, OREGANO, PARSLEY TO TASTE

You can add more or less of anything. Cook at least 1 hour; the longer the better. You can also add any other vegetable to make it more like vegetable soup.

Kathy Dowda, *Kingsport*

Chili

4 POUNDS GROUND BEEF, BROWNED	3 CANS KIDNEY BEANS
6 LARGE ONIONS, CHOPPED	6 TABLESPOONS CHILI POWDER
4 CUPS WATER	SALT TO TASTE
6 CLOVES GARLIC, MINCED	1/2 TEASPOON RED PEPPER
6 SMALL CANS TOMATOES	

Simmer ground beef, onions, water and minced garlic in a large kettle for 1 1/2 hours. Simmer tomatoes, kidney beans, chili powder, salt, red pepper with other ingredients for 1 hour. Sit down and eat with crackers.

Robbie J. Melton, *Allons*

Five Hour Beef Stew

1 1/2 POUND CHUCK ROAST, CUT IN BITE SIZE CHUNKS	1 NO. 2 CAN TOMATOES
1 CUP CELERY, CHUNKED	1 TABLESPOON SALT
4 CARROTS, CHUNKED	2 TABLESPOONS SUGAR
2 OR 3 MEDIUM POTATOES, CHUNKED	3 TABLESPOONS MINUTE TAPIOCA
1 ONION, SLICED	2 OR 3 GENEROUS SPLASHES OF WORCESTERSHIRE SAUCE
1/2 CUP FRESH BREAD CRUMBS	SPRINKLE OF OREGANO (OPTIONAL)

Do not brown meat. Mix all ingredients together in baking dish with a tight fitting lid, or cover securely with aluminum foil. Bake in a 250 degree oven for 5 to 6 hours. Do not try to hurry this stew. The slow oven is the key to its success.

Lorraine Whitler, *Nashville*

Swiss Vegetable Stew

1/4 CUP BUTTER OR MARGARINE, MELTED	1 TEASPOON SALT
1 1/2 CUPS YELLOW SQUASH, SLICED	1/4 TEASPOON DRY MUSTARD
1 1/2 CUPS BROCCOLI, SLICED IN 1-INCH PIECES	1/2 CUP SWISS CHEESE
1 EGG	1/4 CUP PARMESAN CHEESE, GRATED
1/4 CUP MILK	

Sauté vegetables in butter until they can be pierced with a fork. In a large bowl, heat egg, stir in milk, salt, mustard and Swiss cheese. Place vegetables in 1-quart casserole. Bake uncovered in a 300 degree oven for 20 minutes, or until thoroughly heated. *Yield:* 8 to 10 servings.

Note: This menu may be prepared ahead of time, refrigerated overnight and baked on the day it is to be served.

Leora McPherson, *Nolensville*

Church Stew

As a farm child growing up in rural Madison County in West Tennessee during the depression years, I experienced very few social events. Our country church 4th of July picnic was such an event. The older men of the community barbecued whole hogs and made stew. My father was a young man then and did not have enough seniority to make that stew, but he knew how it was done. Years later when our family began a tradition, he was the authority and to this day (he is 81) he makes stew in a black iron "wash pot" every 4th of July.

10 POUNDS CHUCK ROAST	1 GALLON FRESH CUT CORN
10 POUNDS PORK ROAST	5 POUNDS ONIONS, SLICED
12 POUNDS STEWING HENS	3 GALLONS FRESH TOMATOES, PEELED
2 POUNDS DRY WHITE BEANS, SOAKED OVERNIGHT	1/2 CUP SALT
	1/4 CUP BLACK PEPPER
1 GALLON FRESH BUTTER BEANS	2 TABLESPOONS CAYENNE PEPPER

Salt meats and cook until tender in moderate amount of water. When cool, skin and bone hens, cut all meat into larger than bite sized pieces and return it to broth. In an outdoor cooking pot, or the equivalent, cook white beans, lima beans and onions until tender but firm in just enough water to cover. Add corn, salt and peppers. Stir continually to keep corn from sticking. Cook 30 minutes. Add tomatoes and cook 30 minutes more. Add meat and broth to the cooked vegetable mixture. The consistency should be rather thick. This makes approximately 8 gallons and can be frozen in whatever serving quantity you prefer.

Note: Ideally this would be made in summer when fresh vegetables are plentiful; however, it can be made with fresh frozen vegetables without losing the unique flavor.

Venis Gee Spencer, *Jackson*

Photographic Services

Photographic Services

Quick Vegetable Stew

Great for freezing leftovers for a quick lunch. Serve with your favorite cornbread recipe. A meal in itself.

1 POUND HAMBURGER MEAT	1 ONION (MEDIUM)
2 TEASPOONS SALT	1 CAN GREEN BEANS, DRAINED
1 TEASPOON BLACK PEPPER	1 CAN GREEN PEAS, DRAINED
1 TEASPOON DRY TACO SEASONING	1 CAN WHOLE KERNEL CORN
1/2 TEASPOON PAPRIKA	1 32-OUNCE CAN TOMATO JUICE
1 TEASPOON WORCESTERSHIRE SAUCE	1 CUPS FROZEN BABY LIMA BEANS
1 7-OUNCE CAN TOMATO PASTE	1 SMALL JAR SLICED MUSHROOMS (OPTIONAL)
1 CARROT	1 LARGE POTATO, DICED
1 STALK CELERY	1 CUP ELBOW MACARONI (OPTIONAL)

Brown hamburger in large Dutch oven. Add spices, seasonings, and tomato paste. Mix well. Grate carrot, celery and onion in blender; add and stir well. Add other ingredients and stir well, mixing thoroughly. Cook on medium high for 10 minutes, stirring once or twice, then reduce heat to low for about 20 to 30 minutes. *Yield:* 4 quarts.

Gloria D. Mangrum, *Fairview*

Spaghetti Pie

1½ POUNDS GROUND BEEF
1 MEDIUM ONION, CHOPPED
1 STALK CELERY, CHOPPED
1 16-OUNCE CAN TOMATOES, CHOPPED
1 6-OUNCE CAN TOMATO PASTE
SALT AND PEPPER TO TASTE
SUGAR TO TASTE

6 OUNCES SPAGHETTI
¼ CUP BUTTER, MELTED
⅓ CUP GRATED PARMESAN CHEESE
2 EGGS, BEATEN
1 CUP COTTAGE CHEESE
1½ CUPS (6 OUNCES) SHREDDED MOZZARELLA CHEESE

Brown meat; drain. Add onion and celery; cook until tender. Stir in tomatoes and tomato paste; season to taste with salt, pepper and sugar. Mix well. Simmer 20 minutes. Cook spaghetti according to package directions; drain. Combine with butter, parmesan cheese and eggs; mix well. Line a greased 10-inch pie plate with spaghetti mixture to form a crust. Spoon cottage cheese over crust. Top with meat sauce and mozzarella cheese. Bake in a 325 degree oven for 45 minutes. *Yield:* 6 to 8 servings.

Nancy Love, *Franklin*

Millie's Hamburger Casserole

1 POUND GROUND HAMBURGER
1 MEDIUM ONION
1 CAN VEG-ALL

1 CAN TOMATO SOUP
4 MEDIUM POTATOES
SALT AND PEPPER TO TASTE

In skillet, brown hamburger and onion. Drain off grease. In 2-quart casserole dish, place sliced potatoes. Add browned hamburger and onion on top of this. In a separate bowl, take liquid from Veg-All and the tomato soup (undiluted) and mix together. Veg-All should be layered on top of hamburger. Top with soup mixture. Place covered casserole dish in a 350 degree oven for 1 hour or until potatoes are cooked.

Vickie Ghee (Mrs. Ron) Stinson, *Chapel Hill*

Texas Hash

1 POUND HAMBURGER
2 MEDIUM ONIONS, SLICED
½ GREEN PEPPER, CUT IN PIECES
1 16-OUNCE CAN TOMATOES
1 CUP TOMATO JUICE

2 CUPS NOODLES, UNCOOKED
1 TO 2 TEASPOON CHILI SEASONING
1 TEASPOON SALT
¼ TEASPOON PEPPER

Brown hamburger and pour off excess fat. Add sliced onions and cook on low for 5 minutes. Add remaining ingredients and place in casserole dish. Cover and bake in a 350 degree oven about 30 minutes.

Mary Mann West, *Columbia*

Charlie's Favorite Lasagna

1 POUND GROUND BEEF	1 PACKAGE LASAGNA NOODLES
1 ONION	1 8-OUNCE CARTON COTTAGE CHEESE
1/2 BELL PEPPER	1/4 CUP PARMESAN CHEESE
1 SMALL JAR MUSHROOMS	1/3 CUP PARSLEY FLAKES
1 JAR RAGU SPAGHETTI SAUCE	2 EGGS
SALT AND PEPPER TO TASTE	1 PACKAGE MOZZARELLA CHEESE, SLICED

Combine ground beef, onion, pepper and mushrooms; brown and remove excess fat. Add spaghetti sauce; salt and pepper to taste. Prepare lasagna noodles according to package. In small bowl mix cottage cheese, Parmesan cheese, parsley flakes and eggs. In a 13 x 9 x 2 inch pan add a layer of ground beef and a layer of noodles. Spread slices of Mozzarella cheese over noodles. Add cottage cheese mixture, layer of noodles, and the rest of the ground beef. You can add more Mozzarella cheese on top. Bake in a 375 degree oven for 30 minutes. Let set for 10 minutes before serving.

Mrs. Charles A. (Renee) Harber, *Bells*

Cheeseburger Pie

1 POUND GROUND BEEF	3/4 TEASPOON SALT
1/2 CUP EVAPORATED MILK	1/2 TEASPOON PEPPER
1/2 CUP CATSUP	1 DEEP DISH UNBAKED PIE SHELL
1/3 CUP DRY BREAD CRUMBS	4 OUNCES AMERICAN CHEESE, GRATED
1/4 CUP OREGANO, CHOPPED	1 TEASPOON WORCESTERSHIRE SAUCE

Combine ground beef, milk, catsup, bread crumbs, oregano, salt and pepper in a large bowl. Mix well with hands. Pat mixture into pie shell. Bake in a 350 degree oven for 30 to 35 minutes. Toss cheese with Worcestershire sauce and sprinkle on top of pie. Bake 10 minutes longer. Cool 10 minutes. Cut in wedges. *Yield:* 6 servings.

Note: A family favorite. Almost like meat loaf, but different because of the cheese and Worcestershire sauce. A good dish to serve company.

Mrs. Sam Durbin, *Jackson*

Ground Beef, Corn and Cheese Bake

This recipe was a First Place Winner in the Dairy Recipe Contest for Monroe County.

3 TABLESPOONS BUTTER	2 TABLESPOONS DRIED OREGANO LEAVES
3 1/2 POUNDS GROUND BEEF	1 TABLESPOON SUGAR
3 3/4 CUPS FRESH WHOLE KERNEL CORN, OR 3 10-OUNCE PACKAGES FROZEN CORN, PARTLY THAWED	16 OUNCES NOODLES (MEDIUM), COOKED
	3 1/2 CUPS COTTAGE CHEESE

3 15-OUNCE CANS TOMATO SAUCE	3 8-OUNCE PACKAGES CREAM CHEESE, SOFTENED
1 TEASPOON GARLIC SALT	1½ CUPS SOUR CREAM
¾ TEASPOON BLACK PEPPER	4½ CUPS CHEDDAR CHEESE, GRATED

Line three 8 x 8 x 2 inch baking dishes with freezer wrap. (Do not line fourth baking dish, which is to be used for food to be served without freezing.) Melt butter in large skillet; add ground beef and cook over medium heat until browned., stirring with a fork to separate. Remove meat with slotted spoon to drain. Pour off pan drippings and put meat back into skillet; stir in corn, tomato sauce, garlic salt, black pepper, oregano and sugar; cook over moderate heat for 5 minutes. Remove skillet from heat. Cook noodles as directed on package; drain. Mix cottage cheese, cream cheese and sour cream in a large mixing bowl; then mix with cooked noodles. Layer half of the noodle-cheese mixture in the bottom of the 4 casserole dishes; cover with half the meat sauce and sprinkle ⅓ cup grated cheese on each casserole. Add remaining noodle-cheese mixture, and then meat sauce. Sprinkle each with remaining grated cheese.

To bake without freezing: heat oven to 350 degrees. Bake casserole uncovered 40 to 45 minutes, or until bubbly and lightly browned.

To freeze: fold and seal freezer wrap on remaining casseroles. Label and freeze.

To bake after freezing: heat oven to 350 degrees. Remove freezer wrap from frozen casserole. Place, still frozen, in original baking dish. Bake uncovered 1 hour and 15 minutes, or until heated through and lightly brown.

Note: The size of the baking dish can be adjusted to the number of servings needed each time.

Lorene Dial, *Madisonville*

Sour Cream Noodle Casserole

1 8-OUNCE PACKAGE MEDIUM NOODLES	1 8-OUNCE CAN TOMATO SAUCE
1 POUND GROUND BEEF	1 CUP CREAMED COTTAGE CHEESE
2 TABLESPOONS BUTTER	1 CUP DAIRY SOUR CREAM
1 TEASPOON SALT	½ CUP GREEN ONIONS, CHOPPED
⅛ TEASPOON PEPPER	¾ CUP SHARP CHEDDAR CHEESE, SHREDDED
¼ TEASPOON GARLIC SALT	

Cook noodles in boiling salted water according to package directions. Rinse and drain. Brown meat in butter in skillet. Add salt, pepper, garlic salt and tomato sauce. Simmer 5 minutes. Combine cottage cheese, sour cream, chopped onion and noodles. Alternate layers of noodle mixture and meat mixture in a 2-quart casserole, beginning with noodles and ending with meat. Top with shredded cheddar cheese. Bake in a 350 degree oven for 25 to 30 minutes, or until cheese is melted and browned. *Yield:* 8 servings.

Mary T. Turner, *Blountville*

Weekend Special

1½ POUND HAMBURGER OR GROUND BEEF	1 CAN PEAS (ENGLISH GREEN PEAS)
1 MEDIUM ONION, CHOPPED	½ CUP ELBOW SPAGHETTI
1 GREEN PEPPER, CHOPPED	1 10-OUNCE CAN TOMATO SAUCE
1 CAN WHOLE TOMATOES	1 TEASPOON CHILI POWDER (OPTIONAL)
1 CAN VEG-ALL	SALT AND PEPPER TO TASTE

Brown ground beef, onion and green pepper until tender. While that is simmering, cook the spaghetti according to box directions and set aside. Add all the canned ingredients to the ground beef mixture and heat thoroughly. Transfer this to a casserole dish, add the spaghetti, mix thoroughly. Place this in a 300 degree oven and bake for 1 hour and 30 minutes. *Yield:* 7 to 8 servings.

Willie Mae Carter, *Lexington*

Pepper Steak

2 POUNDS FILET STEAK, THINLY SLICED	3 SMALL TOMATOES, QUARTERED
¼ CUP ALL-PURPOSE FLOUR	1½ CUPS BEEF BOUILLON
1 CUP BUTTER	2 TABLESPOONS CORNSTARCH
2 GREEN PEPPERS, SLICED	¾ CUP RED COOKING WINE
2 ONIONS, SLICED	2 TABLESPOONS SOY SAUCE
2 CLOVES GARLIC, MINCED	SALT AND PEPPER TO TASTE
½ POUND MUSHROOMS, SLICED	

Dip steak in flour. In large skillet, sauté in half the butter; sauté peppers, onions, garlic and mushrooms in remaining butter for 5 minutes. Add tomatoes and bouillon. Bring to a boil, then reduce heat; simmer 10 minutes. Mix cornstarch, red cooking wine and soy sauce. Add to skillet, cook and stir until thickened. Add meat. Simmer 5 minutes. Serve with rice or noodles. *Yield:* 4 to 6 servings.

Note: To use less tender cuts of meat such as round or flank steak, slice meat paper thin. Brown as above, without flour; but return to skillet with bouillon.

Mrs. Sam Durbin, *Jackson*

Lois's Swiss Steak with Vegetable Sauce

1½ POUNDS ROUND STEAK	1 STALK CELERY, CHOPPED
¼ CUP ALL-PURPOSE FLOUR	2 MEDIUM-SIZED ONIONS, CHOPPED
¼ TEASPOON SALT	1½ CUPS CANNED TOMATOES
¼ TEASPOON PEPPER	¼ CUP ALL-PURPOSE FLOUR
2 TABLESPOONS SHORTENING	SALT AND PEPPER TO TASTE
½ CUP WATER	1 GREEN PEPPER, CHOPPED
3 STRIPS BACON	2 CARROTS, DICED

Pound beef thoroughly with meat mallet. Roll in flour which has been seasoned with salt and pepper. Brown well on both sides in a heavy skillet with plenty of shortening to keep meat from sticking. Then pour into a casserole and pour 1/2 cup of water into the skillet to loosen up the crusted juices and cook until slightly thick. Pour this over meat in casserole. Cover and bake in slow oven (300 degrees) for 1 1/2 to 2 hours, or until the meat is very tender. Cut the bacon into small pieces and fry; add the celery, onions, canned tomatoes, pepper and carrots. Season well and cook until chopped vegetables are tender. Serve the sauce with the meat.

Gail N. Steele, *Knoxville*

For years, refrigerated cars carrying bananas stopped in South Fulton, Tennessee, and its twin city of Fulton, Kentucky, to be re-iced. In 1962, the two towns began the annual International Banana Festival to promote friendship between banana-producing countries and the United States. The World's Largest Banana Pudding, made of 3,000 sliced bananas, 250 pounds of vanilla wafers, and 950 pounds of boiled custard, is served to 10,000 visitors each year.

Barbecued Beef

1 4 OR 5-POUND BEEF ROAST	2 TABLESPOONS BROWN SUGAR
1 CUP MEAT STOCK, OR 1 BOUILLON CUBE DISSOLVED IN 1 CUP BOILING WATER	1 TABLESPOON LEMON JUICE
1 CUP CATSUP OR CHILI SAUCE	2 TABLESPOONS VINEGAR
1 TABLESPOON WORCESTERSHIRE SAUCE	1 TEASPOON CELERY SALT
1 TEASPOON SALT	1 TEASPOON ONION SALT

Cook roast until tender. Shred the meat and put in a skillet. Add meat stock, catsup, Worcestershire sauce, salt, brown sugar, lemon juice, vinegar, celery salt and onion salt. Cook over low heat about 30 minutes. Serve on hamburger buns. *Yield:* 6 to 8 servings.

Mrs. Barbara Long, *Elizabethton*

Mexican Casserole

1 PACKAGE FROZEN TORTILLAS	1 13¼-OUNCE CAN CREAM OF MUSHROOM SOUP
2 POUNDS HAMBURGER	1 13¼-OUNCE CAN CREAM OF CHICKEN SOUP
SALT, PEPPER AND GARLIC POWDER TO TASTE	1 SMALL CAN TACO SAUCE
1 ONION, CHOPPED	1 SMALL CAN CHOPPED CHILI PEPPERS
½ CUP WATER	1 POUND SHARP CHEDDAR CHEESE, GRATED
1 LARGE CAN EVAPORATED MILK	

Place a layer of tortillas in bottom of casserole. Brown hamburger with salt, pepper and garlic powder; add remaining ingredients except cheese. Place a layer of meat mixture over the tortillas, then place another layer of tortillas; place meat mixture on top. Add grated cheese. Bake in a 350 degree oven for 45 minutes or until bubbly.

Joni Compton, *Madison*

Round Steak Casserole

1 CUP ONION, CHOPPED	1½ SOUP CANS WATER
1 CUP BELL PEPPER, CHOPPED	2 CUPS INSTANT RICE
1 CUP CELERY, CHOPPED	½ CUP ALMONDS (OPTIONAL)
¼ CUP MARGARINE	1 SMALL CAN MUSHROOMS (OR ½ POUND FRESH MUSHROOMS)
1 1-POUND ROUND STEAK, CUT INTO BITE-SIZED PIECES	SALT AND PEPPER TO TASTE
1 CAN GOLDEN MUSHROOM SOUP	3 SLICES AMERICAN CHEESE OR ½ CUP GRATED CHEESE

Brown onion, bell pepper and celery in margarine. In separate skillet, brown the round steak; combine with onion, bell pepper and celery. Stir in soup and water. Add uncooked rice, almonds and mushrooms; salt and pepper to taste. Cook 10 minutes over low heat. Pour into 1½-quart casserole dish and cover. Bake in a 325 degree oven about 20 minutes. Remove lid. Top with cheese and bake again until cheese melts, about 8 minutes.

Darlene Spoon, *Lenoir City*

Down-Home Beef Casserole

1 POUND GROUND BEEF	1 CAN TOMATO SOUP
SALT TO TASTE	½ SOUP CAN OF WATER
1 ONION, CHOPPED	1 CUP SELF-RISING MEAL
1 GREEN PEPPER, CHOPPED	1 TEASPOON SUGAR
1 CAN WHOLE KERNEL CORN (WATER AND ALL)	1 EGG
1 CAN RED KIDNEY BEANS	MILK AS NEEDED

Brown ground beef, salting to taste. Add onion, green pepper, corn, kidney beans, soup and water and stir; cook mixture until pepper and onion are done. Put into casserole dish. In a medium mixing bowl, mix together meal, sugar and egg; add milk to thin batter so it can be spooned over beef mixture. Bake in a 400 degree oven until cornbread is done.

Patricia Wilds, *Newport*

Yumzetti

1 POUND HAMBURGER	1 CAN TOMATO PASTE
1 CAN CREAM OF CELERY SOUP	1 PACKAGE WIDE NOODLES
1 CAN CREAM OF MUSHROOM SOUP	6 TO 8 SLICES OF VELVEETA CHEESE

Brown hamburger. Cook noodles until tender. Mix together soups and tomato paste. Put in layers in casserole. Bake in a 350 degree oven for 45 minutes, then remove and add cheese on top. Return to oven until cheese has melted.

Susan D. Gratz, *Morristown*

Porky Pines Hamburger

2 POUNDS GROUND CHUCK OR HAMBURGER MEAT	1 TABLESPOON WORCESTERSHIRE SAUCE
2 EGGS, WELL BEATEN	1 13-OUNCE OR LARGE 16-OUNCE CAN TOMATO SAUCE
1 LARGE ONION, DICED	1 13-OUNCE CAN TOMATO PASTE, DILUTED WITH WATER
1½ TEASPOON GARLIC SALT OR 1 GARLIC BUD	1 CUP UNCLE BEN'S RICE, UNCOOKED
1 TEASPOON SEASONED SALT OR SEASON-ALL	1 16-OUNCE CAN TOMATO JUICE
1 CUP BREAD CRUMBS OR CRACKER CRUMBS	½ CUP WATER

Mix hamburger, eggs, onions, garlic, seasoned salt, Worcestershire sauce, tomato sauce (part of can), tomato paste (part of can) and uncooked rice. Mix well. Roll meat mixture into balls about egg size. In hot electric skillet add tomato juice, rest of tomato paste with water and rest of tomato sauce. Let it come to a good boil. Drop meat balls in, let boil a few minutes then turn to simmer. Cover meat balls with juice and cover with lid. Stir a little and turn over lightly. Check now and then; don't let it get too dry. Cook 40 minutes to be sure rice is done. *Yield:* 6 to 8 servings.

Mrs. Mary E. Handley, *Chattanooga*

Tennessee Pot-Roast

1 3 TO 3½-POUND BONELESS BEEF ROAST	1 BEEF BOUILLON CUBE, CRUSHED
3 TABLESPOONS ALL-PURPOSE FLOUR	4 CARROTS, CUT IN 3-INCH PIECES
1 TEASPOON SALT	1 CUP CELERY, 2-INCH PIECES
¼ TEASPOON ALLSPICE	3 MEDIUM SIZE POTATOES, CUT IN QUARTERS
2 TABLESPOONS SHORTENING	1 TEASPOON THYME
2 CUPS APPLE JUICE	

Combine flour, salt, pepper and allspice. Dredge meat, reserving excess flour. Brown meat in shortening. Remove meat to Dutch oven or large pan. Heat apple juice and crushed bouillon cube and stir to dissolve. Pour liquid over meat, cover tightly and cook slowly 2 hours. Add carrots, celery, potatoes and thyme; cover and continue cooking for 30 minutes, or until meat and vegetables are tender. Remove meat and vegetables to warm platter. *Yield:* 8 to 10 servings.

Mrs. George Lance, *Madison*

Barbecued Pot Roast

1 4 TO 5-POUND BEEF SHOULDER OR CHUCK ROAST	2 TABLESPOONS WORCESTERSHIRE SAUCE
2 TABLESPOONS VEGETABLE OIL	1 TEASPOON SALT
2 MEDIUM ONIONS, SLICED	½ CUP CATSUP
2 CLOVES GARLIC, MINCED	¼ CUP RED WINE VINEGAR
½ CUP WATER	1 TEASPOON ROSEMARY LEAVES
	1½ POUNDS SMALL POTATOES, PEELED

Brown roast on all sides in hot oil in a large Dutch oven; add onion and garlic. Combine remaining ingredients except potatoes; mix well and pour over roast. Cover and simmer 2 hours; add potatoes and cook an additional 30 minutes. *Yield:* 8 servings.

Mrs. Dennis H. Donovan, *Nashville*

German Style Steak

2 POUNDS ROUND STEAK (MINUTE STEAKS)	1 CAN GOLDEN MUSHROOM SOUP
ALL-PURPOSE FLOUR	1 CAN CREAM OF CHICKEN SOUP
WESSON OIL	1 4-OUNCE CAN MUSHROOMS
ONIONS TO COVER STEAK, SLICED	SALT AND PEPPER TO TASTE

Spread prepared mustard on both sides of meat. Flour both sides. Brown in oil on both sides. Slice onions over top of meat. Mix soups, mushrooms and liquid. Add water as desired. Pour over meat and simmer 45 minutes or until tender. Season to taste. *Yield:* 6 servings.

Mrs. Nathan Fox, *Columbia*

Company Meatballs

1 POUND GROUND CHUCK	1/4 TEASPOON PEPPER
2 SLICES BREAD, IN CRUMBS	1 TEASPOON WORCESTERSHIRE SAUCE
1/2 CUP OATS	4 OUNCES TOMATO SAUCE
1/2 CUP MILK	6 TABLESPOONS CATSUP
1 EGG, BEATEN	1 HEAPING TABLESPOON DRIED ONION FLAKES
1 TEASPOON SALT	

Combine all ingredients, using hands to mix well. Form into balls and place in baking dish. Cover with sauce.

Sauce:

4 OUNCES TOMATO SAUCE	2 TABLESPOONS MOLASSES
ENOUGH CATSUP TO MAKE 1 1/4 CUPS LIQUID	1 HEAPING TEASPOON PREPARED MUSTARD

Mix well and pour sauce over meatballs. Bake in a 350 degree oven for approximately 1 hour or until meatballs begin to brown.

Mrs. Jo Ann King, *Knoxville*

Beef Stroganoff

2 MEDIUM ONIONS	1/8 TEASPOON PEPPER
1/4 CUP SALAD OIL	1/4 TEASPOON WORCESTERSHIRE SAUCE
1/2 POUND MUSHROOMS	DASH TABASCO SAUCE
1 POUND ROUND, SIRLOIN OR FLANK STEAK	DASH GARLIC POWDER
2 TABLESPOONS ALL-PURPOSE FLOUR	2 CUPS TOMATO JUICE
1 LARGE CAN TOMATOES, CHOPPED	1/2 CUP SOUR CREAM
1 1/2 TEASPOONS SALT	

Slice onions thin as possible, and cook slowly in salad oil. Slice mushrooms and add to golden brown onions. Cook 5 minutes more; remove to small bowl. Remove all fat from steak, and cut in bite size cubes and brown in same skillet. Sprinkle flour over meat and blend in well. Add chopped tomatoes with their juice and add salt, pepper, Worcestershire, Tabasco and garlic powder. Add 2 cups tomato juice. Cover skillet and let simmer 1 hour, stirring occasionally. Then add onions, mushrooms and sour cream and cover. Simmer 1/2 hour longer. Serve from chafing dish with noodles or rice. *Yield:* 4 servings.

Rose S. Vaughn, *Manchester*

Red River Stroganoff

2 POUNDS SIRLOIN STEAK, REMOVE FAT	1 TEASPOON SWEET BASIL
ALL-PURPOSE FLOUR FOR ROLLING STEAK	1 CUP WATER
¼ CUP BUTTER	1 TABLESPOON WORCESTERSHIRE SAUCE
2 LARGE ONIONS, CHOPPED	SALT AND PEPPER TO TASTE
1 CAN CONSOMMÉ	1 LARGE CAN MUSHROOMS (OPTIONAL)

Cut meat into ¼-inch cubes and roll in flour; brown in butter. Add onions, consommé, basil, water and Worcestershire mixture. Salt and pepper to taste. Cook slowly uncovered until meat is tender. Before serving add sour cream to taste. Serve over hot rice.

Note: Can be made from lean ground round steak. If using this, sprinkle about ¼ cup flour over meat as it browns and stir well before adding liquid.

Mary Alice Cox, *Clinton*

Italian Beef

6 POUND BEEF ROAST (SIRLOIN TIP OR BOTTOM ROUND)	1 CLOVE GARLIC, MINCED
SALT AND PEPPER TO TASTE	2 BAY LEAVES
3 CUPS WATER	2 TABLESPOONS VINEGAR
3 GREEN PEPPERS, SLICED	½ TEASPOON OREGANO
1 TEASPOON CARAWAY SEED	2 MEDIUM ONIONS, SLICED

Salt and pepper beef roast; cook for 2 hours. Cool and slice very thin. Add remaining ingredients to sliced beef and cook 2 more hours. Remove bay leaves. Serve on hard rolls with green pepper. Dip in au jus.

Ina Linderman, *Rogersville*

Fillet of Beef With Port Butter

3 CUPS BEEF STOCK	2 TABLESPOONS PORT WINE
1 CUP PORT WINE	2 TABLESPOONS RED WINE VINEGAR
1 6-POUND BEEF FILLET AT ROOM TEMPERATURE, TRIMMED	8 TABLESPOONS UNSALTED BUTTER, MELTED
2 TABLESPOONS MINCED SHALLOTS OR ONION	½ TEASPOON SALT
	¼ TEASPOON COARSELY GROUND BLACK PEPPER

Combine stock and 1 cup port in a saucepan. Boil until reduced to approximately ¾ cup. Set aside. Place meat in oven that has been preheated to 450 degrees. Immediately reduce heat to 375 degrees. Roast meat to 125 degrees on meat thermometer, about 1 hour and 15 minutes. Set meat aside. Drain all but 1 tablespoon of fat from roasting pan. Add shallots or onion, 2 tablespoons port and vinegar. Bring to a boil scraping sides and bottom of pan. Boil over moderate heat for 1 minute. Add original sauce and boil another 2 minutes. Remove from heat and mix in butter, 2 tablespoons at a time with a wire whisk. Add salt and pepper. Slice fillet and spoon sauce over slices. *Yield:* 12 to 14 servings.

Daisy King, *Nashville*

Sloppy Joes

2 TABLESPOONS SHORTENING	1 TEASPOON GARLIC POWDER
1¼ POUNDS GROUND BEEF	2 TABLESPOONS ALL-PURPOSE FLOUR
½ CUP ONION, CHOPPED	1⅔ CUP (1 LARGE CAN) EVAPORATED MILK
1 TEASPOON SALT	1 CUP CATSUP
1 TABLESPOON CHILI POWDER	DASH LIQUID SMOKE (OPTIONAL)

Cook beef and onion in shortening until beef is browned and onion is tender. Drain off excess fat. Sprinkle in seasonings and flour; stir well. Gradually add milk. Cook over low heat stirring constantly until thickened. Add catsup and smoke. Heat to serving temperature.

Mrs. Calvin (Ruth) Borden, *Fairfield Glade*

Roast 'Sharon Style'

1 2½ TO 3-POUND BONELESS CHUCK ROAST	1 MEDIUM ONION, CHOPPED
GARLIC POWDER	1 32-OUNCE BOTTLE SAUERKRAUT, DRAINED
CAYENNE PEPPER	1 28-OUNCE CAN TOMATOES, RESERVE JUICE
ALL-PURPOSE FLOUR	1 CUP BROWN SUGAR
1 TABLESPOON OIL	

Season meat with garlic powder and cayenne pepper to taste; lightly flour meat. Heat oil in Dutch oven and sauté onions. On top of onions, brown meat on both sides. Put sauerkraut on top of meat. Mash tomatoes and put on top of sauerkraut. Put brown sugar on top of tomatoes and then gently pour reserved tomato juice on top. Cover and bake in a 350 degree oven for about 2½ to 3 hours. Remove cover for the last ½ hour of cooking.

Sharon Abroms, *Nashville*

Sweet and Sour Meat Loaf

1½ POUNDS GROUND BEEF	¼ TEASPOON PEPPER
1 CUP BREAD CRUMBS	1 8-OUNCE CAN TOMATO SAUCE
1 TEASPOON SALT	1 SMALL ONION, CHOPPED

Combine the above; form a loaf and bake in a 350 degree oven for 50 minutes.

Sauce:

1 8-OUNCE CAN TOMATO SAUCE	½ CUP SUGAR
2 TABLESPOONS BROWN SUGAR	2 TEASPOONS PREPARED MUSTARD
2 TABLESPOONS VINEGAR	

Combine all ingredients in a saucepan and bring to a boil. Pour over meat loaf and bake another 10 minutes.

Mrs. Lee Vance, *Erwin*

Perry Masseingill hunts squirrels on the Cumberland Plateau. Here it's more than sport, for the game Perry and others shoot will be eaten.

Meat Loaf

1 POUND GROUND BEEF

1 POUND GROUND PORK

1 CUP FINE DRY BREAD CRUMBS

2 EGGS, BEATEN

1/3 CUP ONION, CHOPPED

2 TEASPOONS SALT

1/4 TEASPOON DRY MUSTARD

1/8 TEASPOON GARLIC SALT

1/8 TEASPOON CELERY SALT

1/8 TEASPOON PAPRIKA

1/4 TEASPOON BLACK PEPPER

Combine the 2 meats thoroughly in a large mixing bowl; then work in bread crumbs. Beat eggs well, add onion and other seasonings, and mix well. Add to meat and stir or knead until blended. Pack into a buttered bread loaf pan and unmold onto a flat baking pan. Bake in a 350 degree oven for 1½ hours, or until well done. *Yield:* 10 servings.

Mrs. Ruth Ramsey, *Piney Flats*

Party Meat Loaf

3 EGGS, SLIGHTLY BEATEN

1/3 CUP EVAPORATED MILK

1/3 CUP PICKLE RELISH, DRAINED

1 TABLESPOON INSTANT MINCED ONION

1 CUP AMERICAN CHEESE, CUT IN 1/4 INCH CUBES

1 POUND GROUND LEAN CHUCK

1 POUND SAUSAGE

1 CUP FINE DRY BREAD CRUMBS

Combine all ingredients thoroughly. Shape into loaf and place in 9 x 5 x 3 inch baking pan. Tuck extra cheese cubes in as much as possible. Top with 1/2 cup Barbecue Sauce. Bake in a 350 degree oven for 70 to 75 minutes. Remove from pan to platter. Serve with remaining Barbecue Sauce.

Barbecue Sauce:

1/2 CUP CATSUP

1 8-OUNCE CAN TOMATO SAUCE

2 TABLESPOONS BROWN SUGAR

2 TABLESPOONS ONION, FINELY CHOPPED

2 TABLESPOONS PICKLE RELISH, DRAINED

2 TABLESPOONS WATER

2 TABLESPOONS VINEGAR

1 TABLESPOON WORCESTERSHIRE SAUCE

DASH PEPPER

Combine all ingredients in a saucepan. Heat until steaming. Serve with Party Meat Loaf. *Yield:* about 2 cups sauce.

Mrs. Rolus Smith, *Nashville*

Company Meat Loaf

1 1/2 TO 2 POUNDS GROUND BEEF

1/4 POUND SAUSAGE

2 EGGS

1 TEASPOON SALT

1 TABLESPOON WORCESTERSHIRE SAUCE

1/2 TEASPOON BLACK PEPPER

PINCH SAGE

DASH GARLIC POWDER

1 CUP BREAD CRUMBS

1 CUP VELVEETA CHEESE, GRATED OR CUBED

1 CARROT, GRATED

1/4 CUP ONION, MINCED

1/4 CUP CELERY, CHOPPED

1/4 CUP SWEET PEPPER, CHOPPED

1 16-OUNCE CAN TOMATOES, DRAINED

Mix all loaf ingredients together. Form loaf and bake uncovered in a 425 degree oven for 45 to 60 minutes, or until almost done. While loaf is baking, mix topping ingredients together.

Topping:

1/4 CUP TOMATO CATSUP

1/2 TEASPOON DRY MUSTARD

3 TABLESPOONS BROWN SUGAR

1/8 TEASPOON ALLSPICE

Combine all ingredients; mix until sugar is dissolved. When loaf is almost done, remove from oven and prick top with fork. Pour on topping and bake another 10 to 15 minutes until lightly browned. Best to let loaf set 5 to 10 minutes before slicing. *Yield:* 6 to 8 servings.

Mrs. Mary Anne Wallace, *Knoxville*

Liver and Gravy

¼ CUP ALL-PURPOSE FLOUR
¼ TEASPOON SALT
⅛ TEASPOON PEPPER
1 POUND BEEF LIVER, THINLY SLICED
2 TABLESPOONS BACON DRIPPINGS
2 MEDIUM ONIONS, CHOPPED
3 TABLESPOONS BACON DRIPPINGS

1 TABLESPOON ALL-PURPOSE FLOUR
1½ CUPS WATER
½ TEASPOON WHOLE BASIL
1 TEASPOON SALT
½ TEASPOON WHOLE THYME
¼ TEASPOON PEPPER

Combine ¼ cup flour, ¼ teaspoon salt, and ⅛ teaspoon pepper. Coat liver in seasoned flour mixture, and brown in 2 tablespoons bacon drippings. Remove liver and place in a shallow 1½-quart baking dish.

Sauté onion in 3 tablespoons bacon drippings. Add 1 tablespoon flour, stirring occasionally until brown. Gradually add all water, stirring until smooth. Stir in seasonings; pour over liver. Bake in a 350 degree oven for 40 minutes or until gravy is thickened and liver is tender. *Yield:* 4 servings.

Mrs. Ruth Ramsey, *Piney Flats*

Liver Casserole

1 CUP ELBOW MACARONI
4 SLICES BACON
2 TABLESPOONS BACON FAT
½ POUND BEEF LIVER, UNCOOKED, CUBED
2 TABLESPOONS ALL-PURPOSE FLOUR
1 TEASPOON SALT

½ CUP ONIONS, SLICED
2 CANS CONDENSED CREAM OF MUSHROOM SOUP, UNDILUTED
¾ CUP MILK
1½ TABLESPOONS BOTTLED MEAT SAUCE
1 CUP CANNED WHOLE KERNEL CORN

Cook macaroni as package directed; drain. Meanwhile, sauté bacon until lightly browned; drain. Pour off all but 2 tablespoons fat. Sprinkle liver with flour and salt; sauté quickly in fat until well browned; add onions and cook until just tender. Pour soup into 1½-quart casserole; slowly stir in milk and meat sauce. Fold in macaroni, liver and onions and corn. Top with bacon strips. Bake in casserole in a 350 degree oven about 50 minutes or until bubbly. This may be prepared ahead and refrigerated before cooking.

Mrs. Eloise Throop, *Mountain City*

Hungarian Stuffed Cabbage

1 LARGE HEAD CABBAGE
1½ POUNDS GROUND CHUCK
1 MEDIUM ONION, FINELY CHOPPED
½ CUP RICE, UNCOOKED
1½ TEASPOONS SALT
¼ TEASPOON PEPPER
1 LARGE ONION, SLICED

2 TABLESPOONS WESSON OIL
1 PINT CAN TOMATO JUICE
1 8-OUNCE CAN TOMATO SAUCE
1 CUP SAUERKRAUT, UNDRAINED
1 TABLESPOON BROWN SUGAR
1 CUP WATER

Wash and core cabbage, put in large pot of boiling water. Cook 10 minutes. Remove from heat, let stand 10 to 15 minutes to soften leaves, then drain. Thoroughly mix meat, minced onion, rice, salt and pepper. Separate cabbage leaves carefully, keeping them whole. Put leaf on a cutting board and cut off rib to thickness of leaf. Put a tablespoon of meat mixture at base of leaf, roll up loosely to permit swelling of rice. Cook sliced onion in oil in Dutch oven until golden. Add tomato juice, tomato sauce and sauerkraut. Sprinkle brown sugar over top. Arrange the cabbage rolls in pot on top of the kraut mixture, and pour water over all. Cover and bake in a 350 degree oven for about 1 hour. *Yield:* about 20 rolls.

Mrs. Willie B. Gilliam, *Lenoir City*

Quick Pizza Casserole

1 POUND GROUND BEEF	¾ CUP BISCUIT MIX
1 14-OUNCE JAR PIZZA SAUCE	1½ CUPS MILK
2 CUPS (8 OUNCES) MOZARELLA CHEESE, SHREDDED	2 EGGS

Cook ground beef until browned, stirring to crumble. Drain off pan drippings. Spoon beef into an 8-inch square baking dish. Top with pizza sauce and cheese.

Combine biscuit mix, milk, and eggs, beat until smooth. Pour mixture over casserole, covering evenly. Bake in a 400 degree oven for 30 to 35 minutes. *Yield:* 6 servings.

Malinda Pafford, *Camden*

Pizza Casserole

1 4-OUNCE PACKAGE PEPPERONI	½ TEASPOON BASIL
1 6-OUNCE PACKAGE SPAGHETTI	½ TEASPOON OREGANO
¼ CUP MARGARINE	1 4-OUNCE CAN SLICED MUSHROOMS, DRAINED
PARMESAN CHEESE	
1 MEDIUM ONION, CHOPPED	1 2-CUP PACKAGE GRATED MOZARELLA CHEESE
1 POUND GROUND BEEF	1 PACKAGE SLICED MOZARELLA CHEESE
2 8-OUNCE CANS TOMATO SAUCE	

Boil pepperoni for 5 minutes; drain on paper towel. Cook and drain spaghetti. Add butter or margarine and a generous amount of Parmesan cheese to spaghetti. Cook onion and ground beef together until meat is browned; drain off grease. Add tomato sauce and seasonings to meat and simmer covered for 20 minutes. Add drained mushrooms to meat sauce after it simmers. Layer in long 9 x 13 inch Pyrex dish in this order: spaghetti, grated Mozarella, pepperoni, meat sauce, and sliced mozarella. Bake uncovered in a 350 degree oven for 20 minutes.

Darlene Spoon, *Lenoir City*

Miscellaneous Meats

Chitterlings (Chittlins)

This recipe was used by J. B. Johnson, a well-known Maury County cook, for many years. He could prepare meals for ten to one thousand persons with ease and extreme efficiency.

25 POUNDS FROZEN OR FRESH CHITTERLINGS	BAY LEAF
WATER	1 BUNCH CELERY, CHOPPED
1 CUP VINEGAR	SEVERAL WHITE ONIONS
RED PEPPER	SALT

If frozen, thaw chitterlings. Remove all fat; clean and wash thoroughly. Scrubbing on an old-fashioned washboard is very helpful. Place cleaned chitterlings in a black wash kettle. Cover with water and add vinegar, red pepper, bay leaf, celery, white onions and salt. Boil outdoors over a wood fire until tender, about 2 to 3 hours. If you prefer stewed chittlins, they are ready to eat when tender. Stewed chittlins may be placed in cold storage for 2 to 3 days, then reheated. Serve accompanied by cole slaw, French fries and hush puppies. *Yield:* 20 generous servings.

Fried: If you prefer chittlins fried, make a batter of the following ingredients:

5 POUNDS ALL-PURPOSE FLOUR	PEPPER
1 DOZEN EGGS	MILK TO MAKE A THICK BATTER
SALT	HOT SAUCE (IF DESIRED)

Combine flour, eggs, salt, pepper and milk to make a batter; drop small amounts of chitterlings into batter until coated thoroughly. Fry in deep fat, preferably Crisco, until golden brown. Drain and serve very hot with hot sauce, if desired.

Dot Sowell, *Columbia*

Squirrel Pot Pie

2 TO 4 SQUIRRELS	½ TEASPOON PARSLEY FLAKES
2 TABLESPOONS ALL-PURPOSE FLOUR	½ TEASPOON GROUND SAGE
2 TABLESPOONS BUTTER	½ BAY LEAF
1 TEASPOON SALT	10 TO 15 UNBAKED BISCUITS

Pressure cook squirrels until tender. Take squirrels from broth, reserving broth. Add water to broth to equal 2 cups liquid. Remove meat from bones and place meat in 9-inch square baking dish. Make thin white sauce of flour, butter and reserved liquid; add salt, parsley, sage and bay leaf. Pour sauce over meat; top with biscuits. Bake in a 450 degree oven for 20 to 30 minutes. Serve steaming hot. This is a good method of preparing squirrels too old to fry. *Yield:* 10 servings.

Mrs. Calvin (Ruth) Borden, *Fairfield Glade*

Lorene's Quail

I am married to an East Tennessee hunter who enjoys hunting quail during the hunting season. I have cooked quail many times and many ways, but this recipe was enjoyed by all hunters to whom I have served it. This recipe is a method, because I never know how many quail my hunter will bring home.

VEGETABLE OIL	QUAIL, DRESSED AND CUT UP AS DESIRED
ALL-PURPOSE FLOUR	ABOUT 1 TABLESPOON ONION, CHOPPED
SALT	1 CAN CREAM OF MUSHROOM SOUP
BLACK PEPPER	1 SOUP CAN MILK

Heat oil in skillet to medium hot. Mix flour, salt and pepper together. Roll quail in flour mixture and fry in oil until golden brown. Remove from oil and arrange in a baking dish. When all quail is browned, pour out remaining oil, leaving browned bits in skillet. Stir in chopped onion, add soup and milk; mix until smooth and thoroughly heated. Adjust salt and pepper to own taste. Pour mixture over browned quail. Bake in a 325 degree oven about 1 hour or until tender. Serve with hot biscuits or cooked rice.

Mrs. Garland (Lorene) Porter, *Evensville*

Venison Pot Roast

With deer becoming more plentiful in Tennessee, more people are interested in venison recipes. My husband has brought home several deer from managed game hunts, but I was the lucky one to first sight 3 deer at the edge of our lawn one Sunday morning — they went on their merry way! If you have venison in your freezer, perhaps you will like this.

3 TO 4 POUND VENISON ROAST, THAWED	1 BAY LEAF
2 CUPS VINEGAR	5 CARROTS, WHOLE
4 CUPS WATER	5 POTATOES, WHOLE
1 ONION SLICE OR CLOVE OF GARLIC	5 ONIONS, WHOLE
2 TEASPOONS SALT	1/4 CUP CELERY, CHOPPED
2 TEASPOONS BLACK PEPPER	MORE WATER IF NEEDED

Place venison in a container with a lid. Mix vinegar, water, onion, salt, pepper and bay leaf; pour mixture over venison and cover. Place in refrigerator to marinate 2 or 3 days; turn. When ready to cook roast, remove, rinse and dry.

Dredge meat in flour and brown in a skillet with hot fat. When golden brown, add small amount of water, cover, lower heat and simmer 2 to 3 hours. When meat is tender, add carrots, potatoes, onions, celery and more water if needed. Cover and cook until vegetables are tender. Arrange on a warmed platter. Make a gravy of the liquid in the skillet and pour over venison and vegetables. *Yield:* 5 servings.

Mrs. Garland (Lorene) Porter, *Evensville*

Homemade Salami

2 POUNDS GROUND BEEF (LEAN CHUCK)	½ TEASPOON GARLIC POWDER
½ TEASPOON SALT	1 TABLESPOON LIQUID SMOKE
¼ TEASPOON FRESH GROUND BLACK PEPPER	1 TABLESPOON MUSTARD SEED
¼ TEASPOON ONION SALT	2 TABLESPOONS TENDERQUICK SALT

Put all ingredients in a large mixing bowl. Mix by hand and shape into 4 long rolls. Wrap in Saran wrap and refrigerate for 24 hours. Unwrap and place on cake rack. Place in jelly roll pan and bake in a 300 degree oven for 1 hour. (The cake rack allows fat to drip off as it bakes.) Cool. Wrap in Saran wrap. Refrigerate or may be frozen.

Mrs. David H. Wallace, *Oak Ridge*

Tennessee Spiced Round

1 10 TO 12-POUND ROUND OF BEEF, 3 TO 4 INCHES THICK	1 OUNCE SALTPETER (AVAILABLE AT MOST DRUG STORES)
1 TABLESPOON GROUND CINNAMON	2 GALLONS WATER
1 TABLESPOON GROUND CLOVES	6 CUPS SUGAR
2 TABLESPOONS GROUND ALLSPICE	1 TABLESPOON GROUND ALLSPICE
2 TABLESPOONS BLACK PEPPER	1 TABLESPOON GROUND CINNAMON
STRIPS OF PORK FAT OR SLAB BACON (ABOUT 2 POUNDS)	1 TABLESPOON GROUND CLOVES
	COLD WATER
1 CUP BROWN SUGAR, FIRMLY PACKED	1 CUP SUGAR

With a stick or steel (used for sharpening knifes) make dime-size vertical holes about 1-inch apart all the way through the beef round. Combine 1 tablespoon cinnamon, 1 tablespoon cloves, 2 tablespoons allspice and pepper; roll pork fat strips in spice mixture, and push strips into holes in beef.

Combine brown sugar and saltpeter; rub into beef round. If necessary, tie beef with string or fasten with small skewers to keep it from unrolling. Wrap beef in cheesecloth to hold fat in place.

Combine 2 gallons water, 6 cups sugar, 1 tablespoon allspice, 1 tablespoon cinnamon and 1 tablespoon cloves to make a brine. Bring brine to a boil; then cool completely.

Place beef in brine and let stand for 3 to 4 weeks in refrigerator or other cool place; do not allow to freeze.

To cook spiced round, remove from brine and soak 1 hour in enough cold water to cover beef; drain and rinse. Place beef in a large container and cover with water again; add 1 cup sugar and simmer 15 minutes per pound. Add water as needed to keep meat completely covered. When beef is done, remove from heat and cool in broth; drain meat and refrigerate. Slice thinly across the grain. It can be kept moist by wrapping tightly in cheesecloth that has been dipped in a solution of 1 part vinegar and 2 parts water. Redampen cloth every 4 to 5 days.

Mrs. William H. Colley, Jr., *Donelson*

Mexican Chop Suey

3 POUNDS VENISON, CLEANED AND CUT IN BITE-SIZE PIECES	2 MEDIUM ONIONS, COARSELY GROUND
MEAT TENDERIZER	2 CUPS CELERY, DIAGONALLY SLICED
SALT, PEPPER AND ALL-PURPOSE FLOUR	1 14-OUNCE CAN MILD OR HOT ENCHILADA SAUCE
2 TO 3 TABLESPOONS BACON FAT	2 8-OUNCE CANS TOMATO SAUCE
1 6-OUNCE CAN CHOPPED GREEN CHILIS	GARLIC SALT TO TASTE
1 4-OUNCE CAN MUSHROOM PIECES	

Sprinkle venison generously with meat tenderizer; refrigerate overnight. Drain mushroom pieces, reserving liquid. Dredge venison in seasoned flour; brown in bacon fat in large heavy skillet or Dutch oven. Add green chilis, mushroom pieces, onions, celery, enchilada sauce, 1 can tomato sauce and garlic salt. Simmer for 1 to 2 hours, stirring occasionally. Add reserved mushroom liquid and remaining can of tomato sauce as needed. Serve over steamed rice. *Yield:* 8 servings.

Mrs. Calvin (Ruth) Borden, *Fairfield Glade*

Corned Beef Patties

2 TABLESPOONS MARGARINE	1¼ CUP (1 CAN) CORNED BEEF
¼ CUP ONION, DICED	1½ CUP CANNED TOMATOES, DRAINED
2 TABLESPOONS ALL-PURPOSE FLOUR	1 RECIPE SHELL PASTRY

Melt margarine, add onion; cook slowly until soft. Add flour; stir until well blended. Add remaining ingredients. Bring to a boil, stir constantly until thick and smooth. Let simmer 10 minutes before placing in shells.

Shells:

2 CUPS ALL-PURPOSE FLOUR	4 LEVEL TABLESPOONS SHORTENING
1 TEASPOON BAKING POWDER	1 EGG YOLK, SLIGHTLY BEATEN
½ TEASPOON SALT	⅓ CUP MILK

Sift dry ingredients; add shortening and mix thoroughly with a fork. Add eggs to milk, add to dry mix to form soft dough. Roll out half the dough ⅛ inch thick; cup into square quarters. Fit each into muffin pan, fill with corned beef mix. Fold edges over into the center. Bake in a 425 degree oven for 20 minutes. *Yield:* 10 servings.

Sue Brummel Harris, *Humboldt*

Seafood

Crab Meat Justine

1 CUP DRY SHERRY
¼ POUND BUTTER
½ POUND FRESH LUMP CRAB MEAT
DASH WORCESTERSHIRE SAUCE

DASH TABASCO SAUCE
SQUEEZE OF LEMON JUICE
HOLLANDAISE SAUCE

Melt the butter. Add all the other ingredients in the order listed, taking care not to burn or boil the mixture. Place about 2 tablespoons of the mixture on a slice of toasted French bread and top with Hollandaise sauce. Lightly brown the Hollandaise in a very hot oven.

Justine's, *Memphis*

Shrimp Creole

1 LARGE ONION, FINELY CHOPPED
¼ BELL PEPPER, FINELY CHOPPED
1 CLOVE GARLIC, MINCED
3 TABLESPOONS MARGARINE
1 CAN TOMATO PASTE

1½ CUPS WATER
SALT AND PEPPER TO TASTE
DASH CAYENNE PEPPER
2 CUPS SHRIMP, COOKED
2 CUPS RICE, COOKED

Sauté onions, pepper and garlic in margarine. Blend in remaining ingredients except shrimp and rice; cook slowly on low heat for 30 minutes in covered saucepan. Stir in shrimp and heat through; serve over hot, cooked rice.

Mrs. Rosalie G. Phelps, *Paris*

Fried Oysters

Select fresh oysters that are greyish-cream colored. The liquid should be thick, not watery.

1 PINT FRESH OYSTERS
1 CUP ALL-PURPOSE FLOUR
1 CUP CORN FLAKE CRUMBS
2 EGGS, SLIGHTLY BEATEN WITH 1 TABLESPOON WATER

¼ TEASPOON SALT
⅛ TEASPOON (OR SLIGHTLY LESS) BLACK PEPPER

In three separate bowls place the flour, corn flake crumbs, and eggs. Add salt and pepper to the flour. Dip oysters in flour, then in egg, then coat with corn flake crumbs. Heat ¼-inch oil in a frying pan (preferably cast iron) and when hot enough to fry, drop oysters into hot oil. Fry until a golden brown. Drain on paper towels.

Mrs. Sanford W. Downs, Jr., *Martin*

Scalloped Oysters

CRACKERS
2 8-OUNCE CANS BULLHEAD OYSTERS

SWEET MILK
1/2 CUP BUTTER OR MARGARINE

Line bottom of 2 or 2½-quart Corning or Pyrex dish with finely crushed crackers. Then place a layer of oysters; then a layer of crackers, doing this until all oysters are used, ending with a medium-crushed layer of crackers on the top. Be sure to reserve juice from oysters until the layers have been completed.

After the layers of oysters and crackers have been completed, pour juice from oysters over the mixture. Then pour sweet milk over the mixture until it nearly covers the top layer of crackers. Slice the stick of butter or oleo and place it over the mixture; when heated it will melt into the casserole. Cook in a 400 degree oven until the butter is melted and the crackers are medium brown.

Note: for no-salt diet, this casserole can be used with no-salt or low-salt crackers and butter and is just as delicious.

Mrs. Harry (Marie) Batey, *Lewisburg*

Minced Oysters

This recipe was handed down from my husband's grandmother, Margaret Micajah Anderson, daughter of the first mayor of Bristol, Tennessee. It has always been a family favorite and now I serve it to our grandchildren at the family holiday dinners.

1 SMALL ONION, FINELY CHOPPED
1/2 CUP BUTTER (NOT MARGARINE)
4 EGGS, SLIGHTLY BEATEN

1 QUART OYSTERS, CUT INTO PIECES
10 SLICES WHITE BREAD, TOASTED AND CRUMBLED
SALT AND PEPPER TO TASTE

In a skillet or heavy stew pan, sauté onion in butter until clear. Mix beaten eggs, oysters, bread crumbs, and seasonings. Add to onions and cook over low heat, stirring frequently, about 15 minutes. Put into baking shells or baking dish and bake in a 350 degree oven about 15 minutes.

Mrs. Craig (Betty Jo) Caldwell, *Bristol*

Cheesy Salmon Loaf

1 CAN SALMON	1 TABLESPOON LEMON JUICE
1/3 CUP CELERY, CHOPPED	1/2 TEASPOON SALT
1/3 CUP ONION, CHOPPED	1/8 TEASPOON PEPPER
3 EGGS	1/2 CUP BREAD CRUMBS
1 CUP CHEDDAR CHEESE, SHREDDED	1/2 CUP MAYONNAISE

Combine and bake in loaf pan in a 350 degree oven for 45 minutes.

Mrs. Charles D. (Myrtle S.) Taylor, *Johnson City*

Salmon Corn Scallops

Canned Salmon is a most delicious food; it is nutritious with a complete protein in each serving.

1/2 CUP ONION, CHOPPED	1 CUP CRACKER CRUMBS
1/2 CUP RED SWEET PEPPER, CHOPPED	1 CUP SHREDDED SHARP CHEDDAR CHEESE
1/2 CUP CELERY, CHOPPED	2 EGGS, SLIGHTLY BEATEN
2 TABLESPOONS BUTTER	1 16-OUNCE CAN CREAM-STYLE CORN
1 CAN (7 3/4 OUNCES) SALMON, FLAKED	

Sauté first three ingredients in butter. Combine all ingredients. Turn into 8 x 8 x 2 inch baking dish. Bake in a 300 degree oven for 30 minutes. *Yield:* 6 servings.

Mrs. Carrie Bartlett, *Gallatin*

Seafood Crepes

3 TABLESPOONS BUTTER	1 TABLESPOON MINCED ONION FLAKES
3 TABLESPOONS ALL-PURPOSE FLOUR	1/2 TEASPOON MUSTARD
2 CUPS CREAM	1 CAN (4 OUNCES) CHOPPED MUSHROOMS
2 EGG YOLKS	2 TABLESPOONS WHITE WINE
2 TABLESPOONS PARMESAN CHEESE	1 CAN SHRIMP OR 1/2 POUND FRESH SHRIMP, COOKED AND PEELED
1/2 TO 1 CUP SWISS OR GRUYERE CHEESE, GRATED	1 CAN CRAB MEAT OR 1/2 POUND FRESH CRAB MEAT, COOKED

Combine butter and flour in saucepan. Heat and gradually stir in cream and beaten egg yolks. Add Parmesan and Swiss or Gruyere cheese, onion flakes, mustard and mushrooms. Stir until base is thickened and cheese melted. Add white wine, shrimp and crab meat. Stir for five minutes more to thoroughly heat and fill crepes. Heat in a 350 degree oven for 25 to 30 minutes. May be prepared and frozen for later use. *Yield:* 6 to 8 crepes.

Ann Cox, *Murfreesboro*

Family Salmon Loaf

2 TABLESPOONS BUTTER
2 TABLESPOONS ALL-PURPOSE FLOUR
2 CUPS MILK
1 CUP MILD CHEESE, GRATED
1/3 CUP BELL PEPPER, FINELY CHOPPED

SALT AND PEPPER
2 EGGS
1 POUND CAN SALMON
1 CUP CRACKER CRUMBS
1/2 CUP ONION, FINELY CHOPPED (OPTIONAL)

Combine butter, flour and milk to make cream sauce. Add cheese, bell pepper and season to taste. Mix eggs with salmon. In buttered casserole dish, place layer of salmon, layer of sauce, layer of crumbs, etc. Bake in a 350 degree oven for 25 to 30 minutes until bubbly and slightly browned.

Mrs. Jessie Harris, *Clarksville*

Tuna-Rice Casserole

1 CAN CREAM OF CHICKEN SOUP
1 SOUP CAN MILK
1 1/2 CUPS MINUTE RICE, UNCOOKED
1 9 1/4-OUNCE CAN TUNA FISH

1/2 CUP GRATED CHEDDAR CHEESE
1 TABLESPOON INSTANT MINCED ONION
CORN FLAKE CRUMBS
BUTTER

Combine soup and milk to make a smooth sauce. Grease 2-quart casserole; place in layers 1/2 cup rice, 1/2 cup tuna, 1/4 cup cheese and onion. Add 1/2 of soup mixture, then repeat previous layers. Pour remaining soup mixture over casserole. Top with corn flake crumbs and dot with butter. Bake in a 350 degree oven for 30 minutes.

Mrs. B. T. Atkisson, Jr., *Columbia*

Jimmie's On Top of Old Smoky Casserole

1 MEDIUM ONION, CHOPPED
3 TABLESPOONS BUTTER, MELTED
1 10 3/4-OUNCE CAN CONDENSED CREAM OF SHRIMP SOUP
1 8-OUNCE CAN SLICED WATER CHESTNUTS, DRAINED
1/2 CUP MILK

1/2 CUP SOUR CREAM
2 6 1/2-OUNCE CANS WATER PACK CHUNK TUNA, DRAINED
1 17-OUNCE CAN PEAS, DRAINED
SALT AND PEPPER
CHOW MEIN NOODLES

Sauté onion in butter until tender. Stir in next 5 ingredients and bring mixture to a boil. Gently fold in peas, salt and pepper to taste. Heat to serving temperature and serve over chow mein noodles. *Yield:* 6 servings.

Marilyn Caponetti, *Knoxville*

Tuna A La King

2 TABLESPOONS GREEN PEPPER, CHOPPED
1 TABLESPOON BUTTER OR MARGARINE
1 CUP MUSHROOM SOUP
1/2 CUP MILK

1 6½-OUNCE CAN TUNA FISH, DRAINED
2 TABLESPOONS CHOPPED PIMENTO
3 HARD COOKED EGGS, COARSELY CHOPPED

Cook green pepper in butter until soft; stir in mushroom soup, add milk. Put mixture in top of a double boiler. When hot, drop in chunks of tuna, pimento and eggs. Serve on toast or Zwieback.

Mrs. M. Duane Smith, Sr., *Chattanooga*

Creole Gumbo

Creole gumbo is one of the cherished possessions of both old and young New Orleans. Filé is the powdered sassafras leaf. It used to be made by the Choctaw Indians, who brought it to the French Market. Their word for sassafras is Kombo, from which we get our word Gumbo.

The filé which they introduced is used instead of okra, and serves the same purpose in the gumbo, but filé is never put in until just a minute before serving, whereas okra is cooked with the soup.

1½ POUNDS LARGE SHRIMP
  BAY LEAVES
  SALT TO TASTE
1/4 POUND VEAL
1 SLICE LEAN HAM
1 TABLESPOON BUTTER
1 LARGE ONION
1 TEASPOON PARSLEY, CHOPPED

1 BAY LEAF
  DASH CAYENNE, THYME, AND BLACK PEPPER
2 TABLESPOONS ALL-PURPOSE FLOUR
1 SMALL CAN TOMATOES
2 QUARTS HOT WATER
2 TABLESPOONS FILÉ

In a separate pot scald the shrimp in water highly seasoned with bay leaves and salt. Let them cool in the water before shelling. If canned shrimp are used they must not be parboiled. While the shrimp are boiling, cut the veal and ham into small bits, dredging with salt and pepper. Put a tablespoon of butter into a frying pan; when it is hot, slice the onion into this. When the onion looks withered, add chopped meat.

Cover this for 10 minutes, stirring it constantly, as anything cooked in butter is apt to burn. Next add the chopped parsley and bay leaf, cayenne, thyme and black pepper; stir in 2 tablespoons flour.

When this is thoroughly mixed and slightly brown, add your tomatoes. Cook for a few minutes and transfer into the soup pot which has in it 2 quarts of hot water. Put in part of the shrimp, broken into pieces, to be absorbed into the soup, giving it flavor. Bring your soup to a slow boil and let it cook 2 hours. Put in the remainder of the shrimp (whole) and let boil for 15 minutes. Sprinkle in 2 tablespoons of filé, and the gumbo is ready for the table.

Serve over cooked dry rice. Serves 6 to 8 people, depending on how hungry they are. A salad, French bread, and wine complete this outstanding gumbo dinner.

Mrs. Gladys S. Bonney, *Oak Ridge*

Chapter Seven

Vegetables

Southern Fried Apples

⅓ CUP SUGAR	⅛ TEASPOON SALT
1 TEASPOON GROUND NUTMEG	4 LARGE COOKING APPLES
½ TEASPOON GROUND CINNAMON	5 TABLESPOONS BUTTER

Mix together sugar, nutmeg, cinnamon and salt. Wash, core and slice apples in ½ inch slices. Heat butter in frying pan. Add apple rings and ½ the sugar mixture. Cook about 3 minutes. Turn, sprinkle with remainder of sugar mixture, and continue cooking until apples are almost transparent. Serve hot. *Yield:* 6 servings.

Mrs. Sherry Ligon Allison, *Cookeville*

Artichoke Bottoms Stuffed with Spinach

4 PACKAGES FROZEN CHOPPED SPINACH, STEAMED UNTIL JUST THAWED	2 TABLESPOONS WORCESTERSHIRE SAUCE
½ CUP BUTTER	2 CANS CREAM OF MUSHROOM SOUP
1 CUP ONIONS, CHOPPED	SALT, PEPPER AND GARLIC POWDER TO TASTE

Squeeze excess water from the spinach. Melt butter in a pan and cook onions in it until they are clear. To this add the Worcestershire sauce, soup and seasonings. Combine this mixture with spinach. Fill each artichoke bottom with the spinach mixture. Sprinkle with Parmesan cheese and bake in a 350 degree oven until hot and brown, about 15 minutes.

Carolyn Barnett, *Humboldt*

125

Asparagus Casserole

3 HARD-BOILED EGGS, CHOPPED
1 MEDIUM ONION, CHOPPED
1 SMALL SWEET PEPPER, CHOPPED
1 CUP GRATED CHEESE

1 CUP RITZ CRACKER CRUMBS
1 LARGE CAN DRAINED ASPARAGUS
1 CAN CREAM OF MUSHROOM SOUP

Mix together eggs, onion, pepper, cheese and crackers. Put alternately in baking dish a layer of mixture and a layer of asparagus, ending with mixture. Cover with the undiluted soup and top with extra grated cheese and cracker crumbs. Bake until soup seeps throughout the casserole. Bake covered in a 300 degree oven for 30 minutes, remove cover for the last 10 minutes and continue baking.

Judith Rhyne, *Clinton*

Asparagus Casserole

2 CANS CUT ASPARAGUS, DRAINED
1 SMALL CAN TINY PEAS, DRAINED
3 GREEN ONIONS, THINLY SLICED
1 CAN CREAM OF MUSHROOM SOUP

1/2 CUP ALMONDS, SLICED
SALT AND PEPPER TO TASTE
2 CUPS SHARP CHEDDAR CHEESE, GRATED

Layer all ingredients in order listed in casserole dish. Sprinkle some crushed almonds on top. Bake in a 350 degree oven for 30 minutes.

Mrs. Billy Ray Viar, *East Ridge*

Three Bean Hot Dish

1 POUND MAYO'S TENNESSEE SMOKED SAUSAGE
1/2 POUND HAMBURGER
3 TABLESPOONS VINEGAR
3/4 CUP BROWN SUGAR
1/2 CUP CATSUP

1 ONION, CHOPPED
1 TEASPOON DRY MUSTARD
1 15-OUNCE CAN BAKED BEANS
1 15-OUNCE CAN KIDNEY BEANS
1 15-OUNCE CAN LIMA BEANS

Fry sausage; remove from pan and crumble. Brown hamburger and add next 5 ingredients. Cook until blended. Place all mixture into casserole and bake in a 350 degree oven for 40 minutes.

Philip R. Graham, *Clarksville*

Combination Baked Beans

1 30-OUNCE CAN PORK AND BEANS
1 30-OUNCE CAN KIDNEY BEANS
2 16-OUNCE CANS BUTTER BEANS
1/2 POUND BACON, CHOPPED
2 MEDIUM ONIONS, CHOPPED

1 CUP BROWN SUGAR
1 CUP CATSUP
2 TABLESPOONS MUSTARD
2 TABLESPOONS VINEGAR

Drain beans and put into a large casserole dish. Fry the bacon. Drain. Add onions, sugar, catsup, mustard and vinegar. Pour over beans and bake in a 350 degree oven for 1 hour.

Mrs. John Featherston, *Madison*

Tennessee Baked Beans

3 SLICES BACON, CUT INTO 1 INCH PIECES
1 SMALL ONION, CHOPPED
2 CANS PORK AND BEANS, DRAINED
⅓ CUP BROWN SUGAR
½ CUP CHILI SAUCE

Fry bacon until crisp, remove and drain. Sauté onion in bacon grease until translucent. Add beans, brown sugar, chili sauce and bacon. Stir. Bake in a 350 degree oven for 45 minutes or until warmed.

Note: If you are in a hurry, forget the oven and use the stove to heat well.

Noelle Hendricks, *Memphis*

Baked Beans

1 POUND GROUND CHUCK
2 CUPS ONIONS
2 CANS PORK AND BEANS
1 CAN KIDNEY BEANS
1 CUP BROWN SUGAR
1 TABLESPOON VINEGAR
1 TEASPOON SALT
1 CUP CATSUP
1 TABLESPOON MUSTARD

Brown ground chuck and onions together and drain. Add remaining ingredients and mix well. Bake in a 400 degree oven for 30 to 40 minutes.

Pam Savage, *Sparta*

Green Beans and Sour Cream

1 16-OUNCE CAN FRENCH STYLE GREEN BEANS, DRAINED
1 CAN FRENCH-FRIED ONION RINGS
1 LARGE CAN MUSHROOMS, DRAINED
1 CUP SOUR CREAM
¼ CUP BUTTER, MELTED
½ CUP CRACKER CRUMBS

Layer beans, onion rings, mushrooms and sour cream in greased casserole dish. Sprinkle with cracker crumbs. Bake in a 350 degree oven for 30 minutes. *Yield:* 6 to 8 servings.

Mrs. Sherry Ligon Allison, *Cookeville*

Vonore Bean Bake

I have a neighbor who never liked baked beans until he tasted these.

1 POUND GROUND BEEF
1 MEDIUM ONION, CHOPPED
1 1-POUND CAN TOMATOES
2 1-POUND CANS BEANS WITH PORK

1 TABLESPOON WORCESTERSHIRE SAUCE
1/4 TEASPOON PEPPER
1 TEASPOON SALT (OPTIONAL)

In large skillet, cook and stir ground beef and onion until onion is tender. Drain off excess fat. Stir in tomatoes, beans with pork, Worcestershire sauce, salt and pepper. Heat thoroughly. Pour into a lightly greased 2-quart casserole. Bake in a 350 degree oven for 30 minutes. Remove cover and bake 15 minutes longer.

Pamela A. Bivens, *Vonore*

Home Baked Beans

2 CUPS (1 POUND) NAVY BEANS
1/4 POUND BACON, UNSLICED
2 TEASPOONS SALT
1/2 TEASPOON MUSTARD

1/2 CUP CHILI SAUCE
1 TABLESPOON VINEGAR
1 MEDIUM SIZE ONION, SLICED
2 CUPS BEAN LIQUID

Wash beans, cover with water (2 inches over beans) and soak overnight. Add bacon, cover and simmer over low heat (but do not boil) until just tender, about one hour. Drain, reserve liquid, remove bacon and cut in 1-inch cubes. Pour beans into a 2-quart casserole or bean pot, bury bacon cubes in beans, add combined remaining ingredients. Add bean liquid or water during baking. Bake 5 hours.

Mrs. Calvin (Ruth) Borden, *Fairfield Glade*

Corn and Green Bean Casserole

2 CANS FRENCH STYLE GREEN BEANS,
    DRAINED
2 CANS SHOE PEG CORN, DRAINED
½ CUP ONION, CHOPPED

½ CUP CELERY, CHOPPED
1½ CUPS SHARP CHEDDAR CHEESE, SHREDDED
½ CUP SOUR CREAM
1 CAN CREAM OF CELERY SOUP

Mix all ingredients together and put into a large shallow casserole dish.

Topping:

½ CUP MARGARINE, MELTED
1 TO 1½ PACKS RITZ CRACKERS, CRUSHED

¼ CUP SLICED ALMONDS, CRUSHED
    (OPTIONAL)

In saucepan melt margarine and mix in crushed Ritz crackers and almonds. Place on top of casserole and bake in a 350 degree oven for 45 minutes.

Shirley Gourley, *Philadelphia*

Robin Hood

The Farmer's Market in Nashville is a place where people from Middle Tennessee can bring their fruit, vegetables, and other food to those in the city.

Broccoli-Cheese Pie

6 CUPS WATER	½ TEASPOON SALT
1 TABLESPOON SALT	4 EGGS
3 OUNCES UNCOOKED MACARONI RINGS (ABOUT ¾ CUP)	1 EGG WHITE
1 EGG YOLK	1 CUP CREAMED COTTAGE CHEESE
1 TABLESPOON SNIPPED CHIVES	1 TABLESPOON SNIPPED CHIVES
1 CUP CHEDDAR CHEESE, SHREDDED	1 TEASPOON SALT
1 10-OUNCE PACKAGE FROZEN CHOPPED BROCCOLI	PAPRIKA

Heat oven to 375 degrees. Heat water and 1 teaspoon salt to boiling, stir in macaroni. Boil until tender, 5 to 8 minutes. Drain, rinse in cold water. Beat egg yolk, stir in macaroni and 1 tablespoon chives. Press mixture against bottom and side of greased 9-inch pie plate with back of spoon. Bake 10 minutes; remove from oven and cool 10 minutes. Increase oven temperature to 425 degrees. Sprinkle cheddar cheese over crust. Prepare broccoli as directed on package, using ½ teaspoon salt, drain. Arrange broccoli on cheese. Beat eggs, egg white, cottage cheese, 1 tablespoon chives and 1 teaspoon salt; pour over broccoli, sprinkle with paprika. Bake uncovered 15 minutes. Reduce temperature to 300 degrees and bake about 30 minutes or until knife inserted 1 inch from edge comes out clean. Cool 10 minutes before serving. *Yield:* 6 servings.

Pat Tyler, *Alamo*

Broccoli Casserole

This is the only broccoli recipe my husband will eat. He doesn't like broccoli but will eat this and go back for seconds. I always take it to a family get-together or to a meal we have at church and never come home with any.

2 LARGE STALKS OR 3 MEDIUM STALKS FRESH BROCCOLI, COOKED (CAN USE 2 PACKAGES FROZEN BROCCOLI)	¼ CUP BUTTER OR MARGARINE
	8 OUNCES AMERICAN CHEESE, CHOPPED OR GRATED
6 EGGS	1 12-OUNCE CARTON COTTAGE CHEESE
6 TABLESPOONS ALL-PURPOSE FLOUR	

Cook broccoli in salt water until tender. Drain. Mix eggs, flour, butter and cheeses together in a bowl. Add drained broccoli. Mix together. Pour into an 8 x 12 x 2 inch glass baking dish and bake in a 350 degree oven for 45 minutes. Before putting in baking dish, grease it on the sides and bottom with butter to keep from sticking. *Yield:* 6 servings.

Mrs. Bonnie Petty, *Jackson*

Broccoli Casserole

2 PACKAGES FROZEN BROCCOLI

¼ CUP MARGARINE

1 CUP VELVEETA CHEESE FOOD, CUT IN SMALL PIECES

½ CUP ONION, CHOPPED

½ CUP CELERY, CHOPPED

1 CAN CREAM OF MUSHROOM SOUP

1 CAN CREAM OF CHICKEN SOUP

1 4-OUNCE CAN ENDS AND PIECES OF MUSHROOMS, DRAINED

2 CUPS RICE, COOKED

Cook broccoli about 10 minutes, add margarine and cheese while broccoli is hot. Stir until melted. Sauté onion and celery together in small amount of margarine, add to broccoli. Add soups, mushrooms and rice. Mix well and bake in greased casserole dish in a 375 degree oven for 30 or 35 minutes.

Mrs. Jessie Harris, *Clarksville*

Cabbage Creole

5 CUPS CABBAGE, CHOPPED

1 LARGE ONION, CHOPPED

1 GREEN PEPPER

1 1-POUND CAN TOMATOES

1 TEASPOON SUGAR

SALT AND PEPPER TO TASTE

1 CUP EXTRA SHARP CHEDDAR CHEESE, GRATED

Cook cabbage in boiling salted water for 10 minutes; drain well and place in pan. In large skillet melt 2 tablespoons margarine and sauté onions and green peppers. Add tomatoes with juice, sugar, salt and pepper and simmer for 5 or more minutes. Sprinkle with cheese and bake in a 325 degree oven about 20 minutes or until cheese melts.

Variation: Place 1 pound of well drained ground beef or sausage over the cabbage. Then add tomato mixture and cheeses. Bake for a main dish dinner.

Judy Jackson, *Blountville*

Carrot Balls

2 CUPS COOKED CARROTS

1½ CUPS BREAD CRUMBS

1 CUP SHARP CHEDDAR CHEESE, SHREDDED

1 EGG WHITE

SALT AND PEPPER TO TASTE

DASH TABASCO SAUCE

CORN FLAKES, CRUSHED

Combine carrots, bread crumbs and cheese; fold in stiffly beaten egg white. Add seasonings. Form into 10 balls; roll in finely crushed corn flakes. Place on greased baking sheet; bake in a 375 degree oven for about 30 minutes or until brown. Good!

Mrs. M. Duane Smith, Sr., *Chattanooga*

Marinated Carrots

2 POUNDS CARROTS, SLICED AND COOKED
2 MEDIUM SWEET ONIONS
1 SMALL GREEN PEPPER
1/2 CUP SALAD OIL
3/4 CUP VINEGAR

1 TEASPOON PREPARED MUSTARD
1 CAN CREAM OF TOMATO SOUP
1 CUP SUGAR
1 TEASPOON PEPPER
1 TEASPOON WORCESTERSHIRE SAUCE

Cook carrots. Cut onion and green pepper in round slices and mix with cooked carrots. Mix other ingredients together and pour over vegetables. Cover and marinate for 12 hours or more. Drain to serve. Will keep for 2 weeks in refrigerator. Serve hot or cold.

Frances Williams, *Newbern*

Baked Celery

10 TO 12 STALKS CELERY
2 TABLESPOONS BUTTER
2 TABLESPOONS ALL-PURPOSE FLOUR
1 1/2 CUPS MILK
1/2 TEASPOON MACE

2 DASHES TABASCO SAUCE
1/2 CUP CHEDDAR CHEESE, GRATED
1 TEASPOON WORCESTERSHIRE SAUCE
  BUTTERED BREAD CRUMBS

Slice celery stalks crosswise. Cook in salted water until firm but tender. In another pan, melt butter, blend in flour. Add milk, mace, Tabasco, cheese and Worcestershire sauce. Cook until thickened, stirring constantly. Drain cooked celery and arrange in a buttered baking dish. Pour sauce over celery, sprinkle top with bread crumbs. Bake in a 325 degree oven for about 25 minutes. Freezes well. *Yield:* 4 to 6 servings.
Note: If you are in a hurry, you can substitute cheese soup for the cheddar cheese.

Mrs. R. G. Nixon, *Gatlinburg*

Scalloped Cauliflower

1 LARGE HEAD OF CAULIFLOWER
4 TABLESPOONS MARGARINE
4 TABLESPOONS ALL-PURPOSE FLOUR
1 1/2 TEASPOONS SALT
2 CUPS MILK

1/4 TEASPOON PEPPER
3 EGGS, BOILED AND CHOPPED
1 CUP BUTTERED TOAST CRUMBS
1/4 CUP CHEDDAR OR AMERICAN CHEESE, GRATED

Cook cauliflower until tender. Break into flowerets. Melt margarine in saucepan, add flour and salt; stir and cook until bubbly. Add milk and pepper; stir until smooth and thickened. Place in layers in greased casserole: cauliflower, eggs and sauce. Top with crumbs and cheese. Bake in a 375 degree oven for 25 minutes. *Yield:* 8 servings.

Margie Flynt, *Madison*

Corn Pudding

10 EARS CORN	3 EGG YOLKS, BEATEN
3 TABLESPOONS REAL BUTTER	3 TABLESPOONS SUGAR
2 TABLESPOONS ALL-PURPOSE FLOUR	1 TEASPOON SALT
1 PINT WHOLE MILK	EGG WHITES, BEATEN

Shave off tips of corn kernels; scrape pulp from cobs. Melt butter and smooth flour in it; add milk, beaten yolks, sugar and salt. Fold in egg whites. Bake in greased casserole in a 350 degree oven until firm. Should take 45 minutes. *Yield:* 8 to 10 servings.

Note: If you must used canned corn instead of ears, use 2 cans of shoe-peg variety.

Mrs. Shields Wilson, *Chattanooga*

Corn Pudding

3 TABLESPOONS MARGARINE	2 CUPS CORN
2 HEAPING TABLESPOONS ALL-PURPOSE FLOUR	1 CUP GREEN AND RED PEPPER, CHOPPED
1¼ CUPS MILK	1 TABLESPOON SUGAR
2 OR 3 EGGS	1 PACKET ROMANOFF MBT ONION BROTH MIX
	½ TEASPOON SALT

In a saucepan make sauce of margarine and flour melted together. Add milk, cook until thickened; remove from heat. Mix together eggs, corn, green and red peppers, sugar, MBT onion mix and salt. Combine with sauce. Pour into buttered baking dish and bake in a 350 degree oven until set and slightly browned.

Variation: Top with buttered bread crumbs before baking.

Sharon Webb, *Knoxville*

Southern Fried Corn

12 EARS WHITE CORN	1 TEASPOON SUGAR
½ CUP BACON GREASE (MORE OR LESS TO TASTE)	SALT AND PEPPER TO TASTE
	WATER

Cut corn from cob and scrape well. If the kernels are large, make several cuttings before scraping. Put in skillet with bacon grease, sugar, salt, pepper and 3 cups water. Cook slowly, stirring frequently and adding water as needed to keep from sticking, for 1 hour.

Mrs. William H. Colley, Jr., *Donelson*

Corn Casserole

This is a wonderful way to dress up a can of corn and make it festive.

1 17-OUNCE CAN WHOLE KERNEL CORN	1/2 CUP MILK
1 2-OUNCE JAR PIMENTOS, CHOPPED	2 TABLESPOONS ALL-PURPOSE FLOUR
1 CUP SHREDDED CHEESE	2 TABLESPOONS SUGAR
1 MEDIUM SIZE GREEN BELL PEPPER	2 TABLESPOONS MARGARINE, MELTED
2 EGGS, SLIGHTLY BEATEN	1 TEASPOON SALT

Combine all ingredients. Mix well and pour into a greased 1 1/2-quart casserole dish. Bake in a 350 degree oven for 45 to 50 minutes. *Yield:* 4 to 6 servings.

Christine McKnight, *Nashville*

Eggplant Supreme

2 MEDIUM TO LARGE EGGPLANTS, SLICED LENGTHWISE	1 MEDIUM ONION, CHOPPED
1 PACKAGE SEASONED CROUTONS	1 CUP SHREDDED CHEDDAR CHEESE
4 RIPE TOMATOES, PEELED, CORED AND CHOPPED	SALT AND PEPPER TO TASTE

Scoop out seeds of eggplant carefully and throw away. Cut or scoop out meat of eggplant carefully to about 1/4 thickness remaining to the peel. Chop eggplant meat that was removed. Mix the tomatoes, eggplant, 2 cups of croutons, and onion together. Salt and pepper.

Place eggplant boats in baking dish that has been very lightly rubbed with 1 tablespoon oil. Spoon mixture into boats to overflowing. Sprinkle tops of each with cheese. If there is mixture left over, place around the outside of eggplant boats. Bake in a 350 degree oven for 40 minutes. *Yield:* 4 servings.

John McCoy, *Ooltewah*

Eggplant Casserole

1 EGGPLANT	4 PIECES CELERY
1 SMALL GREEN PEPPER, DICED	1/3 CUP CRACKER CRUMBS
1/2 CUP MILK	2 TABLESPOONS BUTTER, MELTED

Peel and slice eggplant. Boil in salt water until tender. Pour off remaining water and mash eggplant. Add diced pepper, onion, milk, celery, cracker crumbs, 2 tablespoons melted butter and 3/4 of the cheese. Place in baking dish and cook about 45 minutes. Sprinkle remaining cheese on top and cook a few minutes.

June B. Baker, *Clarksville*

Cheesy English Pea Casserole

1 10-OUNCE PACKAGE FROZEN ENGLISH PEAS
1 5-OUNCE PACKAGE MEDIUM EGG NOODLES
1 8-OUNCE PACKAGE CREAM CHEESE, CUBED AND SOFTENED
2 CUPS (8 OUNCES) SHREDDED SHARP CHEDDAR CHEESE

1 TABLESPOON BUTTER
1 2½-OUNCE JAR SLICED MUSHROOMS, UNDRAINED
½ CUP ONIONS, CHOPPED
½ TEASPOON WHITE PEPPER
5 ROUND BUTTERY CRACKERS, CRUSHED

Cook peas according to package directions, drain and set aside. Cook noodles according to package directions, drain. Add next 3 ingredients, stirring gently until melted. Stir in peas, mushrooms, onion and pepper.

Spoon into a greased 10 x 6 x 2 inch baking dish. Sprinkle cracker crumbs around edge of casserole. Bake in a 325 degree oven for 20 minutes or until thoroughly heated. *Yield:* 6 servings.

Elizabeth Frazier, *Greenbrier*

Mushroom Soufflé

Use as an extra item on your menu, much the same way you might use scalloped oysters.

⅓ CUP CHOPPED ONIONS
½ MEDIUM SIZE GREEN PEPPER, CHOPPED
6 SLICES BREAD, CUBED, DISCARD CRUSTS
3 EGGS, BEATEN
1 POUND FRESH MUSHROOMS (OR 2 3- OR 4-OUNCE CANS INCLUDING LIQUID)

1¼ CUPS MILK
½ TEASPOON SALT
¼ TEASPOON THYME
½ TEASPOON DRY MUSTARD

Cook onions and green peppers in margarine until tender. Combine with remaining ingredients. Pour into a 1½-quart flat baking dish. Bake in a 350 degree oven for 50 to 60 minutes. *Yield:* 6 servings.

Mrs. Shields Wilson, *Chattanooga*

Okra Patties

1 PINT OKRA, COOKED
1 EGG
1 TEASPOON SALT
2 TABLESPOONS MEAL

¼ TEASPOON BAKING POWDER
4 TABLESPOONS ALL-PURPOSE FLOUR
¼ TEASPOON BLACK PEPPER

Drain okra, mash well. Add egg and beat. Sift dry ingredients together and add to okra; mix well. Drop by spoonsful into very hot oil. Fry until golden, turning once.

Mary Alice Cox, *Clinton*

French Fried Onion Rings

½ CUP BUTTERMILK

½ CUP MILK

3 OR 4 MEDIUM ONIONS, THICKLY SLICED

1 CUP ALL-PURPOSE FLOUR

Combine milks and soak onions in milk mixture. Dip into flour; shake off excess. Re-dip into milk and then into flour again; shake. Fry in deep fat. *Yield:* 4 to 6 servings.

Mrs. M. Duane Smith, Sr., *Chattanooga*

Robin Hood

Molasses is made in the fall by an age-old process. Sorghum stalks are fed into a mill that extracts a sweet, sticky juice which is then cooked for hours. As the mixture boils, the thickening syrup is worked constantly to insure the flavor and quality of the molasses.

Green Onions

6 LARGE GREEN ONIONS
1/4 CUP BACON DRIPPINGS

1 CUP WATER
1 TEASPOON SALT

Chop onions up coarsely, head and blades. Melt bacon drippings in skillet and add onions with salt water. Cook until tender and water is absorbed.

Mrs. Geraldine Garner, *Maryville*

Spicy Hot Black-Eyed Peas

1 17-OUNCE CAN BLACK-EYED PEAS
1 16-OUNCE CAN WHOLE TOMATOES, UNDRAINED AND CHOPPED
1 MEDIUM ONION, CHOPPED
1/2 BELL PEPPER, CHOPPED
1 TEASPOON DRY MUSTARD

1/2 TEASPOON CHILI POWDER
1 TEASPOON SALT
1/2 TEASPOON PEPPER
1 TABLESPOON SOY SAUCE
1 1/2 TEASPOON LIQUID SMOKE
3 SLICES BACON
PARSLEY

Cook bacon until crisp. Remove bacon and sauté onions and bell pepper, drain. Crumble bacon and reserve for later. Mix remaining ingredients and heat to boiling, then simmer for 20 minutes. Pour mixture into serving dish; sprinkle with bacon and parsley over top. *Yield:* 8 servings.

Lettie C. Cardy, *Normandy*

Nashville Hopping John

From A GRANNY WHITE COOKBOOK. Granny White was an early settler of Nashville, and lived on what is now Granny White Pike.

2 CUPS DRIED BLACK-EYED PEAS, SOAKED OVERNIGHT IN WATER
1/2 CUP ONION, CHOPPED
1/2 GREEN PEPPER, CHOPPED
1 CLOVE GARLIC, CHOPPED
1/4 TEASPOON RED CRUSHED PEPPER OR TABASCO SAUCE

4 CUPS WATER
1/4 POUND BOILING PORK
2 CUPS COOKED RICE
1 CUP DRY RICE
2 TABLESPOONS OIL

Place first 7 ingredients in pot; boil for 10 minutes. Drain off liquid. Add dry rice and oil to boiling water; add pork mixture and cook for 12 minutes. Drain until dry. Place in skillet, mix in peas and cook a few seconds to heat, then serve.

Mrs. John Featherston, *Madison*

Baked Pineapple with Cheese

20 OUNCE CAN PINEAPPLE CHUNKS
½ CUP SUGAR
1 CUP SHARP CHEDDAR CHEESE

3 TABLESPOONS ALL-PURPOSE FLOUR
½ CUP MARGARINE, MELTED
½ CUP RITZ CRACKERS, CRUMBLED

Drain pineapple, keep 3 tablespoons juice. Combine sugar and flour and stir in 3 tablespoons pineapple juice. Add grated cheese and pineapple chunks. Mix well. Spoon into greased 1-quart casserole. Combine margarine and Ritz crackers. Sprinkle over. Bake in a 350 degree oven for 20 to 30 minutes or until brown.

Mrs. William H. Colley, Jr., *Donelson*

Poke Casserole

Poke is a native plant in Tennessee. Every spring, parboil and freeze for use during the year. This is very good to people who say they don't eat poke. You can substitute two 10-ounce packages of spinach, but try the poke.

2 CUPS PARBOILED POKE, DRAINED AND
  SQUEEZED OF JUICE
½ CUP MARGARINE, MELTED
6 EGGS, HAND BEATEN
1 TABLESPOON ALL-PURPOSE FLOUR

1 LARGE CONTAINER COTTAGE CHEESE
1 STICK CRACKER BARREL SHARP CHEDDAR
  CHEESE, CUBED
1 PACKAGE GRATED CHEDDAR CHEESE

Mix all together, adding poke last. Put in greased Pyrex dish. Bake in a 350 degree oven for 1 hour. Let set 20 minutes before serving.

Mabel Hester, *Dover*

Susan's Stuffed Baked Potatoes

Version 1:

4 BAKING POTATOES
8 OUNCES VELVEETA CHEESE
4 TABLESPOONS MILK
1 10-OUNCE PACKAGE FROZEN BROCCOLI (OR
  10 OUNCES FRESH BROCCOLI, COOKED)

4 TABLESPOONS BUTTER
4 TABLESPOONS SOUR CREAM
2 TABLESPOONS CHIVES
SALT AND PEPPER TO TASTE

Version 2:

4 BAKING POTATOES
4 OUNCES VELVEETA CHEESE
4 OUNCES SWISS CHEESE
4 TABLESPOONS MILK
4 OUNCES CANNED CORNED BEEF, HEATED

4 TABLESPOONS BUTTER
4 TABLESPOONS SOUR CREAM
2 TABLESPOONS CHIVES
SALT AND PEPPER TO TASTE

Conventional stove oven: Bake potatoes at 400 degrees for 1 to 1½ hours until fluffy. While keeping potatoes warm, melt cheese with milk until smooth.

Placing each potato in a soup bowl, split lengthwise, place 1 tablespoon butter on each potato; allow to melt. Add 1 tablespoon sour cream on top of each potato, then top with broccoli (or corned beef), dividing in four equal portions. Pour an equal portion of the cheese sauce over each potato. Sprinkle with chives. Salt and pepper to taste. Serve immediately.

Microwave oven: Pierce each potato with a fork, place on a paper towel and bake on high setting 3 minutes per potato. Test for doneness, continue cooking potato not done at 1 minute intervals until done. Melt cheese and milk together in a glass container by cooking on high for 3 minutes, stirring at $1\frac{1}{2}$ minutes, or until smooth. Top potato as instructed under the conventional method.

Susan D. Gratz, *Morristown*

Crab and Mushroom Stuffed Potatoes

I serve this as a main course, adding a salad and a green vegetable.

4 MEDIUM BAKED POTATOES	1 3-OUNCE CAN CHOPPED BROILED MUSHROOMS
¼ CUP BUTTER, MELTED	1 TABLESPOON ONION, GRATED
¼ CUP HEAVY CREAM, HEATED	1 CUP SHARP CHEDDAR CHEESE, GRATED
1 TEASPOON SALT	1 6½-OUNCE CAN CRAB MEAT, DRAINED AND FLAKED
⅛ TEASPOON PEPPER	

Cut hot potatoes in half lengthwise. Scoop out all pulp without breaking the skin. Mash or whip pulp and add butter, cream, salt and pepper. Beat until light and fluffy. Drain mushrooms, reserving broth for use in soup. Add mushrooms, onion, ⅔ cup grated cheese and crab meat to potato mixture. Pile into potato shells and sprinkle with remaining cheese.

Bake in a 350 degree oven for 20 minutes or until cheese melts. *Yield:* 8 stuffed potato halves.

Sherron De Vos, *Fairfield Glade*

Cheese Scalloped Potatoes

4 TO 5 MEDIUM POTATOES, PARED AND DICED	½ TEASPOON SALT
1 11-OUNCE CAN CONDENSED CHEDDAR CHEESE SOUP	DASH PEPPER
1 PACKAGE SOUR CREAM SAUCE MIX	1 TABLESPOON BUTTER, MELTED
½ CUP MILK	¼ CUP DRY FINE BREAD CRUMBS

Cook potatoes in boiling water, salted, until tender; drain. Combine soup, sour cream sauce mix, milk, salt and pepper. Place half of the potatoes in a $1\frac{1}{2}$-quart casserole. Top with half the soup mixture. Repeat with remaining potatoes and soup mixture. Combine melted butter or margarine, bread crumbs. Sprinkle on top. Cover and bake in moderate oven at 375 degrees for 25 minutes. Uncover and bake for an additional 10 to 30 minutes. *Yield:* 6 servings.

Mrs. Parvon (Linda) Reed, *Bristol*

Hash Brown Potato Casserole

2 CUPS (8 OUNCES) AMERICAN OR CHEDDAR CHEESE, SHREDDED

1 10¾-OUNCE CAN CONDENSED CREAM OF CHICKEN SOUP

1 CUP DAIRY SOUR CREAM

½ CUP ONION, FINELY CHOPPED (OPTIONAL)

¼ CUP BUTTER, MELTED

¼ TEASPOON SALT

¼ TEASPOON PEPPER

1 32-OUNCE PACKAGE FROZEN LOOSE-PACK HASH BROWN POTATOES, THAWED

1 CUP CORN FLAKES, CRUSHED

1 TABLESPOON BUTTER, MELTED

Grease a 13 x 9 x 2 inch baking dish; set aside. In a large mixing bowl combine shredded cheese, chicken soup, sour cream, chopped onion, ¼ cup butter, salt and pepper. Mix well. Fold in thawed hash brown potatoes. Turn mixture into prepared baking dish. Toss together corn flakes and 1 tablespoon melted butter. Sprinkle over potato mixture. Bake in a 350 degree oven about 1 hour or until casserole is golden brown and potatoes are tender. *Yield:* 8 to 10 servings.

Cora Veal, *Madisonville*
Celia R. Billingsley, *Oneida*

Sweet Potato Honey Casserole

5 LARGE SWEET POTATOES

1 8-OUNCE CAN CRUSHED PINEAPPLE, UNDRAINED

1 CUP HONEY

1 CUP FLAKED COCONUT

1 CUP PECANS, CHOPPED

1½ CUPS MINIATURE MARSHMALLOWS

Cook sweet potatoes in boiling water 20 to 25 minutes or until tender. Let cool to touch; peel and mash.

Combine sweet potatoes and next four ingredients. Spoon into a lightly greased shallow 2-quart casserole. Remove from oven and top with marshmallows; bake uncovered for an additional 5 minutes or until marshmallows are golden brown. *Yield:* 8 servings.

Mrs. Elveta B. Croft, *Madisonville*

Jamaican Yam Casserole

1 16-OUNCE CAN YAMS, DRAINED

½ MEDIUM BANANA, THICKLY SLICED

¼ CUP ORANGE JUICE

½ TEASPOON SALT

⅛ TEASPOON PEPPER

2 TABLESPOONS PECANS, COARSELY CHOPPED

2 TABLESPOONS TOASTED FLAKED COCONUT

In a buttered 1-quart casserole dish, arrange yams and banana. Pour juice over all. Sprinkle with salt and pepper. Top with pecans and coconut. Bake covered in a 350 degree oven for 30 minutes. *Yield:* 2 servings.

Mrs. Sherry Ligon Allison, *Cookeville*

Sinfully Rich Sweet Potatoes
(Sweet Potato Casserole)

3 CUPS SWEET POTATOES, MASHED	1 CUP EVAPORATED MILK
3/4 CUP SUGAR	1/4 CUP MARGARINE
2 EGGS, BEATEN	1 TEASPOON VANILLA

Beat all ingredients together and pour into a greased 2-quart casserole. Cover with topping and bake in a 375 degree oven for 30 minutes.

Topping:

1 CUP BROWN SUGAR	1 CUP FLAKED COCONUT
1/3 CUP MARGARINE, MELTED	1 CUP PECANS, CHOPPED

Combine ingredients and mix well until crumbly. Sprinkle over potatoes.

Sue Bucy, *Paris*
Jane D. Rader, *Sevierville*
Nelson Hamm, *Ramar*
Mary T. Turner, *Blountville*
Mrs. Willie B. Gilliam, *Lenoir City*

Sweet Potato Creole

8 SWEET POTATOES, COOKED	1 1/4 CUPS PINEAPPLE JUICE
1 LEMON, SLICED WITH RIND REMOVED	1 CUP BROWN SUGAR
3 ORANGE SECTIONS, SLICED	1/2 TEASPOON SALT
1 1/3 CUPS CRUSHED PINEAPPLE	5 TABLESPOONS BUTTER

Peel sweet potatoes and cut into 4 lengthwise strips. Place alternate layers of sweet potatoes, lemon, orange and pineapple into a greased casserole. Combine remaining ingredients and cook into a thick syrup. Pour syrup over potatoes. Bake in a 350 degree oven 30 to 40 minutes. *Yield:* 8 servings.

Mark C. Griffin, *Memphis*

Sweet Potato Pudding

6 MEDIUM RAW SWEET POTATOES, GRATED	1/4 CUP BUTTER, MELTED
1 CUP BROWN SUGAR	1 EGG, SLIGHTLY BEATEN
PINCH SALT	

Combine ingredients. Pour into greased casserole and bake in a 350 degree oven.

John and Barbara Ward, *Knoxville*

Fried Ramps

WHITE RAMPS
BACON GREASE

SALT TO TASTE
2 OR 3 EGGS

Pull off outer skin around bulb of ramps to clean them. Chop ramps fine and fry in an iron skillet in bacon grease, adding salt to taste. When done, break the eggs into the ramps and scramble them. Cook until done. For a milder taste, substitute chopped green onions for the ramps in this recipe.

Diana Parks, *Madisonville*

Rice Casserole

2 TABLESPOONS BUTTER
2 SMALL OR 1 LARGE ONION, CHOPPED
½ CUP RICE, UNCOOKED
⅛ TEASPOON PEPPER

1 POUND CAN TOMATOES (OR JUICE)
1 TEASPOON SALT (OR LESS IF DESIRED)
1 CAN FRENCH STYLE GREEN BEANS
⅓ CUP WATER (OPTIONAL)

Sauté onions in butter until brown. Add rice, tomatoes, green beans and other ingredients. Cook covered on top of stove 30 minutes.

Mrs. Jean Hood, *Santa Fe*

Pork and Yellow Rice

1 POUND GROUND PORK OR UNSEASONED SAUSAGE
1 MEDIUM ONION, CHOPPED
1 CLOVE GARLIC, CHOPPED
1 BELL PEPPER, CHOPPED
1 4-OUNCE CAN MUSHROOMS, DRAINED
1 CUP RAW RICE

½ TEASPOON PEPPER
1 TABLESPOON MINCED PARSLEY
¼ TEASPOON TUMERIC
2 CUPS CHICKEN BROTH (OR 2 CHICKEN BOUILLON CUBES IN 2 CUPS WATER)
½ TEASPOON HOT PEPPER SAUCE
JUICE OF 1 LEMON

Fry sausage in large skillet over medium heat until brown. Drain excess fat. Add onion, garlic, pepper, mushrooms and rice and sauté until onion is golden and rice is lightly browned. Add pepper, parsley, tumeric, broth, hot sauce and lemon juice and bring to boil. Stir and cover. Reduce heat to simmer and let cook until liquid is absorbed and rice is done. Add water if needed.

MaryAnn Rohm, *Tennessee Ridge*

Squash Fritters

¼ TEASPOON ONION, GRATED

FEW GRAINS PEPPER

SUGAR TO TASTE

2 TABLESPOONS SALT

6 TABLESPOONS ALL-PURPOSE FLOUR

2 EGGS, BEATEN

2 CUPS RAW SQUASH, GRATED

2 TEASPOONS BUTTER OR MARGARINE, MELTED

Combine onion, pepper, sugar, salt, flour and beaten eggs. Add squash. Add butter. Drop by tablespoons on oiled griddle. Brown quickly.

Rebecca Byrd, *Dover*

Squash Puffs

1 POUND YELLOW SQUASH, SLICED

1 EGG, BEATEN

½ CUP ALL-PURPOSE FLOUR

½ CUP CORN MEAL

1 TEASPOON BAKING POWDER

½ TEASPOON SALT

1 MEDIUM ONION, FINELY CHOPPED

VEGETABLE OIL

Cook squash, covered, in boiling water until tender. Drain. Mash enough to measure 1 cup; reserve any remaining squash for use in other recipes. Combine the one cup mashed squash and egg; stir well. Combine flour, cornmeal, baking powder and salt; mix well. Add squash mixture and onion, stir until blended. Drop squash mixture by level tablespoonsful into hot oil. Cook until golden brown, turning once. Drain well on paper towels. These puffs may be cooled and frozen. When ready to serve, set out at room temperature for about 30 to 40 minutes, then crisp in 350 degree oven for about 10 minutes. *Yield:* about 2 dozen.

Mrs. Willie B. Gilliam, *Lenoir City*

Summer Squash Patties

1½ CUPS SELF-RISING FLOUR

½ TEASPOON SUGAR

¾ TEASPOON SALT

½ CUP SOUR CREAM

1 EGG

1 TABLESPOON VEGETABLE OIL

3 CUPS YELLOW SQUASH, COARSELY GRATED

1 MEDIUM ONION, GRATED

PEPPER TO TASTE

Combine first six ingredients, beating until smooth. Stir in squash; add onion and pepper. Drop mixture by tablespoons into a hot greased skillet. Cook until golden brown, turning once. Drain.

Becky Makamson, *Lebanon*

In late April, visitors from all over make their way to Cosby's Ramp Festival—the smelliest celebration in Tennessee. The ramp, which has edible white roots, is a cousin of the onion and flourishes in the moist woodlands of East Tennessee. One can eat the cooked ramps at the Festival or just enjoy chicken and entertainment.

Photographic Services

Photographic Services

Squash Casserole

½ CUP CHOPPED ONION
½ CUP CHOPPED CELERY
2 TABLESPOONS MARGARINE
4 CUPS COOKED SQUASH

1 CUP HOLLANDAISE SAUCE, PREPARED (PACKAGED MIX)
½ CUP TOASTED BREAD CRUMBS
PARMESAN CHEESE

Sauté onions and celery in margarine, add to squash. Stir in Hollandaise sauce. Pour squash mixture into 1½-quart casserole dish. Cover with toasted bread crumbs and sprinkle parmesan cheese on top. Cover and bake in a 350 degree oven for 35 to 40 minutes. Uncover last 5 minutes and brown slightly.

Kathy Sweeney, *College Grove*

Squash Casserole

8 TO 10 SQUASH
6 CRACKERS, CRUMBLED
½ CUP SWEET MILK
2 EGGS
1 ONION, GRATED
1 BELL PEPPER, GRATED

½ CUP LONGHORN CHEESE, GRATED
¼ CUP MARGARINE
1 TEASPOON SUGAR
CRACKER CRUMBS
SALT AND PEPPER TO TASTE

Parboil squash in salted water until tender. Drain and mash well. Add crackers. Beat milk and eggs together and add to squash. Grate onion and pepper. Grate cheese. Add all 3 to squash. Add butter and sugar. Salt and pepper to taste. Pour in buttered casserole, top with crackers. Bake in a 325 degree oven for 1 hour. May be prepared ahead.

Helen L. Garner, *Chattanooga*

Spinach Casserole

2 PACKAGES FROZEN CHOPPED SPINACH, COOKED AND DRAINED
2 CUPS ONION, CHOPPED
1 CUP MAYONNAISE

2 EGGS, BEATEN
1 CUP SHARP CHEDDAR CHEESE, SHREDDED
1 CAN CREAM OF MUSHROOM SOUP, UNDILUTED

Mix together and place in a 9 x 12 inch baking dish. Toast 4 slices of rye or whole wheat bread and crumble over top. Sprinkle with butter. Bake in a 350 degree oven for 45 minutes.

Georgia Verble, *Clinton*

Spinach Parmesan

4 10-OUNCE PACKAGES CHOPPED SPINACH, COOKED AND DRAINED
½ CUP GRATED PARMESAN CHEESE
6 TABLESPOONS ONION, FINELY CHOPPED
6 TABLESPOONS HEAVY CREAM
5 TABLESPOONS BUTTER, MELTED
½ TEASPOON SALT
½ CUP CRACKER CRUMBS
2 EGGS, HARD BOILED

Combine spinach, cheese, onion, cream, 4 tablespoons of butter and salt. Turn into 8-inch square baking dish. Combine remaining 1 tablespoon of butter and cracker crumbs. Sprinkle over spinach. Bake in a 350 degree oven for 15 to 20 minutes. If desired, garnish with the egg slices. *Yield:* 10 servings.

Mrs. Theresa Sanchez, *Franklin*

Scalloped Tomatoes

4 SLICES WHITE TOAST
2 TABLESPOONS BUTTER
  GARLIC SALT
¼ CUP ONION, FINELY CHOPPED
1 TEASPOON SALT
¼ TEASPOON PEPPER
2½ CUPS TOMATOES
2 TABLESPOONS MELTED BUTTER

Spread toast with 2 tablespoons butter; sprinkle with garlic salt and cut into cubes. Add onion, salt and pepper to tomatoes. Place a layer of cubes in greased casserole dish. Add tomatoes and top with remaining cubes. Pour melted butter over top. Bake in a 375 degree oven for 20 minutes.

Cathy Moran, *Cookeville*

Tomato Pudding (A Sweet Vegetable)

This recipe has come down through my family for four generations. It is very hard to put it on paper because we have always fixed it to taste. Some people may like it sweeter than others. I prefer to use bacon drippings since it gives it a better flavor and the original recipe called for drippings.

1 QUART CANNED TOMATOES
1½ CUPS BROWN SUGAR
¼ CUP BUTTER (OR 1 TABLESPOON BACON DRIPPINGS)
6 SLICES BREAD

Place tomatoes, sugar and butter or (bacon drippings) in saucepan and bring to boil. Break bread into pieces and add to tomato mixture. Add extra bread until all liquid is absorbed.

Christine McKnight, *Nashville*

Baked Zucchini and Tomatoes

2 MEDIUM ZUCCHINI	SALT AND PEPPER TO TASTE
2 MEDIUM FRESH TOMATOES	BUTTER
1 MEDIUM MILD ONION	1 CUP BUTTER CRACKERS, CRUSHED

Wash zucchini; do not peel unless the skin is hard. Peel the tomatoes and onion. Slice all vegetables into very thin crosswise slices. In a greased baking dish make alternate layers of zucchini, tomatoes and onions, sprinkling each layer with a little salt and pepper, dotting with butter. Cover the top with crushed cracker crumbs. Bake in a 350 degree oven until vegetables are tender.

Mrs. Donald (Rolene) Pake, *Nashville*

Tomato Delights

My job at Opryland USA leaves me little time for cooking. This is one dish that I can prepare quickly that is delicious and very attractive. My guests always love it. A salad, wine and your favorite dinner roll completes the dinner.

6 FIRM, RIPE TOMATOES	1 EGG, WELL BEATEN
1 MEDIUM SIZE GREEN PEPPER, CHOPPED	1/4 TEASPOON DRIED WHOLE OREGANO
1 SMALL ONION, CHOPPED	1/4 TEASPOON DRIED WHOLE BASIL
1/4 CUP BUTTER OR MARGARINE, MELTED	1/4 TEASPOON SALT
1 CUP (4 OUNCES) CHEDDAR CHEESE, SHREDDED	4 SLICES BACON, COOKED AND CRUMBLED
1 CUP REGULAR RICE, COOKED	SMALL BIT OF PARSLEY

Cut a slice from the top of each tomato; scoop out pulp, leaving shells intact and reserving pulp. Sprinkle inside of tomato shells lightly with salt, invert to drain. Chop tomato pulp up.

Sauté green pepper and onion in butter. Add tomato pulp and remaining ingredients, except parsley; stir well. Spoon mixture into tomato shells and place in a shallow baking dish. Bake in a 350 degree oven for 25 to 30 minutes. Garnish with parsley. *Yield:* 6 servings.

Ms. Denise L. Dunlap, *Nashville*

Turnip Greens

TURNIP GREENS	SALT TO TASTE
SEVERAL NEW POTATOES	BACON GREASE

Wash and drain greens. Put in a large iron skillet and cover with water. Scrape several small, new potatoes and place on top of the greens. Add salt to taste. Put cover on skillet and cook 1 to 2 hours until tender. Drain off any remaining water. Add bacon grease and simmer until hot, 15 to 20 minutes.

Diana Parks, *Madisonville*

Turnips

3 POUNDS WHITE TURNIPS
1/4 POUND BACON, DICED
2/3 CUP ONION, FINELY CHOPPED
1 TABLESPOON ALL-PURPOSE FLOUR

1 CUP CANNED BEEF BOUILLON (OR 1 CUBE DISSOLVED IN 1 CUP HOT WATER)
1 TEASPOON SUGAR
1/4 TEASPOON RUBBED SAGE
1/4 TEASPOON BLACK PEPPER

Peel and cube or slice turnips. Drop into boiling water and cook 5 minutes. Drain. Sauté bacon, add all other ingredients. Cook until tender. *Yield:* 6 servings.

Mrs. J. W. Bragg, *Arlington*

Baked Vegetable Casserole

1 1/2 CUPS MILK, SCALDED
1 CUP DRY BREAD CRUMBS
1/4 CUP BUTTER, MELTED
1/2 TABLESPOON SALT
1 TABLESPOON PARSLEY, CHOPPED

2 PIMENTOES, CHOPPED
DASH OF PAPRIKA
1 1/2 TABLESPOONS ONIONS, CHOPPED
3 EGGS, BEATEN
1 TO 2 CUPS FROZEN VEGETABLES
1 1/2 CUPS CHEESE, SHREDDED

Pour scalded milk over bread crumbs; stir to moisten. Add butter, salt, parsley, pimentos, paprika, onion and eggs. Mix well. Place thawed vegetables in a 1-quart baking dish. Pour sauce over vegetables. Sprinkle shredded cheese on top. Place dish in a pan of water and bake in a 325 degree oven for 1 1/4 hours.

Pam Smith, *Nashville*

Vegetable Casserole Delight

This is my original recipe. It was the state winner in the Dairy Recipe Contest in 1984 over 4,000 entries statewide.

2 14 1/2-OUNCE CANS CUT ASPARAGUS SPEARS, DRAINED
10 OUNCES EXTRA SHARP CHEDDAR CHEESE
1 17-OUNCE CAN SMALL, SWEET ENGLISH PEAS, DRAINED
4 OUNCES PIMENTO, FINELY DICED
SALT AND PEPPER TO TASTE
1 10 1/2-OUNCE CAN CREAM OF CELERY SOUP

1/2 CUP WHOLE MILK
8 OUNCES SOUR CREAM
8 OUNCES SLICED SWISS CHEESE
4 BOILED EGGS, FINELY CHOPPED OR DICED
1 CUP SEASONED CROUTONS, FINELY GROUND
5 TABLESPOONS BUTTER, MELTED

Generously butter bottom and sides of 3-quart glass elongated baking dish. Pour asparagus evenly in bottom of baking dish. Grate or cut cheddar cheese into very slim slices and place evenly on top of asparagus layer. Cover with English peas and diced pimento.

In a separate dish, dilute cream of celery soup with milk and mix. Add sour cream and mix together. Pour mixture over last vegetable layer. Arrange Swiss cheese evenly for next layer. Sprinkle boiled eggs on top. Cover with buttered bread crumbs. Bake in a 350 degree oven for about 25 minutes or until dish is bubbly and crumbs slightly brown on top. *Yield:* 8 servings.

Note: I garnished with a tomato rose surrounded by greenery.

Variation: Dish could be made a main dish by adding 2 cups chopped cooked chicken.

Pamela S. Jones, *Cottage Grove*

Bean Casserole

This makes a large dish and is nice for a picnic. Men especially like this dish.

1 1-POUND CAN GREEN LIMA BEANS	1 CUP BROWN SUGAR, PACKED
1 1-POUND CAN LARGE BUTTER BEANS	2 HEAPING TEASPOONS PREPARED MUSTARD
1 1-POUND CAN RED BEANS	1 TEASPOON VINEGAR
1 1-POUND CAN CUT GREEN BEANS	1/2 POUND BACON, CHOPPED
1 LARGE CAN PORK AND BEANS	1 ONION, SEPARATED INTO RINGS

Drain all the beans, except the pork and beans, and mix in large long casserole dish. Rinse the pork and beans can out with 1/2 cup water, and add to casserole. Mix together the brown sugar, prepared mustard and vinegar; mix thoroughly with beans. On top of mixture put 1/2 pound raw chopped bacon. Separate the onion into rings and place on top of bacon. Bake in a 350 degree oven for 1 1/2 hours. Serve hot or cold.

Mrs. Claud T. Pearce, *Nashville*

Vegetable Casserole

1 16-OUNCE CAN SHOE PEG CORN	1 CUP CHEDDAR CHEESE, GRATED
1 16-OUNCE CAN FRENCH STYLE GREEN BEANS	1 8-OUNCE CONTAINER SOUR CREAM
1 CUP CELERY, CHOPPED	1 CAN CREAM OF CELERY SOUP
1 CUP ONION, CHOPPED	4 CUPS CHEESE CRACKERS
1 CUP GREEN PEPPER, CHOPPED	1 2-OUNCE PACKAGE SLICED ALMONDS
	1/2 CUP BUTTER, MELTED

Drain vegetables and mix together with cheese, sour cream, and soup. Place in a 9 x 13 inch pan. Crumble crackers and mix with almonds and melted butter. Sprinkle on top of casserole mixture. Bake in a 350 degree oven for 35 to 45 minutes. *Yield:* 16 servings.

Betty J. Anglin, *Jonesborough*

Zucchini in Cream

6 SMALL ZUCCHINI, CUT INTO ½ INCH SLICES	6 TABLESPOONS SHARP CHEDDAR CHEESE, GRATED
⅔ CUP SOUR CREAM	½ TEASPOON SEASONED SALT
1 TABLESPOON BUTTER OR MARGARINE	3 TABLESPOONS FRESH BREAD CRUMBS

Simmer zucchini in enough water to cover for 10 minutes; drain. Turn into 8-inch baking dish. Combine sour cream, butter, 4 tablespoons cheese and salt in small saucepan; heat and stir until blended. Pour over zucchini. Top with bread crumbs and remaining grated cheese. Bake in a 375 degree oven for 10 minutes or until crumbs are golden. Let stand for 5 minutes; serve. *Yield:* 4 servings.

Regina Albright, *Clarksville*

Zucchini Casserole

5 OR 6 ZUCCHINI SQUASH	⅛ TEASPOON ONION SALT (OR TO TASTE)
3 OUNCES CREAM CHEESE, DICED	½ CUP BUTTERED BREAD CRUMBS
⅛ TEASPOON GARLIC POWDER	⅛ TEASPOON PAPRIKA
	PARMESAN CHEESE

Slice squash into 2-inch pieces, cook in small amount of boiling water 8 to 10 minutes. Drain zucchini well, mix in cream cheese, add garlic and onion salt. Put in a buttered casserole and top with buttered bread crumbs. Sprinkle with paprika and cheese. Bake in a 350 degree oven for 30 minutes.

Mrs. Sue Gray Walker, *Knoxville*

Chapter Eight

Eggs, Cheese, and Pasta

Breakfast Before

Make a day ahead, refrigerate, pop in oven 45 minutes before breakfast or brunch.

1 POUND SPICY PORK SAUSAGE, BULK	1 TEASPOON DRIED MUSTARD
6 EGGS	2 SLICES WHITE BREAD, CUBED
2 CUPS MILK	1 CUP CHEDDAR CHEESE, GRATED
1 TEASPOON SALT	

Sauté sausage. Drain all the grease off. Beat eggs with milk, salt and mustard. Layer the cubes of bread, sausage and cheese in a 9 x 13 inch baking dish. Pour liquid mixture on top. Refrigerate overnight. Bake in a 350 degree oven for 45 minutes. Serve with fresh fruit cups and English muffins. *Yield:* 6 to 8 servings.

Deborah Rinehart, *Talbott*
Margaret Hogshead, *Nashville*
Marie H. Hunter, *Kingsport*
Karen Peters, *Bristol*

Sausage Strata

6 SLICES WHITE BREAD, TRIMMED	¼ TEASPOON PEPPER
1 CUP SWISS CHEESE, GRATED	4 EGGS, BEATEN
1½ POUNDS SAUSAGE, CRUMBLED, BROWNED AND DRAINED	¾ CUP HALF AND HALF
1 TEASPOON PREPARED MUSTARD	1 TEASPOON WORCESTERSHIRE SAUCE
	¼ TEASPOON NUTMEG

Butter a 9 x 12 inch glass baking dish. Place bread to fit on bottom. Next, combine sausage with remaining ingredients, place on bread crumbs and top with cheese. Bake in a 350 degree oven for 30 to 35 minutes. Great as an appetizer or as part of a luncheon.

Eleanor M. Fleenor, *Lenoir City*

Breakfast Pizza

1 POUND PORK SAUSAGE	6 EGGS
1 CAN CRESCENT DINNER ROLLS	SALT AND PEPPER TO TASTE
1 POUND CHEESE, GRATED (1/2 POUND EACH MOZZARELLA AND SHARP CHEDDAR)	1/2 CUP SWEET MILK
	1 TEASPOON OREGANO

Crumble sausage in a skillet and fry until done, but not hard. Stir occasionally while frying to keep crumbled fine. Put sausage into a collander and let drain and cool. Spray a baking pan, 13 1/2 x 9 1/2 x 2 inch (or thereabouts) with Pam and unroll the crescent rolls in the pan in 2 strips; pinch together the middle seam and perforated places, spread with fingers to cover bottom of pan. Crumble sausage over the roll crust evenly. Sprinkle cheese over sausage, beat eggs, milk, salt, oregano together and pour this egg mixture as evenly as possible over cheese. Bake in a 350 degree oven for 30 to 35 minutes. Let pizza set for 5 to 10 minutes, cut into squares and serve hot. This is delicious with fresh fruit cut up together or fresh home grown sliced tomatoes, or both.

Mary E. Marcum, *Morristown*

Country Breakfast

6 SLICES BACON, DICED	3 CUPS POTATOES, RAW AND DICED
1 ONION, CHOPPED	1 TEASPOON SALT
6 EGGS	1/4 TEASPOON PEPPER
1/2 CUP CREAM	

Partially cook bacon in heavy skillet. Combine potatoes, onion, salt and pepper. Spread over bacon, cover skillet tightly and cook over low heat for about 20 minutes or until potatoes are done.

Beat eggs with cream, pour over potatoes. Lift gently with spatula as it cooks underneath and let uncooked eggs run under. Put back on heat and let cook until eggs set.

Ethel Schultz, *Lafayette*

Sausage Quiche

1 POUND SAUSAGE	1 9-INCH PIE SHELL, UNCOOKED
2 TABLESPOONS SAUSAGE DRIPPINGS	2 EGGS, BEATEN
1/2 CUP ONIONS, CHOPPED	1 CUP EVAPORATED MILK
1/3 CUP GREEN PEPPER, CHOPPED	1 TABLESPOON PARSLEY FLAKES
1 TABLESPOON ALL-PURPOSE FLOUR	3/4 TEASPOON SEASONED SALT
1 1/2 CUPS SHARP OR MEDIUM CHEDDAR CHEESE, GRATED	1/4 TEASPOON GARLIC SALT
	1/4 TEASPOON BLACK PEPPER

Sauté sausage and drain off grease into measuring cup. Using 2 table-spoons of drippings, sauté onions and green pepper. To flour, add the grated cheese. Put the sausage, onion and pepper mixture in the pie shell; then layer the cheese mixture. Combine remaining ingredients and pour over cheese. Bake in a 350 degree oven for 35 to 40 minutes. Let set a few minutes before cutting. Can also be made with ground beef instead of sausage.

Marcella T. Epperson, *Johnson City*

Photographic Services

Many generations ago, the Phillips family migrated to West Tennessee from North Carolina. Today it is a large family. A reunion at the Whiteville home of Charles Phillips one July 4 brought more than forty family members from as far away as Los Angeles to renew old acquaintances, eat lots of good food including homemade ice cream, and enjoy a sense of belonging to each other.

Spring Asparagus and Egg Bake

2 14½-OUNCE CANS ASPARAGUS, DRAINED

¼ CUP BUTTER

¼ CUP ALL-PURPOSE FLOUR

½ TEASPOON SALT

1½ CUPS MILK

1 CUP MILD CHEDDAR CHEESE, SHREDDED

⅛ TEASPOON RED PEPPER

4 EGGS, HARD COOKED AND SLICED

½ CUP CRACKER CRUMBS

¼ CUP MARGARINE OR BUTTER

In a saucepan, melt butter, stir in flour and salt; blend in enough milk to make a smooth paste. Stir in remainder of milk and cook over medium heat until sauce is thick, stirring constantly. While sauce is hot, stir in shredded cheese and red pepper. Stir until cheese is melted. In a greased 1½-quart baking dish layer half of asparagus, eggs and sauce. Repeat ingredients to make a second layer. Top with cracker crumbs mixed with ¼ cup butter. Bake in a 350 degree oven for 30 minutes or until mixture bubbles. Place under broiler 2 minutes to brown top. *Yield:* 5 servings.

Note: To double the recipe, use twice as much of each ingredient and bake 45 to 50 minutes in a 3-quart casserole.

Mrs. Mae Hallum, *Memphis*

Baked Egg Casserole

6 TO 8 EGGS, BOILED

  SALAD DRESSING

3 TABLESPOONS BUTTER

4 TABLESPOONS ALL-PURPOSE FLOUR

2 CUPS MILK

½ CUP AMERICAN CHEESE, GRATED

1 CUP CORNFLAKES, CRUSHED

Cut the eggs lengthwise and dress using salad dressing. Melt butter, stir in flour and milk to make white sauce; pour over dressed eggs in a casserole dish. Add cheese and cornflakes. Bake in a 350 degree oven for 10 minutes. *Yield:* 6 to 8 servings.

Mrs. Jim Gassaway, *Woodbury*

Eggs Galore

Eat three out of seven mornings per week!

2 MEDIUM EGGS

½ CUP MOZZARELLA, SWISS, OR FARMERS CHEESE, GRATED

¼ CUP WHEAT GERM

2 DILL PICKLE SPEARS, CHOPPED

1 TABLESPOON MUSTARD

2 TEASPOONS BARBECUE SAUCE

½ TEASPOON MAYONNAISE

  DASH OF SOY SAUCE

  DASH VINEGAR

Combine ingredients and beat to death. Then scramble in frying pan until cooked to desired consistency. Serve with a toasted English muffin. *Yield:* 1 serving (for a person with a strong constitution!).

Hank "Eggs" Allison, *Nashville*

Egg and Bacon Casserole

2 TABLESPOONS BUTTER OR MARGARINE, MELTED

2 TABLESPOONS ALL-PURPOSE FLOUR

2 CUPS MILK

1/8 TEASPOON BLACK PEPPER

2 CUPS AMERICAN CHEESE, SHREDDED

1 CUP BACON, BROKEN INTO BITE-SIZED PIECES

12 EGGS

2 CUPS BUTTERED BREAD CRUMBS

1/2 TEASPOON PAPRIKA

Combine butter and flour, blending until smooth. Cook over low heat until bubbly. Gradually stir in milk, cooking until smooth and thickened, stirring constantly. Remove from heat and add pepper and cheese. Set aside.

Cook bacon until crisp. Drain and break into pieces. Pour off bacon drippings, leaving about 1 tablespoon. Add eggs and cook until set, stirring occasionally to scramble. Fold in cheese sauce. Spoon mixture into a lightly greased 12 x 7 x 2 inch baking dish. Top with bread crumbs and sprinkle with paprika. Bake uncovered in 350 degree oven for approximately 30 minutes until top is brown and casserole bubbles around the edges. *Yield:* 8 servings.

Note: May be prepared ahead and refrigerated until ready to bake.

Mrs. George Lance, *Madison*

Tennessee Grits

At times our weather makes news. A little boy from the deep south, who had never seen snow, was visiting his grandparents in Tennessee when an unexpected snow fell that night. Looking excitedly out the window the next morning, he called to his grandmother, "Grandma, look! The whole world is covered with grits!" Try this recipe and you may enjoy more "grits" in your life.

3 CUPS WATER

1 TEASPOON SALT

1 CUP QUICK COOKING GRITS

1/2 CUP MARGARINE

1 GARLIC CHEESE ROLL

2 EGGS

MILK

Cook grits in salted water according to directions on grits package. Melt margarine and cheese roll over low heat in a sauce pan. Beat eggs well and place in a measuring cup, fill to 1 cup with milk. Combine grits, cheese and egg mixtures, stirring well. Pour into a buttered 1 1/2-quart baking dish. Sprinkle top with paprika, buttered bread crumbs or grated cheese. Bake in a 350 degree oven for about 40 minutes. *Yield:* 4 to 6 servings, according to appetite.

Variation: Crushed corn flakes may be spread on top before baking if desired.

Note: A good substitute for potatoes, also if any is left over, we cut into squares, warm it in the microwave oven and enjoy it with our bacon and scrambled eggs for breakfast.

Mrs. Garland (Lorene) Porter, *Evensville*
Mrs. Edward M. (Virginia) Lindsey, *Lawrenceburg*

Macaroni Cheese Deluxe

1 7-OUNCE PACKAGE ELBOW MACARONI
2 CUPS COTTAGE CHEESE
1 CUP SOUR CREAM
1 EGG, SLIGHTLY BEATEN

3/4 TEASPOON SALT
DASH BLACK PEPPER
8 OUNCES (2 CUPS) SHARP AMERICAN CHEESE, GRATED
PAPRIKA TO TASTE

Cook macaroni according to package directions. Drain well. Combine cottage cheese, sour cream, egg, salt and black pepper. Add grated cheese and mix well; stir in cooked macaroni. Bake in 9-inch baking dish. Sprinkle with paprika. Bake in a 350 degree oven for 45 minutes. *Yield:* 6 to 8 servings.

Lorene Dial, *Madisonville*

Special Company Macaroni and Cheese

1 1/2 CUPS ELBOW MACARONI, UNCOOKED
1 4-OUNCE CAN MUSHROOM STEMS AND PIECES, DRAINED
1/4 CUP PIMENTO, FINELY CHOPPED
1 1/2 CUPS (8 OUNCES) PROCESSED AMERICAN CHEESE, CUBED

2/3 CUP EVAPORATED SKIMMED MILK
3 TABLESPOONS ONION, CHOPPED
1 TEASPOON SALT
1 TEASPOON DRY MUSTARD
1 TEASPOON WORCESTERSHIRE SAUCE
1/8 TEASPOON BLACK PEPPER

Cook macaroni as directed on package. In greased 1 1/2-quart casserole, mix macaroni, mushrooms and pimento. In a 2-quart saucepan over low heat, stir in remaining ingredients until cheese melts. Stir into macaroni; if desired, top with more cheese. Bake in a 350 degree oven for 20 to 25 minutes or until bubbly. *Yield:* 6 servings.

Mrs Calvin (Ruth) Borden, Fairfield Glade

Cheese Pudding

12 SLICES BREAD, CUBED
1 POUND CHEDDAR CHEESE, GRATED
3 CUPS MILK
4 EGGS, WELL BEATEN

2 TEASPOONS DRY MUSTARD
1 TEASPOON SALT
1/3 CUP BUTTER, CUT INTO SMALL PIECES

Butter casserole dish. Break bread into cubes and spread in casserole dish. Beat eggs well. Add grated cheese, milk, dry mustard and salt. Pour over bread. Cut butter into small pieces and put on top of egg mixture. Refrigerate overnight. Bake in slow oven (300 degrees) for 1 hour. *Yield:* 14 servings.

Mrs. David H. Wallace, *Oak Ridge*

Creamy Rice Mold

Delicious accompaniment for most any main dish.

2 ENVELOPES (2 TABLESPOONS) UNFLAVORED GELATIN

1/2 CUP COLD WATER

2 13¾-OUNCE CANS (3½ CUPS) CHICKEN BROTH

¾ CUP MAYONNAISE OR SALAD DRESSING

2 TABLESPOONS LEMON JUICE

1 CUP WHIPPING CREAM, WHIPPED

2½ CUPS COOKED RICE

¾ CUP CELERY, CHOPPED

¼ CUP GREEN ONION, SLICED

CURLY ENDIVE FOR GARNISH

Soften gelatin in cold water. Bring chicken broth to boiling; add gelatin, stirring until dissolved. Beat in mayonnaise and lemon juice. Chill until partially set; whip until light and fluffy. Fold in whipped cream, cooked rice, celery and green onion. Turn into 8-cup ring mold. Chill 6 hours or until firm. Unmold; garnish with curly endive. *Yield:* about 10 servings.

Mary J. Barnes, *Fairfield Glade*

Mexican Rice Casserole

3 SLICES BACON

1/2 CUP GREEN PEPPER, CHOPPED

1 SMALL ONION, CHOPPED

1/2 CUP RICE, UNCOOKED

1 POUND LEAN GROUND BEEF

1 SMALL CLOVE GARLIC, MINCED, OR 1/2 TABLESPOON GROUND GARLIC

1¾ CUPS WATER

1 8-OUNCE CAN TOMATO SAUCE

1 TABLESPOON CHILI POWDER

2½ CUPS CHEDDAR OR VELVEETA CHEESE, GRATED

Sauté bacon in large skillet until crisp. Remove from pan and drain on absorbent paper. Add green pepper and onions to skillet and cook until tender. Add rice and continue to cook until golden color. Stir in ground beef and garlic. Cook until meat is no longer pink.

Add water, tomato sauce and seasonings. Cover and simmer for 25 minutes. Spray 2-quart casserole with Pam, or use margarine. Spoon half the mixture into casserole dish, sprinkle with half of the cheese and half of the bacon, crumbled. Add remaining meat mixture and top with remaining cheese and crumbled bacon. Bake in a 450 degree oven for about 10 minutes or until cheese bubbles. *Yield:* 6 servings.

Marie Grimes, *Linden*

City Butter

1 POUND MARGARINE

1 CUP BUTTERMILK

1 CUP SEASONED OIL

Mix these ingredients and put in containers.

Mrs. Rolus Smith, *Nashville*

Fettucini

1 BOX COOKED FETTUCINI NOODLES	1½ TO 2 CUPS MILK OR CREAM
1 BOX FROZEN SPINACH, THAWED	½ STICK MARGARINE, MELTED
2 EGGS	SALT, PEPPER, RED PEPPER TO TASTE
2 CUPS MONTEREY JACK, CHEDDAR OR OTHER CHEESE, GRATED	

Mix all ingredients in 9-inch pan (it can be a little soupy). Sprinkle with Parmesan or other cheese. Bake in a 350 degree oven for 15 to 20 minutes.

Phyllis Hunt, *Clarksville*

Homemade Cottage Cheese

Annabel Harr Faust is a native of East Tennessee, as were her parents, the late Charles Edgar Harr and Lelia Latture Harr. She resides on the farm where she and her husband (the late Thomas Wesley Faust) started housekeeping in April of 1922. "Mis"Annie has been quite active in the community of Sullivan County. Writing poetry (published), crafts, quilting and numerous other talents abide in great abundance with this lady.

Her homemade cottage cheese was considered a "real delicacy" in earlier days. The town folks regularly made the long, dusty drive out to the country for Annabel's cottage cheese. In later years the local Farmer's Market was the recipient of the creamy delicacy.

Submitted by an "impartial"daughter (in law).

Home produced clabber milk is best for making cottage cheese (not homogenized). By this I mean milk that is drawn from the cow, carefully strained into clean crocks, and preferably kept in cold spring water (in a spring house) well covered by clean boards or plates. After setting 2 or 3 days in the cold water, depending somewhat on the weather, the cream is skimmed off by hand; the resulting "clabber" milk will be thick and ready for making cheese.

Simply pour the sour clabber milk into a vessel of sufficient size. Any quantity may be made, according to the amount of milk on hand or the amount of cheese desired. With the old wood stove the vessel was set farthest away from the heat, as too much heat toughens the curd. On an electric stove one would use the lowest heat. As the milk heats, the curd separates from the whey. The whey will be fairly warm, but not really hot. Remove from heat and pour into a colander (or cheesecloth bag if you choose) and allow the whey to drain off. I often used a large square cloth, bringing the 4 corners together and hanging it on the outside clothesline. If it hangs too long, it could become a little too dry. The curd is then ready to season as desired. I use sweet cream and a little salt to taste. Mayonnaise and paprika are also good.

Annabel Harr Faust, *Kingsport*

Chapter Nine

Candies and Cookies

Candies

Granola

A great breakfast cereal!

8 CUPS OLD-FASHIONED OATS	½ CUP WATER
1 CUP WHEAT GERM	½ CUP OIL
1 CUP SESAME SEEDS	½ CUP HONEY
1 CUP UNSWEETENED COCONUT	1½ TEASPOON SALT
1 CUP RAW CASHEWS OR ALMONDS	2 TEASPOONS VANILLA
½ CUP CHOPPED BRAZIL NUTS (OPTIONAL)	

In large baking pan combine oats, wheat germ, sesame seeds, coconut and nuts; mix well. Combine water, oil, honey, salt and vanilla; add to dry ingredients. Bake in a 325 degree oven for 45 minutes. Stir every 15 minutes. When cool add raisins.

Mrs. Sanford W. Downs, Jr., *Martin*

Spiced Pecans

1 EGG WHITE	¼ TEASPOON ALLSPICE
2½ TABLESPOONS WATER	¼ TEASPOON GROUND CLOVES
¾ CUP SUGAR	¾ TEASPOON SALT
1 TEASPOON CINNAMON	3 CUPS PECANS, SHELLED
¼ TEASPOON NUTMEG	

Beat egg white and water until frothy. Add remaining ingredients except pecans and blend well. Stir in pecans gently to avoid breaking and coat well. Remove pecans from egg white mixture and place on a foil-covered cookie sheet. Spread in thin layer, keeping pecans from touching as much as possible. Bake in a 275 degree oven for 45 minutes, stirring pecans gently after the first 20 minutes. Stir again 15 minutes later to be sure pecans cook on all sides. After cooking, spread on waxed paper to cool, keeping pecans from touching. Store in airtight container.

Mrs. Michael (Susan) Renshaw, *Old Hickory*

Peanut Brittle

1½ CUPS SUGAR
¼ CUP MARGARINE
½ CUP KARO SYRUP

2 CUPS RAW PEANUTS (SHELLED, OF COURSE)
PINCH SALT
1 TEASPOON VANILLA
1 ROUNDED TEASPOON SODA

Mix all together except soda. In a heavy stewer, let come to a boil. Cook 7 minutes or slightly less if the color changes. Add teaspoon baking soda; stir and pour very thin on aluminum foil.

Mrs. Repps Knox, *Trenton*

Every October, waltz tunes, knockwurst—big juicy sausages—sauerkraut, German potato salad, apple strudel, and beer are enjoyed in the area around Seventh Avenue and Monroe Street in Nashville at the Germantown Oktoberfest.

Bob Schatz/Photo Fair

Chocolate Oatmeal Candy

1/2 CUP MILK	2 1/2 CUPS OATMEAL
2 CUPS SUGAR	1/2 CUP PEANUT BUTTER
1/2 CUP MARGARINE	1/2 CUP NUTS
4 TABLESPOONS COCOA, SIFTED	2 TEASPOONS VANILLA

Boil milk, sugar, margarine and cocoa for 1 1/2 minutes. Add remaining ingredients, mix well and pour into greased pan. No further cooking necessary. *Yield:* 2 dozen squares.

Lib Byck, *Oak Ridge*

Coconut Delight Candy

1/2 CUP MARGARINE	1 CUP VANILLA WAFER CRUMBS
1/2 CUP CANNED MILK (PET OR CARNATION)	1 CUP NUTS (PECANS OR OTHER FAVORITE)
2 CUPS SUGAR	1/2 CUP COCONUT
20 LARGE MARSHMALLOWS	

Mix margarine, milk and sugar together; let come to a boil and stir constantly for 2 1/2 minutes rapidly. Take off heat and add marshmallows, stir until dissolved. Add crumbs, nuts and coconut; drop by teaspoons onto wax paper. No further cooking neccessary.

Cynthia McVay, *Memphis*

Pecan Clusters

1 7-OUNCE JAR MARSHMALLOW CREME	5 CUPS SUGAR
1 1/2 POUNDS MILK CHOCOLATE KISSES	1 13-OUNCE CAN EVAPORATED MILK
6 CUPS PECANS	1/2 CUP BUTTER OR MARGARINE

Place marshmallow creme and kisses in a large bowl; set aside. Place pecans on a baking sheet and place in a warm oven until they are warm. Keep warm until time for use.

Combine sugar, milk and butter in a saucepan. Bring mixture to a boil, then cook for 8 minutes. Pour over kisses and marshmallow creme, stirring until well-blended. Stir in warm pecans. Drop by teaspoonfuls onto waxed paper. *Yield:* 12 dozen.

Mrs. Robert (Myrtle) Hutcheson, *Columbia*

Spiders

1 6-OUNCE PACKAGE CHOCOLATE CHIPS

1 8-OUNCE PACKAGE BUTTERSCOTCH CHIPS

1 8-OUNCE CAN PLANTERS PEANUTS

1 SMALL CAN CHOW MEIN NOODLES

Melt chips over hot water, add nuts and noodles. Blend well, drop by spoonfuls onto wax paper.

Mrs. Joe Sam Savage, *Hampshire*

Bachelor's Fudge

2¾ CUPS GRANULATED SUGAR

¼ CUP BUTTER

1 SMALL CAN CARNATION MILK

1 6-OUNCE JAR MARSHMALLOW CREME

PINCH SALT

1 TEASPOON VANILLA

1 CUP CHOPPED NUTS

1 6-OUNCE PACKAGE CHOCOLATE CHIPS

Mix all ingredients except nuts and chocolate chips. Cook on medium heat. Stir constantly. Bring to a boil; boil for 3 minutes. Remove from heat; stir in nuts and chocolate chips. Pour in buttered dish. Let cool at least 30 minutes before cutting into squares.

Mrs. Lowell K. Maynard, *Joelton*

Peanut Butter Fudge

2 CUPS SUGAR

3 TABLESPOONS MARGARINE

1 CUP EVAPORATED MILK

1 CUP MINIATURE MARSHMALLOWS

1⅓ CUPS PEANUT BUTTER

1 TEASPOON VANILLA

Combine sugar, butter and evaporated milk in electric skillet and set temperature at 280 degrees. Bring to a boil for 5 minutes, stirring constantly. Turn off. Add marshmallows, peanut butter and vanilla. Stir until melted. Blend. Pour into buttered 8 x 8 inch pan. Let set.

Vicki Sue Dean, *Clarksville*

Aunt Gela's Bourbon Balls

1 CUP VANILLA WAFERS, FINELY CHOPPED

1 CUP CONFECTIONERS' SUGAR, SIFTED

1 CUP CRUSHED PECANS

2 TEASPOONS COCOA

2 TABLESPOONS LIGHT CORN SYRUP

¼ CUP BOURBON WHISKEY

Mix all ingredients until uniformly moist. Roll each ball in more confectioners' sugar. Wrap in foil. Keeps for weeks. *Yield:* 3½ dozen balls.

Mrs. Andrew P. Davis, *Nashville*

Classic Bonbons

2 CUPS NUTS, FINELY CHOPPED
2 POUNDS CONFECTIONERS' SUGAR
1 14-OUNCE PACKAGE FLAKED COCONUT
1/2 CUP BUTTER, SOFTENED AT ROOM
    TEMPERATURE

1 CAN SWEETENED CONDENSED MILK
1/4 POUND PARAFFIN
2 12-OUNCE PACKAGES CHOCOLATE CHIPS
2 TEASPOONS VANILLA

Combine nuts, sugar and coconut; add butter, vanilla and milk. Mix well; form into balls. Chill balls until firm (overnight) in an airtight container. Melt paraffin and chocolate chips together in double boiler. Insert wooden picks into candy balls; dip into chocolate mixture. Place on waxed paper to harden. Chocolate will coat better if it is only warm, not hot.

Mrs. Mary Bennett, *Nashville*

Frosted Date Balls

1 1/4 CUPS ALL-PURPOSE FLOUR, SIFTED
1/4 TEASPOON SALT
1/2 CUP BUTTER OR MARGARINE
1/3 CUP CONFECTIONERS' SUGAR, SIFTED
1 TABLESPOON MILK

1 TEASPOON VANILLA
2/3 CUP DATES, CHOPPED
1/2 CUP NUTS, CHOPPED
    CONFECTIONERS' SUGAR

Combine flour and salt, sift twice. Cream butter and gradually add sugar. Add milk and vanilla; stir in the sifted flour. Blend in dates and nuts. Roll in 1-inch balls. Place about 3 inches apart on ungreased baking sheet. Bake in a 300 degree oven for 18 to 20 minutes. While warm, roll in confectioners' sugar.

Reba A. Jones, *Clinton*

Cookies
Mrs. Williamson's Big Orange Cookies

1 POUND CANDY ORANGE SLICES, FINELY CUT
2 3 1/2-OUNCE CANS FLAKED COCONUT
1 TEASPOON ORANGE FLAVORING
1 TEASPOON VANILLA

2 CANS BORDENS SWEETENED CONDENSED MILK
1 CUP PECANS, FINELY CHOPPED
    CONFECTIONERS' SUGAR, SIFTED

Combine all ingredients except confectioners' sugar, and mix well. Spread mixture in a lightly-oiled 10 x 15 x 1/2 inch baking pan and bake in a 275 degree oven for 30 minutes. Remove from oven; while still hot, spoon mixture into a medium-sized bowl of sifted confectioners' sugar. (Not too much of the hot mixture at a time.) Roll into balls the size of small walnuts and place on waxed paper to cool. Store in airtight container. *Yield:* 6 dozen cookies. Good for gift giving.

Marilyn Caponetti, *Knoxville*

Oatmeal Cookies

1 CUP SHORTENING (SUCH AS SPRY OR SNOWDRIFT)	1/2 TEASPOON SALT
	3/4 TEASPOON SODA
2 CUPS SUGAR	4 TABLESPOONS BUTTERMILK (OR SWEET MILK WITH 1 TABLESPOON VINEGAR ADDED)
2 EGGS	
1 1/2 CUPS ALL-PURPOSE FLOUR (A LITTLE MORE MAY BE ADDED IF NEEDED)	2 CUPS QUICK-COOKING OATMEAL
1 TEASPOON CINNAMON	1 CUP RAISINS, CHOPPED

Cream shortening and sugar, add beaten eggs. Sift flour, cinnamon and salt together. Stir soda into buttermilk. Add flour mixture alternately with buttermilk to the first mixture, saving the oatmeal and raisins until last. Drop from teaspoon onto greased cookie sheet, leaving 1 1/2 inches between drops. Bake in preheated 350 degree oven about 7 minutes. Do not overcook. Remove with spatula from pan after cookies have been out of oven 2 or 3 minutes. Good! Good! *Yield:* 5 dozen cookies.

Mrs. Campbell M. Sowell, *Columbia*

Mimi's Chocolate No-Bake Cookies

2 CUPS SUGAR	2 CUPS MINUTE OATS
1/2 TEASPOON SALT	1/2 CUP PEANUT BUTTER
1/4 CUP COCOA	1 TEASPOON VANILLA
1/2 CUP MILK	1/2 CUP COCONUT OR NUTS (OPTIONAL)
1/4 CUP BUTTER	

Mix sugar, salt and cocoa in saucepan. Add milk and butter; bring to a boil over medium heat. Boil 1 minute and 30 seconds. Remove from heat and add remaining ingredients; mix well. Drop by spoonfuls onto wax paper; let cool.

Cathie Hamilton, *Dickson*

Josella's Sugar Cookies

This is a recipe from Josella, who has cooked at the First Baptist Church in Milan for many years.

1/2 CUP BUTTER	2 CUPS ALL-PURPOSE FLOUR
1 CUP SUGAR	1 TEASPOON BAKING POWDER
2 EGGS	1/2 TEASPOON VANILLA
1/4 TEASPOON SALT	

Cream butter and sugar, add eggs one at a time and beat well. Add vanilla and sifted dry ingredients. Chill 2 hours and spoon onto cookie sheet. Bake in a 400 degree oven until slightly colored.

Mrs. Dot Jones, *Milan*

Blender Almond Cookies

²⁄₃ CUP SOFT BUTTER

³⁄₄ CUP SUGAR

1 EGG

2 TEASPOONS ALMOND EXTRACT

¹⁄₄ CUP WATER

¹⁄₄ CUP GRANULATED SUGAR

¹⁄₄ CUP CONFECTIONERS' SUGAR

¹⁄₂ TEASPOON LEMON JUICE

³⁄₄ CUP BLANCHED ALMONDS

2 CUPS ALL-PURPOSE FLOUR

¹⁄₂ TEASPOON SALT

Cream butter, add ³⁄₄ cup sugar, egg and flavoring; beat until light. Combine water, remaining sugars, lemon juice and almonds to make almond paste. Add almond paste, flour and salt. Mix well; chill dough. Shape into 1-inch balls and press each into a flat cake about ¹⁄₃-inch thick. Top each with an almond. Bake in a 325 degree oven for about 25 minutes or until edges are slightly golden.

Mrs. Edward (Joyce) Turner, *Sevierville*

Seven Layer Cookies

¹⁄₄ CUP BUTTER

1 CUP GRAHAM CRUMBS

1 CAN FLAKED COCONUT

1 6-OUNCE PACKAGE CHOCOLATE CHIPS

1 6-OUNCE PACKAGE BUTTERSCOTCH CHIPS

1 CAN SWEETENED CONDENSED MILK

1 CUP PECANS, CHOPPED

Melt butter in 9 x 12 inch baking pan. Add ingredients by layers. Bake in a 325 degree oven for 30 minutes.

Pam Savage, *Sparta*

Old-Fashioned Tea Cakes

I am an 81-year-old retired elementary school teacher who has happy memories of childhood days, when my paternal grandmother baked old-fashioned tea cakes for me whenever I was expected for a visit. My family went for a visit at least twice a month, and sometimes more often. There were always tea cakes as long as grandma was able to cook them, even into my early teen years.

1¹⁄₂ CUPS SUGAR

1 CUP SHORTENING

2 EGGS

1 TEASPOON VANILLA

1 TEASPOON BAKING POWDER

¹⁄₄ TEASPOON SODA

ALL-PURPOSE FLOUR

¹⁄₃ CUP BUTTERMILK

Cream sugar and shortening; add eggs and vanilla. Mix well. Stir baking powder and soda in 1 cup flour. Add alternately with buttermilk. Beat well. Then put in bowl and gradually work in enough flour to roll. Cut and bake in a 375 degree oven until lightly brown.

Edna Wagoner, *Selmer*

Chocolate Chip Cookies

½ CUP CRISCO SHORTENING
¾ CUP BROWN SUGAR, PACKED
½ CUP WHITE SUGAR
2 EGGS
1 TEASPOON VANILLA

2 CUPS ALL-PURPOSE FLOUR
1 TEASPOON SODA
1 TEASPOON SALT
1 CUP CHOCOLATE CHIPS

Cream shortening and sugars until creamy; add eggs and flavoring and mix well. Add dry ingredients, then stir in chips. Spoon onto cookie sheet and bake in a 325 degree oven for 10 to 12 minutes. Do not overcook.

Julia Cooper, *Oak Ridge*

Lemon Cornmeal Cookies

½ POUND BUTTER OR MARGARINE, ROOM
   TEMPERATURE
1 CUP SUGAR
2 EGG YOLKS

1 TEASPOON GRATED LEMON PEEL
1½ CUPS ALL-PURPOSE FLOUR
1 CUP YELLOW CORNMEAL

Beat butter and sugar with mixer until lighter in color and well-blended. Add egg yolks and mix well. Stir in lemon peel, flour, and meal to mix well. Wrap dough in plastic bag and chill 3 to 4 hours. Heat oven to 350 degrees. Roll out dough on lightly floured surface or between sheets of waxed paper. Cut into heart shapes. Place on an ungreased baking sheet and sprinkle with additional sugar. Bake in center of oven 8 to 10 minutes until edges are browned. Or dough may be rolled into a 2-inch cylinder before chilling and cut into rounds ¼ inch thick before baking. *Yield:* 3 dozen.

Corinne Wells, *Columbia*

Double Chocolate Walnut Brownies

1 CUP BUTTER
4 SQUARES UNSWEETENED CHOCOLATE
2 CUPS SUGAR
3 EGGS
1 TEASPOON VANILLA

1 CUP ALL-PURPOSE FLOUR, SIFTED
1½ CUPS COARSELY CHOPPED WALNUTS
1 6-OUNCE PACKAGE SEMISWEET CHOCOLATE
   PIECES

Melt butter and chocolate squares. Remove from heat. Beat in sugar, add eggs, stir in vanilla, flour, and 1 cup walnuts. Spread in a 13 x 9 x 2 inch pan. Combine remaining ½ cup walnuts with chocolate pieces and sprinkle over the top of the cookie mixture pressing down lightly. Bake in a 350 degree oven for 35 minutes. *Yield:* 2 dozen.

Barbara Vaughn, *Livingston*

Miss Wattie's Brownies

This is a different kind of brownie. Although I am allergic to chocolate and have never eaten it, my family and friends think it is the best brownie they have ever eaten.

1 CUP MARGARINE	1/2 CUP BUTTERMILK
8 TABLESPOONS COCOA	2 TEASPOONS VANILLA
1/2 CUP OIL	1 TEASPOON CINNAMON
1 CUP WATER	1 TEASPOON SODA
2 CUPS SUGAR	6 TABLESPOONS SWEET MILK
2 CUPS ALL-PURPOSE FLOUR	1 PACKAGE CONFECTIONERS' SUGAR
2 EGGS	1 CUP NUTS

Bring to a boil 1/2 cup margarine, 4 tablespoons cocoa, 1/2 cup oil and 1 cup water. Pour over a mixture of 2 cups sugar and 2 cups sifted flour. Mix well. Add 2 eggs, 1/2 cup buttermilk, 1 teaspoon vanilla, 1 teaspoon cinnamon, 1 teaspoon soda. Beat well. Pour into long greased and floured pan and bake in a 350 degree oven for 45 minutes.

For icing: Boil 4 tablespoons cocoa, 1/2 cup margarine and 6 tablespoons sweet milk. Pour over 1 package confectioners' sugar, 1 cup chopped nuts and 1 teaspoon vanilla. Beat well and ice the cake while hot.

Mrs. Bill (Freda) Wilson, *Puryear*

Dream Bars

1/2 CUP SOFT SHORTENING	1 CUP ALL-PURPOSE FLOUR
1/2 CUP BROWN SUGAR, PACKED	

Mix shortening and sugar thoroughly. Stir in flour. Flatten into bottom of ungreased oblong pan. Bake in a 350 degree oven for 10 minutes. Then spread with topping.

Almond-Coconut Topping:

2 EGGS, WELL BEATEN	1 TEASPOON BAKING POWDER
1 CUP BROWN SUGAR, PACKED	1/2 TEASPOON SALT
1 TEASPOON VANILLA	1 CUP COCONUT
2 TABLESPOONS ALL-PURPOSE FLOUR	1 CUP NUTS

Mix eggs, sugar and vanilla. Mix with flour, baking powder and salt. Stir in coconut and nuts, pour over first layer. Return to oven and bake 25 more minutes. Cool and cut in bars. *Yield:* 2 1/2 dozen.

Mrs. Rolus Smith, *Nashville*
Mrs. Paul Clabough, *Maryville*

Special K Bars

I find this an economical "candy bar" when my large family wants something sweet to munch on.

½ CUP WHITE KARO SYRUP	3 CUPS SPECIAL K CEREAL
½ CUP SUGAR	1 CUP CHOCOLATE CHIPS
¾ CUP CHUNK PEANUT BUTTER	1 CUP BUTTERSCOTCH CHIPS

Bring Karo syrup and sugar just to a boil, add the peanut butter. Pour over Special K. Pour into a buttered 9-inch square or similar pan. Press gently to even it out. Melt the chocolate chips and the butterscotch chips together. Spread on top of the cereal mixture and cool. Cut into desired size squares.

Diann Melton, *Humboldt*

Redi-Frosted Raisin Bars

1 CUP SUGAR	¼ TEASPOON SALT
1 CUP RAISINS	1 TEASPOON VANILLA
1 CUP WATER	1 CUP BROWN SUGAR
½ CUP MARGARINE	¼ CUP ALL-PURPOSE FLOUR
2 CUPS ALL-PURPOSE FLOUR	½ CUP NUTS
1 TEASPOON SODA	2 TABLESPOONS MARGARINE
½ TEASPOON BAKING POWDER	

Boil sugar, raisins, water and ½ cup margarine gently for 3 minutes, then cool. Add 2 cups flour, soda, baking powder, salt and vanilla. Spread in a 10 x 15 inch flat pan. Mix brown sugar, ¼ cup flour, nuts and 2 tablespoons margarine, put on top of batter and gently press in. Bake in a 325 degree oven for 30 minutes or until toothpick comes out clean. Cut into bars (2 x 3 inches). *Yield:* 25 bars.

Mrs. Dale Montgomery, *Middleton*

Chapter Ten

Cakes, Pies, and Desserts

Cakes

German Chocolate Sour Cream Fudge Cake

1 BOX GERMAN CHOCOLATE CAKE MIX WITH
PUDDING

3 EGGS

1 CUP MILK

¾ CUP WESSON OIL

Mix together and pour in 2 round cake pans. Bake in a 350 degree oven for 30 minutes. Let cool.

Filling:

2 CUPS SOUR CREAM

1½ CUPS SUGAR

3 CUPS COCONUT

3 CUPS COOL WHIP, ROOM TEMPERATURE

1 TEASPOON VANILLA (OPTIONAL)

Mix together, adding vanilla if desired. Split cake layers in half. Put filling on top of each layer; stack and cover cake on top and sides with filling. Keep in refrigerator.

Mable Swafford, *Atwood*

Fresh Apple Cake

2 CUPS ALL-PURPOSE FLOUR

3 TEASPOONS CINNAMON

1 TEASPOON SALT

2 TABLESPOONS BAKING POWDER

1½ CUPS WESSON OIL

2 CUPS SUGAR

4 EGGS

3 CUPS APPLES, CHOPPED

1 CUP PECANS, CHOPPED (OR 1 CUP SEEDLESS RAISINS)

Sift together dry ingredients. In a large bowl combine oil, sugar and eggs; add dry ingredients. Fold in apples and pecans. Bake in a greased bundt pan in a 350 degree oven for 40 to 50 minutes.

Frosting:

3 OUNCE PACKAGE CREAM CHEESE

¼ CUP MARGARINE

1 BOX CONFECTIONERS' SUGAR

1 TEASPOON VANILLA

Mix all together; frost Fresh Apple Cake.

Mrs. Eloise Throop, *Mountain City*

Hummingbird Cake

3 CUPS ALL-PURPOSE FLOUR	1½ TEASPOONS VANILLA
2 CUPS SUGAR	2 CUPS BANANAS, CHOPPED
1 TEASPOON SODA	2 CUPS NUTS, CHOPPED
1 TEASPOON SALT	1 SMALL CAN CRUSHED PINEAPPLE WITH JUICE
1 TEASPOON CINNAMON	3 EGGS, BEATEN
1½ CUPS CRISCO OIL	

Sift together flour, sugar, soda, salt and cinnamon. Stir in remaining ingredients, but do not beat. Bake in a tube pan in a 350 degree oven for 1 hour and 15 minutes (or in 3 greased and floured 9-inch round cake pans for 25 to 30 minutes). Cool.

Frosting:

1 8-OUNCE PACKAGE CREAM CHEESE	1 TEASPOON VANILLA
½ CUP MARGARINE, SOFTENED	½ CUP PECANS, CHOPPED
1 BOX CONFECTIONERS' SUGAR	

Mix together and frost cake.

Mary T. Turner, *Blountville*
Mrs. Michael (Susan) Renshaw, *Old Hickory*
Ms. Lila Jean Seal, *Sneedville*
Mrs. Jean Pierce, *Manchester*

Blue Ribbon Carrot Cake

2 CUPS ALL-PURPOSE FLOUR	2 TEASPOONS VANILLA
2 TEASPOONS SODA	1 8-OUNCE CAN CRUSHED PINEAPPLE, DRAINED
2 TEASPOONS CINNAMON	2 CUPS RAW CARROTS, GRATED
½ TEASPOON SALT	3½ OUNCES SHREDDED COCONUT
3 EGGS	1 CUP (4 OUNCES) WALNUTS, COARSELY CHOPPED
¾ CUP VEGETABLE OIL	BUTTERMILK GLAZE
¾ CUP BUTTERMILK	CREAM CHEESE FROSTING
3 CUPS SUGAR	

Generously grease a 13 x 9 inch baking dish or two 9-inch cake pans; set aside. Sift flour, soda, cinnamon and salt together, set aside. In a large bowl, beat eggs, add oil, buttermilk, sugar and vanilla; mix well. Add flour mixture, pineapple, carrots, coconut and walnuts. Stir well. Pour into prepared baking dish or pans. Bake in a 350 degree oven for 55 minutes or until wooden toothpick inserted in center comes out clean. While cake is baking, prepare Buttermilk Glaze. Remove cake from oven and slowly pour glaze over hot cake. Cool cake in pan until glaze is totally absorbed, about 15 minutes. Prepare Cream Cheese Frosting and frost cake. Refrigerate until set; serve chilled. May be refrigerated several days. *Yield:* 20 to 24 servings.

Buttermilk Glaze:

1 CUP SUGAR
1/2 TEASPOON SODA
1/2 CUP BUTTERMILK

1/2 CUP BUTTER OR MARGARINE
1 TABLESPOON CORN SYRUP
1 TEASPOON VANILLA

In a small saucepan, combine sugar, soda, buttermilk, butter or margarine and corn syrup. Bring to a boil. Cook 5 minutes, stirring occasionally. Remove from heat and stir in vanilla.

Cream Cheese Frosting:

1/2 CUP BUTTER OR MARGARINE, ROOM TEMPERATURE
1 8-OUNCE PACKAGE CREAM CHEESE, ROOM TEMPERATURE

1 TEASPOON VANILLA
2 CUPS CONFECTIONERS' SUGAR
1 TEASPOON ORANGE JUICE
1 TEASPOON GRATED ORANGE PEEL

Cream butter or margarine and cream cheese until fluffy. Add vanilla, powdered sugar, orange juice and orange peel. Mix until smooth.

Sandra Futrell, *Hendersonville*

Banana Chiffon Cake

2 EGGS, SEPARATED
1 1/3 CUPS SUGAR
2 CUPS ALL-PURPOSE FLOUR
1 TEASPOON BAKING POWDER
1 TEASPOON SODA
1 TEASPOON SALT

1/3 CUP VEGETABLE OIL
1 CUP VERY RIPE BANANAS, MASHED
2/3 CUP BUTTERMILK
1 TEASPOON VANILLA
1/2 CUP NUTS, CHOPPED
WHIPPED CREAM

Grease well and dust with flour 2 8-inch round pans. Beat egg whites until frothy. Gradually beat in 1/3 cup of the sugar. Continue beating until very stiff and glossy. Sift remaining sugar, flour, baking powder, soda and salt into another bowl. Add oil, mashed bananas, half of buttermilk, flavoring. Beat 1 minute at medium speed on mixer. Scrape sides and bottom of bowl constantly. Add remaining buttermilk, egg yolks. Beat 1 more minute. Fold in meringue. Fold nuts in gently. Pour into prepared pans and bake in a 350 degree oven for 30 to 35 minutes. Cool. Frost with seven-minute frosting or whipped cream. Decorate with sliced bananas.

Mrs. James G. Phelps, *Paris*
Georgia Thomas, *Lenoir City*

Banana Split Cake

This recipe makes a lot, and it is good for a big group. You can easily half it for a smaller family. It keeps well for a day or two in the refrigerator, but not any longer or the bananas will turn dark. It has a lot of ingredients and takes a little time to make, but it is worth it. Sissy Rankin

2 CUPS GRAHAM CRACKER CRUMBS	3 TO 4 BANANAS, SLICED
1/2 CUP MARGARINE, MELTED	1 9-OUNCE CONTAINER COOL WHIP
2 EGGS	1 NO. 2 CAN CRUSHED PINEAPPLE, DRAINED
1 CUP MARGARINE, MELTED	3/4 CUP PECANS, CHOPPED
2 CUPS POWDERED SUGAR	1 SMALL JAR CHERRIES, CHOPPED
1 TEASPOON VANILLA	

Mix graham cracker crumbs and 1/2 cup melted margarine. Press into bottom of 13 x 9 inch pan. In mixing bowl, cream 2 eggs, 1 cup melted margarine, 2 cups powdered sugar and 1 teaspoon vanilla. Beat with mixer for 15 minutes, no less. Spread over crumbs. Thinly slice 3 or 4 bananas, and layer with crushed pineapple. Top with Cool Whip; spread over top of all. Sprinkle chopped pecans and chopped cherries over Cool Whip. Cover and refrigerate overnight.
Variation: Drizzle chocolate syrup over all toppings.

Betty Jo Short, *Eidson*
Holly Osborne Davison, *Watauga*
Sissy Rankin, *Clarksville*

Old-Fashioned Stack Cake

This is an old recipe.

4 CUPS SELF-RISING FLOUR	2 EGGS
1 TEASPOON ALLSPICE	1 CUP MOLASSES
1 TEASPOON CINNAMON	1/2 CUP SHORTENING
1 TEASPOON CLOVES	1/4 CUP MILK

Put sifted flour in bowl, add remaining ingredients in order given. Mix to a soft dough. Divide dough into 5 parts. Shape into round balls. Put some flour on dough board. Roll out to fit bottom of 9-inch pans. Bake in a 450 degree oven until brown. As you take the cakes from the oven, spread each cake with apple mixture. Do not put apples on top layer. Store in container for a few hours before cutting.

Apple Mixture:

1 POUND DRIED APPLES	1 CUP BROWN SUGAR
3 CUPS WATER	1/2 CUP WHITE SUGAR

Wash apples, cook in water until tender. Add sugar; mash and cool slightly.

Mamie Carson, *Jefferson City*

Old-Fashioned Molasses Stack Cake

This Molasses Stack Cake recipe is the one my mother used when I was a child. She always made one of these cakes for our Christmas breakfast. I still make one each Christmas, but I do not serve it for breakfast as she did. I dry my own apples each summer, for they are so much better than those bought in the supermarket.

²/₃ CUP SHORTENING	1 TEASPOON CINNAMON
²/₃ CUP SUGAR	3 TEASPOONS BAKING POWDER
²/₃ CUP MOLASSES	2 TEASPOONS SODA
2 EGGS	¼ TEASPOON SALT
6 CUPS ALL-PURPOSE FLOUR	²/₃ CUP BUTTERMILK
1 TEASPOON GINGER	

Cream together shortening, sugar and molasses. Add eggs, one at a time. Beat well after each egg is added. Sift flour, ginger, cinnamon, baking powder, soda and salt. Add dry ingredients and buttermilk alternately to egg mixture. Divide batter into 5 or 6 parts. Pat into greased and floured 9-inch pans. Bake in a 400 degree oven until lightly browned. Spread each layer with dried apple filling. Do not put apples on top layer.

Apple Filling:

1 POUND DRIED APPLES, COOKED AND MASHED	1½ TEASPOONS CINNAMON
1 CUP BROWN SUGAR	½ TEASPOON CLOVES
	½ TEASPOON ALLSPICE

Combine ingredients. Cool before spreading between cake layers.

Nella Walters, *Knoxville*

Blue Ribbon Angel Food Cake

1¼ CUPS SWANSDOWN CAKE FLOUR, SIFTED	¼ TEASPOON SALT
½ CUP SUGAR	1 TEASPOON VANILLA
1½ CUPS EGG WHITES, ROOM TEMPERATURE (ABOUT 12)	¼ TEASPOON ALMOND EXTRACT
1¼ TEASPOONS CREAM OF TARTAR	1⅓ CUPS SUGAR

Measure sifted flour, add ½ cup sugar, and sift 4 times. Combine egg whites, cream of tartar, salt, and flavorings in large bowl. Beat at high speed of electric mixer or rotary beater, until soft peaks form; about 5 minutes. Sprinkle in remaining sugar in 4 additions, beating until blended after each addition. Sift in flour mixture in 4 additions, folding in with mesh beater, turn bowl often. Pour into ungreased 10-inch tube pan. Bake in a 375 degree oven for 35 to 40 minutes. Cool cake upside down in pan on cake rack. When cold, loosen with a large, long round-edged knife.

Carrie Treichel, *Johnson City*
Mrs. Jean Pierce, *Manchester*
Ina Linderman, *Rogersville*

Fresh Coconut Cake

2 CUPS SUGAR	4 EGGS
1 CUP CRISCO	2 TEASPOONS VANILLA
2½ CUPS SELF-RISING FLOUR	1 CUP SWEET MILK

Combine ingredients. Line the bottom of 3 round 9-inch pans with wax paper. Grease and flour pans. Bake in a 350 degree oven for 30 minutes or until done.

Filling:

1½ CUPS FRESH COCONUT	1 CUP SUGAR
1 CUP EVAPORATED MILK (OR ½ CUP FRESH COCONUT WATER AND ½ CUP EVAPORATED MILK)	

Cook until thick and spread between layers.

Frosting:

1 CUP SUGAR	3 EGG WHITES
½ CUP WHITE SYRUP	¼ TEASPOON CREAM OF TARTAR
3 TABLESPOONS HOT WATER	¼ TEASPOON SALT
1½ TEASPOONS VANILLA	

Mix with electric mixer while cooking. Beat until stiff peaks are formed. Spread on cake on top of filling. Sprinkle with coconut. Fresh coconut should always be used for this cake.

Nancy B. Chambers, *Cumberland Furnace*

Butter Nut Cake

1 CUP SHORTENING	½ CUPS SELF-RISING FLOUR
2 CUPS SUGAR	1 CUP MILK
5 EGGS	2 TO 3 TEASPOONS BUTTERNUT FLAVORING
2½ CUPS ALL-PURPOSE FLOUR	

Cream shortening and sugar 10 minutes. Add eggs and beat slowly 1 minute. Add 1 cup flour. Beat 1 minute. Add remaining flour and milk alternately, mix until creamy. Add flavoring, mixing well, and pour in tube pan and bake in a 325 degree oven for 1 hour. Then increase temperature to 350 degrees for 10 to 20 minutes.

Icing:

1 8-OUNCE PACKAGE CREAM CHEESE	1 TO 2 TEASPOONS BUTTERNUT FLAVORING
½ CUP MARGARINE	1 CUP PECANS, CHOPPED
1 BOX CONFECTIONERS' SUGAR	

Mix ingredients well and spread on cool cake.

Helen L. Garner, *Chattanooga*

Red Velvet Cake

2 CUPS ALL-PURPOSE FLOUR	1 1-OUNCE BOTTLE RED FOOD COLORING
1 TEASPOON BAKING POWDER	1 CUP BUTTERMILK
1 TEASPOON SALT	1 TEASPOON SODA
1 TEASPOON COCOA	1 TEASPOON VINEGAR
3/4 CUP OIL	1 TEASPOON VANILLA
1 1/2 CUPS SUGAR	3/4 CUP MILK
2 EGGS	1/2 CUP SUGAR

Sift flour, baking powder, salt and cocoa in bowl. Cream oil and 1 1/2 cups sugar. Add eggs one at a time; beat well after each. Add food coloring; mix until well blended. Combine buttermilk and soda. Mix well; add to oil-sugar mixture alternately with dry ingredients. Add vinegar and vanilla. Mix well. Spoon into 2 greased 9-inch round pans. Preheat oven to 350 degrees and bake for 25 to 30 minutes. Combine milk and remaining sugar in a saucepan. Bring to a boil. Spoon evenly on each layer. Cool and frost.

Frosting:

1 8-OUNCE PACKAGE CREAM CHEESE	1 POUND CONFECTIONERS' SUGAR
1/2 CUP MARGARINE	1 CUP COCONUT
1 TEASPOON VANILLA	4 TO 5 DROPS RED FOOD COLORING

Combine cream cheese, butter and vanilla in mixing bowl. Beat until smooth. Gradually add sugar while beating. Add 3/4 cup coconut. Mix well. Spread between layers and on top and sides of cake. Combine remaining coconut with red food coloring. Mix and sprinkle over cake.

Mrs. Wanda Powers, *Old Hickory*

Strawberry Cake

1 BOX YELLOW CAKE MIX	1/4 CUP OIL
1 BOX STRAWBERRY JELLO	1/4 CUP WATER
1 CUP STRAWBERRIES, FRESH OR FROZEN	4 EGGS

Mix all ingredients well. Pour in 3 greased and floured layer pans. Bake in a 350 degree oven until done. Cool cake, then ice.

Icing:

1 8-OUNCE PACKAGE CREAM CHEESE	1 CUP COCONUT
1/4 CUP MARGARINE	1 CUP PECANS, CHOPPED
1 CUP CONFECTIONERS' SUGAR	1 CUP STRAWBERRIES, FRESH OR FROZEN

Melt cream cheese and margarine together and add sugar. Remove from heat. Add coconut, pecans and strawberries. Mix well. If thicker icing is desired, add more confectioners' sugar.

May McMurtry, *Humboldt*

Coconut Yellow Cake

I have used this cake recipe for over forty years, on all holidays, church dinners and for "company" visits, also family feasts.

2 CUPS SELF-RISING FLOUR	1 CUP MILK
1½ CUPS SUGAR	2 EGGS, UNBEATEN
½ CUP BUTTER	1 TEASPOON VANILLA

Measure flour, sugar, butter, and ⅔ cup milk in bowl. Mix on medium speed 2 minutes. Add eggs, ⅓ cup milk, and vanilla. Mix 2 minutes. Pour in three 9-inch greased and floured pans. Bake in a 375 degree oven for 25 to 30 minutes.

Coconut Milk:
Add that extra moist touch to your cake.

¾ CUP WATER	4 TABLESPOONS COCONUT
½ CUP SUGAR	PINCH SALT

Put in pan and bring to boil. Strain out coconut. Pour ⅓ cup on each layer of cake before icing. After icing sprinkle on coconut.

White Mound Icing:

1½ CUPS SUGAR	DASH SALT
⅓ CUP WATER	3 EGG WHITES
¼ TEASPOON CREAM OF TARTAR	1 TEASPOON VANILLA

Combine sugar, water, cream of tartar, and salt in a saucepan. Cook covered for 3 minutes. Remove cover and boil to soft ball stage (242 degrees). Beat egg whites until stiff but not dry. Slowly add hot syrup, beating all the time. Add vanilla and beat until mixture holds stiff peaks. Ice cake.

Nancy P. Wortham, *Indian Mound*

Italian Cream Cake

5 EGGS	2 CUPS ALL-PURPOSE FLOUR, SIFTED 2 TIMES
½ CUP MARGARINE	1 3½-OUNCE CAN COCONUT
½ CUP VEGETABLE SHORTENING	1 CUP NUTS, CHOPPED
2 CUPS SUGAR	1 TEASPOON VANILLA EXTRACT
1 TEASPOON SODA	1 TEASPOON COCONUT FLAVOR
1 CUP BUTTERMILK	

Separate eggs and beat whites until stiff. Set aside. Cream margarine, vegetable shortening and add sugar. Add egg yolks, one at a time, beating well after each addition. Dissolve soda in buttermilk; add alternately with flour.

Beat well. Add coconut, nuts, and extracts. Fold in stiffly beaten egg whites. Pour into 3 greased and floured 9-inch cake pans. Bake in a 350 degree oven for 25 minutes.

Cream Cheese Icing:

1 8-OUNCE PACKAGE CREAM CHEESE, SOFTENED
½ CUP MARGARINE

1 1-POUND BOX CONFECTIONERS' SUGAR
1 TEASPOON ALMOND EXTRACT

Combine ingredients and beat well. Spread between layers and on top of cooled cake.

Betty Jo Short, *Eidson*

Bob Schatz/Photo Fair

Oktoberfest in Munich, Germany, began in order to celebrate the fall harvest. When the residents of the Germantown section of Nashville wanted to commemorate their neighborhood, such a celebration seemed natural, and so in 1980 members of the Church of the Assumption and the Monroe Street United Methodist Church began what has become an annual event.

Old-Fashioned Prune Cake

This is an old family recipe that was most always baked at Christmas time.

1 CUP LIGHT BROWN SUGAR	1 TEASPOON SODA
¾ CUP SHORTENING	1 TEASPOON ALLSPICE
3 TABLESPOONS SOUR CREAM	2 TEASPOONS CINNAMON
3 EGGS	1 CUP PRUNES, COOKED AND CHOPPED
2 CUPS ALL-PURPOSE FLOUR, SIFTED	

Blend sugar, shortening, sour cream and eggs. Add dry ingredients and blend well; then add prunes. Divide into 3 cake layer pans. Bake in a 350 degree oven for approximately 25 minutes or until cake comes out clean.

Filling:

2 EGGS	½ CUP HEAVY CREAM
1 CUP LIGHT BROWN SUGAR	1 CUP PRUNES, COOKED AND CHOPPED
2 TABLESPOONS MARGARINE	

Cook mixture until thick. Fill between layers and on top. Let set overnight before cutting. Keep in a tight container to retain moisture. Garnish with pecan halves if desired.

Mrs. Clifford Gresham, *Tullahoma*

Oatmeal Cake

3 CUPS BOILING WATER	1 CUP SHORTENING
2 CUPS OATS	3 CUPS WHITE FLOUR
4 EGGS	2 TEASPOONS CINNAMON
2 CUPS GRANULATED SUGAR	2 TEASPOONS SODA
2 CUPS BROWN SUGAR	1 TEASPOON SALT

Cook oats in water; set aside. Cream eggs, sugars and shortening, add remaining ingredients and beat well; stir in oatmeal. Beat well and stir in oatmeal. Bake in two 13 x 9 inch cake pans in a 350 degree oven until done (approximately 35 minutes).

Topping:

1 POUND BROWN SUGAR	1 CUP MILK
1 CUP BUTTER	2 CUPS COCONUT

Mix together and bring to a rapid boil. Pour over hot cake.
Variation: Add 1 tablespoon vanilla and 1 cup chopped pecans to topping.

Ralph Waldo Emerson IV, *Clarksville*
Pam Oliver, *Bluff City*

Mississippi Mud Cake

3 SQUARES UNSWEETENED CHOCOLATE	1½ CUPS ALL-PURPOSE FLOUR
1 CUP MARGARINE OR BUTTER	1 TEASPOON BAKING POWDER
4 EGGS	1 TEASPOON VANILLA
2 CUPS SUGAR	1 CUP NUTS, CHOPPED

Melt chocolate and butter in double boiler, beat eggs until foamy, then add sugar. Add all other ingredients to chocolate mixture. Put in greased 13 x 9 inch pan. Bake in a 325 degree oven for 30 minutes. While cake is hot, put marshmallows all over top. When cake is cool, pour following cooked mixture over marshmallows.

½ CUP MARGARINE	1 BOX CONFECTIONERS' SUGAR
3 SQUARES UNSWEETENED CHOCOLATE	1 TEASPOON VANILLA
1 SMALL CAN EVAPORATED MILK	

Cook margarine, chocolate, milk and sugar in double boiler until blended. Beat in confectioners' sugar and vanilla.

Norma Jean Vawter, *Milan*

Fruit Cocktail Cake

2 EGGS	2 TEASPOONS SODA
1½ CUPS SUGAR	1 TEASPOON VANILLA
2 CUPS ALL-PURPOSE FLOUR, SIFTED	1 NO. 303 CAN FRUIT COCKTAIL
1 TEASPOON SALT	

Mix eggs, sugar, flour and salt in bowl; beat until smooth. Add vanilla and fruit cocktail. Bake in a greased 8½ x 12 inch pan in a 300 degree oven for 40 minutes.

Icing:

1 SMALL CAN PET MILK	1 TEASPOON VANILLA
¾ TO 1 CUP SUGAR	1 CAN COCONUT (OPTIONAL)
½ CUP MARGARINE	

Mix milk, sugar, and margarine in a pan. Bring to boil and simmer 2 minutes. Take off stove and add vanilla and coconut. Pour over cake (in pan) while hot. Sprinkle with coconut.

Helen Williams, *Newbern*
Mrs. Cartis A. Reed, *Grandview*

Upside-down Cake

2 TABLESPOONS BUTTER
1/2 CUP BROWN SUGAR

5 SLICES PINEAPPLE
MARASCHINO CHERRIES

Melt butter in a round skillet and add brown sugar. Place 5 slices of pineapple on top of the sugar and place a maraschino cherry in center of the pineapple. Pour the Cake Batter on top and bake in a 350 degree oven until browned. Turn out on a large plate to cool.

The Cake Batter:

3 EGGS, BEATEN
1 CUP SUGAR
4 TABLESPOONS SWEET MILK

1 CUP ALL-PURPOSE FLOUR
1 TEASPOON BAKING POWDER
1 TEASPOON LEMON OR VANILLA FLAVORING

Beat eggs together, add sugar, sweet milk, and the flour and baking powder that have been sifted together. Add the flavoring last.

Lois M. Hadley, *Nashville*

Sour Cream Pound Cake

1 CUP BUTTER OR MARGARINE, SOFTENED
2 1/2 CUPS SUGAR
6 EGGS
3 CUPS ALL-PURPOSE FLOUR

1/4 TEASPOON SODA
1 8-OUNCE CARTON SOUR CREAM
1 TEASPOON VANILLA
1 TEASPOON LEMON EXTRACT

Cream butter; gradually add sugar, beating until light and fluffy. Add eggs, one at a time, beating well after each addition. Combine flour and soda; add to creamed mixture alternately with sour cream, mixing well after each addition. Stir in flavorings. Pour batter into a greased and floured 10-inch tube pan. Bake in a 350 degree oven for 1 hour and 15 minutes, or until a wooden pick inserted in center comes out clean. Cool in pan 10 minutes, remove from pan and cool completely. Yummy!!! Do not overbake. *Yield:* 1 10-inch cake.

Mrs. Albert F. (Christine) Houser, *Bristol*
Dixie Sykes, *Dover*
Dixie Gray, *Clarksville*

Pineapple Pound Cake

1/2 CUP SHORTENING
1 CUP BUTTER OR MARGARINE
2 3/4 CUPS SUGAR
6 EGGS
3 CUPS ALL-PURPOSE FLOUR

1 TEASPOON BAKING POWDER
1/4 CUP SWEET MILK
1 TEASPOON VANILLA
3/4 CUP CRUSHED PINEAPPLE, UNDRAINED
PINEAPPLE GLAZE

Combine shortening, butter, and sugar; cream until light and fluffy. Add eggs, one at a time, beating after each addition. Combine flour and baking powder; add to creamed mixture alternately with milk and vanilla, beating well after each addition. Stir in crushed pineapple. Pour batter into a well-greased and floured 10-inch tube pan, bundt pan or 2 loaf pans. Place in a cold oven; bake in a 350 degree oven for 1 hour and 15 minutes or until cake tests done. Cool 10 to 15 minutes in pan. Invert onto serving plate; drizzle Pineapple Glaze over top and sides.

Pineapple Glaze:

¼ CUP MELTED BUTTER OR MARGARINE   1 CUP CRUSHED PINEAPPLE, DRAINED
1½ CUPS CONFECTIONERS' SUGAR

Combine butter and sugar, mixing until smooth. Stir in pineapple. Punch holes in cake and drizzle over top.

Mrs. Claud T. Pearce, *Nashville*

Chocolate Pound Cake

½ CUP SHORTENING   ½ TEASPOON SALT
1 CUP MARGARINE, SOFTENED   ½ CUP COCOA
3 CUPS SUGAR   1¼ CUPS MILK
5 EGGS   1 TEASPOON VANILLA
3 CUPS ALL-PURPOSE FLOUR   CREAMY CHOCOLATE GLAZE
½ TEASPOON BAKING POWDER   PECANS, CHOPPED

Cream shortening and margarine; gradually add sugar, beating until light and fluffy. Add eggs, one at a time, beating well after each addition. Combine flour, baking powder, salt and cocoa; mix well. Add to creamed mixture alternately with milk, beginning and ending with flour mixture. Stir in vanilla. Pour batter into a greased and floured 10-inch tube pan; bake in a 350 degree oven for 1 hour and 15 minutes or until a wooden pick inserted in center comes out clean. Cool in pan 10 to 15 minutes; invert onto serving plate. Spoon Creamy Chocolate Glaze over top of warm cake, allowing it to drizzle down sides. Sprinkle with chopped pecans.

Creamy Chocolate Glaze:

2¼ CUPS CONFECTIONERS' SUGAR, SIFTED   ¼ CUP MARGARINE, SOFTENED
3 TABLESPOONS COCOA   3 TO 4 TABLESPOONS MILK

Combine sugar and cocoa, mixing well. Add remaining ingredients. Beat until smooth. *Yield:* about 2 cups.

Marie McDonald, *Athens*

Pecan Fruit Cake

This cake is good to eat as soon as it is completely cool. It does not need to be aged as so many fruit cakes do.

8 OUNCES CANDIED CHERRIES (RED OR GREEN)
8 OUNCE BOX PITTED DATES (MAY BE PRE-CHOPPED)
6 SLICES CANDIED PINEAPPLE
1 POUND (4 CUPS) PECANS
1 CUP SELF-RISING FLOUR
4 EGGS
3/4 CUP GRANULATED SUGAR
1 TEASPOON VANILLA
3 TEASPOONS CHERRY BRANDY (OPTIONAL)

Chop cherries in half. Chop dates and pineapple coarsely. Leave pecans in as large pieces as possible. Sift flour over fruits and nuts to coat well. Beat eggs until yolks and whites are well blended, then add sugar and flavoring. Beat until dissolved. Add to fruit-nut mixture and mix thoroughly (until all flour is moistened). Pack into lined, well-greased tube pan. Bake in a 350 degree oven for 1 hour and 45 minutes with a pan of water on lower shelf during the last 15 minutes of baking time. Turn out of pan onto rack to cool completely. Slice thin to serve.

Ruth S. Hoover, *Martin*

Tennessee Strawberry Jam Cake

1 CUP BUTTER
1½ CUPS SUGAR
3 EGGS
1 CUP THICK STRAWBERRY JAM
3¼ CUPS ALL-PURPOSE FLOUR
1 TABLESPOON BAKING POWDER
½ TEASPOON SALT
1 TEASPOON CINNAMON
1 TEASPOON NUTMEG
½ TEASPOON CLOVES
1 CUP BUTTERMILK
½ TEASPOON SODA

Cream butter and sugar; add eggs, one at a time. Add jam. Sift flour with baking powder, salt, and spices; add alternately with buttermilk (with dissolved soda in it) and mix well. Pour into a large bundt pan and bake in a 325 degree oven for 1 hour. Or use 3 9-inch round layer pans and bake in a 350 degree oven for 35 to 40 minutes.

White Frosting:

3/4 CUP SUGAR
1 TABLESPOON WATER
½ CUP LIGHT CORN SYRUP
3 EGG WHITES
1/8 TEASPOON SALT
1½ TEASPOONS VANILLA

Boil sugar, water, and syrup until mixture spins a thread, about 10 minutes. Pour this hot syrup over beaten egg whites, add salt and vanilla; beat until it looses its shine and holds its shape. Frost cake; then spoon strawberry jam on top of cake.

Estelle Shepherd, *Woodlawn*

Funnel Cakes

3 EGGS
2 CUPS MILK
¼ CUP SUGAR

3 TO 4 CUPS ALL-PURPOSE FLOUR
½ TEASPON SALT
2 TEASPOONS BAKING POWDER
   VEGETABLE OIL

Beat eggs and add sugar and milk. Sift 2 cups of the flour, salt and baking powder together. Add to milk and egg mixture. Beat batter (with beater, in blender or with food processor) until smooth, adding only as much of the other 1 to 2 cups flour as needed. Batter should be thin enough to go through a funnel, but not too runny.

Heat vegetable oil to about 375 degrees in an 8- or 9-inch skillet about ¾-inch deep. It is important to have and keep the oil hot. Pour about ¼ cup batter into funnel, keeping finger over bottom of funnel until ready to drizzle batter in hot oil. Then swirl and criss-cross batter in oil in lace-like pattern. The frying can become an art, since all sorts of shapes can be made with twists and turns of the funnel.

Let cake brown on one side, turn and brown on the other side; it takes 1 minute or less to bake. Lift from oil, place on plate and sprinkle with powdered sugar (or syrup, molasses, jelly or jam). *Yield:* 6 to 8 funnel cakes.

Jean Nelson, *Knoxville*

No Fault Cheesecake

Crust:

2 CUPS GRAHAM CRACKER CRUMBS, ROLLED
   AND PACKED
½ CUP SUGAR

1 TEASPOON CINNAMON
½ CUP MARGARINE OR BUTTER, MELTED

Mix all ingredients well and press in greased cake pans. Pack sides well; set aside.

Filling:

3 8-OUNCE PACKAGES CREAM CHEESE,
   SOFTENED
1 CUP SUGAR
3 EGGS, WHOLE

   PINCH SALT
1 TEASPOON VANILLA
1 CUP DAIRY SOUR CREAM

Mix all ingredients except sour cream; mix well, then add sour cream. Mix will be liquidy. Pour into crumbed pans. Bake in a 350 degree oven for 20 minutes. Remove and sprinkle tops with leftover crumbs (optional). Bake 10 more minutes, not more than 30 minutes in all. Turn oven off and leave cake in oven for 1 hour with oven door open. Eat or refrigerate.

Anne Skiles, *Humboldt*

Old Fashioned Jam Cake

This recipe has become a Christmas tradition in our family. My mother, who is 80 years old, can still make the biggest and best Jam Cake I have ever tasted.

¾ CUP SHORTENING	2 TEASPOONS CINNAMON
2 CUPS SUGAR	2 TEASPOONS ALLSPICE
6 EGGS, SEPARATED AND BEATEN	2 TEASPOONS CLOVES
2 CUPS BLACKBERRY JAM	1 CUP BUTTERMILK
4 CUPS ALL-PURPOSE FLOUR	1½ CUPS RAISINS
½ TEASPOON SALT	1 CUP NUTS, CHOPPED
2 TEASPOONS SODA, MIXED WITH BUTTERMILK	

Cream sugar and shortening. Add beaten egg yolks, then jam. Add sifted dry ingredients alternately with milk, beating well after each addition. Add raisins and nuts; fold in beaten egg whites. Cook in three 9-inch pans. Bake in a 350 degree oven for 45 minutes. Use a wood toothpick to test whether done; may require a few additional minutes.

Filling:

1½ TABLESPOONS ALL-PURPOSE FLOUR	1½ CUPS RAISINS
2 CUPS SUGAR	1½ CUPS NUTS, CHOPPED
2 CUPS EVAPORATED MILK	2 CUPS COCONUT

Mix flour and sugar, then add milk. Mix all ingredients together and cook until thick; set aside until cold. Spread between layers of cake and outside cake.

Mrs. Luther Webb, Sr., *Nashville*

St. Timothy's Coffee Cake

1 CUP BUTTER OR MARGARINE	¼ TEASPOON SALT
2 CUPS SUGAR	1 TEASPOON CINNAMON
½ TEASPOON VANILLA	½ CUP GOLDEN RAISINS
2 EGGS	1 CUP CHOPPED NUTS
2 CUPS ALL-PURPOSE FLOUR, UNSIFTED	1 CUP SOUR CREAM
1 TEASPOON BAKING POWDER	CINNAMON SUGAR

Cream butter or margarine until light and fluffy. Add sugar gradually and continue to cream. Blend in vanilla. Add eggs, one at a time, beating well after each addition. Sift together flour, baking powder, salt and cinnamon. Add raisins and nuts and coat well. Add dry ingredients to creamed mixture alternately with sour cream. Blend well. Batter will look like whipped cream tinged with honey. Turn into greased and floured bundt pan. Sprinkle with cinnamon sugar. Bake in a 350 degree oven for 60 minutes or until the cake tests done. Leave in pan for at least 1 hour before turning out. Turn out and sprinkle with more cinnamon sugar.

Mrs. H. C. (Mary) Elliott, *Maryville*

The Dogwood Arts Festival is a 17-day extravaganza in Knoxville celebrating the sudden explosion of pink and white dogwoods. More than 200 events and activities make the end of April special in Knoxville. Becky Nelson serves up a funnel cake at one of the booths downtown at Market Square Mall.

Fudge Frosting

6 TABLESPOONS MARGARINE	1/3 CUP LIGHT CREAM
1/2 CUP COCOA	1/8 TEASPOON SALT
4 CUPS CONFECTIONERS' SUGAR, SIFTED	1 1/2 TEASPOONS VANILLA

Melt margarine in large saucepan over low heat. Add cocoa and stir until well-blended. Add 2 cups sifted confectioners' sugar, cream and salt all at once and beat until smooth. Place over low heat. Cook and stir until mixture bubbles up well around edges. Remove from heat. Add vanilla and 2 cups sifted confectioners' sugar in thirds, beating well after each addition until smooth. If too thick for spreading, add small amount of cream and beat. Enough to fill and frost 9-inch cake.

Note: If chocolate is preferred, use 3 squares chocolate and 3 tablespoons margarine.

Mrs. David G. Stone, *Hixson*

Caramel Icing

2 CUPS BROWN SUGAR, PACKED
1/2 CUP MILK
1/2 CUP SHORTENING

1/4 TEASPOON SALT
1 TEASPOON VANILLA

Mix all ingredients, except vanilla, thoroughly. Stir over low heat until shortening is melted. Then, stirring constantly, bring rapidly to a full boil. Boil 1 minute; remove from heat and beat until lukewarm. Add vanilla and continue beating until icing begins to lose its gloss and is of consistency to spread. Will ice a 2-layer cake or a rectangular cake.

Mrs. Brenda Poole, *Andersonville*

Fluffy White Frosting

1 CUP SUGAR
1/4 TEASPOON CREAM OF TARTAR
1/8 TEASPOON SALT
1/3 CUP WATER

6 LARGE MARSHMALLOWS, CUT IN QUARTERS
1 EGG WHITE
1/2 TEASPOON VANILLA

Bring sugar, cream of tartar, salt and water to boiling; let cook until sugar dissolves. Add unbeaten egg white and quartered marshmallows, beating constantly with rotary or electric beater until frosting is in peaks. Add vanilla and spread on cake.

Mrs. Martin Wynia, *Martin*

Caramel Frosting

No taste can beat this old-fashioned recipe for caramel frosting. It was my great-grandmother's recipe, and she used to beat the frosting by hand.

2 CUPS WHITE SUGAR
1 CUP WHOLE MILK
1 CUP WHITE SUGAR

3 TABLESPOONS BUTTER OR MARGARINE
1 TEASPOON VANILLA

Put 2 cups sugar and milk in saucepan and cook slowly. In a saucepan or iron skillet, put 1 cup white sugar and cook over medium heat until sugar begins to turn amber in color; then stir sugar until all of it is amber. Pour this into a pan large enough to hold the entire recipe. Add sugar and milk mixture very slowly, stirring constantly. Cook to 230 degrees (soft ball stage), without stirring. Remove from heat and add butter and vanilla. Beat frosting until it is of consistency to spread on cake.

Karen Barger, *Jackson*

Maple Frosting for Banana Cake

6 TABLESPOONS MARGARINE	1 BOX CONFECTIONERS' SUGAR
1 EGG	1/2 TEASPOON MAPLE FLAVORING
1 EGG WHITE	1/4 CUP BLACK WALNUTS (OPTIONAL)

Cream margarine. Add eggs, then the sifted sugar and flavoring. Mix until the right consistency to spread. Spread walnuts over top, if desired.

Mrs. Paul K. (June) Premo, *Johnson City*

Chocolate Fudge Frosting

2 POUNDS CONFECTIONERS' SUGAR	1/2 CUP BUTTER OR MARGARINE
1/3 CUP CRISCO	4 OR 5 HEAPING TABLESPOONS COCOA
1/2 CUP WATER	1 TEASPOON VANILLA

Put confectioners' sugar and Crisco in mixer. In a small saucepan put water and butter or margarine. Heat until butter (or margarine) melts; remove from heat. Add cocoa and mix. Pour hot chocolate mixture over confectioners' sugar and Crisco and beat until smooth. Add vanilla if desired. Add more sugar if too thin, more water if too thick.

Anita F. Coward, *Clinton*

Pies

Angel Pie

Pie Shell:

2 EGG WHITES	1/2 CUP SUGAR
1/8 TEASPOON SALT	1/2 TEASPOON VANILLA
1/8 TEASPOON CREAM OF TARTAR	1/2 CUP NUTS

Beat egg whites with salt and cream of tartar until foamy. Add sugar, 2 tablespoons at a time, beating well. Beat to form stiff peaks. Fold in vanilla and nuts. Spoon into lightly greased pan. Bake in a 300 degree oven for 50 to 55 minutes. Cool.

Filling:

1 BAR GERMAN CHOCOLATE	2 CUPS WHIPPING CREAM
3 TABLESPOONS WATER	1/2 CUP SUGAR
1 TEASPOON VANILLA	

Stir chocolate over low heat with water; melt. Cool until thickened. Add vanilla. Whip cream; fold half of cream into chocolate mixture. Pile into shell. Add sugar to remaining whipped cream and pile on top. Chill 2 hours or more. You may freeze and then defrost when ready to serve.

Weejee Miller, *Brentwood*

Raw Apple Pie

This recipe was given to me by my mother-in-law, Ruth Alexander Key. The recipe was used in Ruth's mother's family (Murfreesboro area) for as long as she could recall. My children take delight in making the pie now.

6 WINESAP OR JUICY APPLES	PASTRY FOR 2-CRUST PIE
2 CUPS SUGAR	BUTTER
CINNAMON, AS DESIRED	

Peel and grate the apples; mix 1 cup sugar and cinnamon and add to apples. Prepare crust and line the pie pan. Pour apple mixture into shell. Cut strips of pastry for the top. Sprinkle the other cup sugar and cinnamon over the latticed top and dot with butter. Bake in a 350 degree oven until apple juice and sugar mixture bubbles through the top and makes a nice light brown crunchy crust, about 30 to 45 minutes.

Note: Apples must be grated. If apples are not juicy, add a little lemon juice. Use oven liner because pie bubbles a lot. It is better the second day, if it lasts that long. Very good with ice cream.

Jane Key, *Knoxville*

Fried Apple Pies

1½ CUPS DRIED APPLES	⅛ TEASPOON GROUND NUTMEG
3 CUPS WATER	3 CUPS UNBLEACHED FLOUR, SIFTED
¼ CUP HONEY	1 TEASPOON SALT
2 TABLESPOONS LEMON JUICE	1 CUP LARD OR SHORTENING
½ TEASPOONS GRATED LEMON RIND	6 TABLESPOONS COLD WATER
½ TEASPOONS GROUND CINNAMON	1 QUART COOKING OIL
⅛ TEASPOON SALT	

Combine apples and 3 cups water in saucepan. Bring to a boil, reduce heat. Cover and simmer for 35 minutes or until apples are tender and water is absorbed. Stir apples until they are smooth and have no lumps. Combine apples with honey, lemon juice, lemon rind, cinnamon, salt and nutmeg; mix well and set aside.

Combine flour and salt in bowl. Cut in shortening until crumbly, sprinkle 6 tablespoons water over surface, stir until moistened. Shape into ball. Divide in half. Roll out on floured surface. Cut with a 5-inch cutter. Place 1 tablespoon apple filling on half of circle, fold over. Dampen edges and seal. Press edges with a fork to seal. Keep pies covered with a damp cloth until fried. Repeat until all dough is used.

Heat 2 cups oil in 10-inch skillet to 375 degrees. Fry pies until golden brown, turning as needed. Drain on paper towels. Add oil as needed. *Yield:* about 32 pies.

Mrs. Carol Mills, *Allred*

Creamy Blackberry Pie

4 OR 5 CUPS BLACKBERRIES, FRESH, FROZEN OR CANNED

1 CAN SWEETENED CONDENSED MILK

1 3-OUNCE CAN PINK LEMONADE FROZEN CONCENTRATE

1 8-OUNCE CARTON COOL WHIP

2 GRAHAM CRACKER CRUSTS

Drain berries if necessary. Add condensed milk, thawed lemonade, and Cool Whip. Combine gently and pour into crusts. Chill thoroughly. *Yield:* 2 pies.

Note: Regular yellow lemonade may be substituted.

Barbara (Mrs. Donald) Pitzer, *Madison*

Buttermilk Pie

½ CUP BUTTER OR MARGARINE

1½ CUPS SUGAR

3 WHOLE EGGS, WELL BEATEN

1 TABLESPOON CORNSTARCH

¼ CUP PLAIN OR SELF-RISING CORN MEAL

1 TEASPOON VANILLA

½ CUP BUTTERMILK

Cream butter and sugar; add eggs that have been well beaten, then cornstarch, cornmeal and vanilla flavoring. Blend well. Add buttermilk and blend well.

Pour into unbaked pie shell and place in a 450 degree oven. Immediately reduce oven temperature to 350 degrees and bake about 35 minutes or until the filling has set and is lightly brown. This pie is good hot or cold.

Jo Ann Meacham, *Erin*

Chess Pie

This recipe has been passed down through the Fitzgerald family of Williamson County for more than 100 years.

1½ CUPS SUGAR

1 TABLESPOON ALL-PURPOSE FLOUR

3 WHOLE EGGS

½ CUP BUTTER OR MARGARINE

1 TEASPOON VANILLA

1 TEASPOON VINEGAR

4 TABLESPOONS MILK

Mix all ingredients and pour into unbaked pie crust. Bake in a 350 degree oven for 40 to 45 minutes or until firm in the middle.

Christine McKnight, *Nashville*

Swiss Chocolate Pie

1/2 CUP SUGAR	6 LARGE MARSHMALLOWS
4 TABLESPOONS ALL-PURPOSE FLOUR	1 TABLESPOON BUTTER
1 CUP MILK	1 PIE SHELL, BAKED
1 SQUARE CHOCOLATE, MELTED	WHIPPED CREAM

Mix sugar and flour together. Add milk and cook until thick. Add melted chocolate, marshmallows and butter. Pour into baked crust. Chill for about 1 hour, serve with whipped cream.

Mrs. Ludie Tolliver, *Manchester*

Chocolate-Coconut Pie

1/4 CUP MARGARINE	2 2/3 CUPS WATER
2 3 1/2-OUNCE CANS FLAKED COCONUT, TOASTED	4 SQUARES UNSWEETENED CHOCOLATE
	6 EGGS, SEPARATED
3 ENVELOPES UNFLAVORED GELATIN	2 TEASPOONS VANILLA
2 CUPS SUGAR	1/2 TEASPOON CREAM OF TARTAR
1 TEASPOON SALT	1 CUP HEAVY CREAM, WHIPPED

Melt margarine. Stir in coconut and remove from heat. Press mixture against side and bottom of 9-inch pie plate. Refrigerate. Combine gelatin, 1 cup of sugar, salt, water and chocolate in saucepan. Place until low heat until chocolate melts and sugar dissolves. Remove from heat. Beat egg yolks in medium bowl. Stir a little chocolate mixture into yolks. Return to saucepan. Heat until boiling, transfer to bowl, cool over ice water. Stir occasionally, until mixture mounds. Add vanilla. Beat egg whites and cream of tartar in large bowl until foamy. Gradually beat in remaining 1 cup of sugar until meringue forms stiff peaks. Do not underbeat. Fold meringue into chocolate mixture, chill briefly. Mound into coconut shell. Refrigerate until firm, about 4 hours. Garnish with whipped cream.

Patsy Leonard, *Martin*

Buttermilk Coconut Pie

1 CUP SUGAR	1/2 CUP BUTTERMILK
DASH SALT	1 TEASPOON VANILLA
1/4 CUP MARGARINE, MELTED	1 SMALL CAN COCONUT
2 EGGS, SLIGHTLY BEATEN	

Mix sugar, salt, add melted margarine and stir well. Add beaten eggs, mix well and add buttermilk, vanilla and coconut. Mix well, pour into pie shell, and bake in a 350 degree oven for about 1 hour.

Carrie Mae Coakley, *Portlant*

Peanut Lovers' Mud Pie

¼ CUP MARGARINE OR BUTTER	1 CUP WHIPPED CREAM OR WHIPPED TOPPING
½ CUP ALL-PURPOSE FLOUR	1 4-SERVING SIZE PACKAGE INSTANT CHOCOLATE PUDDING MIX
½ CUP ROASTED PEANUTS, CHOPPED	
4 OUNCES CREAM CHEESE, SOFTENED	2 CUPS MILK
¼ CUP SMOOTH PEANUT BUTTER	2 CUPS WHIPPED CREAM OR WHIPPING CREAM
½ CUP CONFECTIONERS' SUGAR	

Melt margarine or butter; mix with flour and nuts and press evenly into an 8 inch square baking pan. Bake in a 350 degree oven for 15 minutes. Cool.

Fold together the cream cheese, peanut butter, powdered sugar and 1 cup whipped topping. Spread over the nut crust. Prepare pudding according to package directions and spread over the cheese layer. Top with the 2 cups whipped cream or topping. Chill 4 hours or more. Cut into squares and garnish with chocolate shavings for serving. *Yield:* 6 servings.

Lois Crenshaw (Mrs. Milton) Mayo, *Milan*

Old-Fashioned Peach Cobbler

This is the best peach cobbler I have ever tested. It has brought me many compliments and has won First Prize at a fair.

Filling:

8 OR 9 PEACHES, PEELED AND SLICED	2 TABLESPOONS SELF-RISING FLOUR
½ CUP WATER	PINCH OF SALT
1½ CUPS SUGAR	½ CUP BUTTER OR MARGARINE, MELTED

Cook peaches in water until tender. Mix flour, salt and sugar. Add to peaches. Mix. Add melted butter or margarine.

Pastry for Cobbler:

1 CUP SELF-RISING FLOUR	⅓ CUP SHORTENING
½ TEASPOON SALT	4 TABLESPOONS SWEET MILK, OR ENOUGH TO MAKE A STIFF DOUGH

Blend flour, salt and shortening to coarse meal texture. Add milk. Roll on floured surface. Pour half of peaches in 9 x 13 inch pan. Cut some dumplings and push dumplings down into the peach juice. Pour remaining peaches in and top with lattice strips. Bake in a 350 degree oven 35 to 40 minutes or until top is golden brown.

Note: I like to sprinkle a little sugar on top before baking. This should be a juicy cobbler, not dry.

Linda Henry, *Knoxville*

Tawny Pumpkin Pie

1¼ CUPS PUMPKIN, COOKED
¾ CUP WHITE SUGAR
½ TEASPOON SALT
¼ TEASPOON GROUND GINGER
1 TEASPOON CINNAMON
1 TEASPOON ALL-PURPOSE FLOUR

½ TEASPOON PUMPKIN SPICE MIX
2 EGGS, BEATEN SLIGHTLY
1 CUP EVAPORATED MILK
2 TABLESPOONS WATER
½ TEASPOON VANILLA
1 9-INCH PIE SHELL, UNBAKED

Combine pumpkin, sugar, salt, spices and flour in mixing bowl. Add eggs; mix well. Add evaporated milk, water and vanilla and mix. Pour into unbaked pie shell. Bake in a 425 degree oven 15 minutes; reduce heat to 350 degrees and bake additional 35 minutes, or until set.

Mrs. Paul Clabough, *Maryville*

Photographic Services

News-Free Press

Photographic Services

Tennessee Mud Pie

¾ CUP VANILLA WAFERS, CRUSHED
2 SQUARES UNSWEETENED CHOCOLATE
⅔ CUPS MARGARINE
2 CUPS CONFECTIONERS' SUGAR
2 EGGS

1 TEASPOON VANILLA
½ GALLON VANILLA ICE CREAM
1 CUP PECANS, CHOPPED
1 CUP HERSHEY'S CHOCOLATE SYRUP
WHIPPED CREAM

Line bottom of an 8 x 12 inch dish with crushed vanilla wafer crumbs. Melt unsweetened chocolate and margarine over low heat and stir in confectioners' sugar, beaten egg yolks and vanilla. Fold in stiffly beaten egg whites and pour over crumbs; freeze until firm. Top with softened ice cream and sprinkle top with chopped pecans. Drizzle top with Hershey's Chocolate Syrup. Cover and freeze. To serve, cut in square blocks and add whipped cream and a cherry if desired. *Yield:* 12 to 16 servings.

Janita H. Brown, *Hendersonville*

Caramel Pecan Pie

½ POUND CARAMELS (28 PIECES)
½ CUP WATER
¼ CUP MARGARINE
¾ CUP SUGAR
¼ TEASPOON SALT

½ TEASPOON VANILLA
2 EGGS, SLIGHTLY BEATEN
1 CUP PECAN HALVES
UNBAKED PIE CRUST

Place caramels, water and margarine in double boiler and heat, stirring until caramels are melted and sauce is smooth. Combine sugar, salt, vanilla and eggs in a separate container. Mix thoroughly. Add pecans and caramel sauce and stir well. Pour into unbaked pie crust and bake in a 400 degree oven for 10 minutes. Reduce heat and finish baking at 350 degrees for 20 minutes.

Betty Coghill, *Clarksville*

Easy Sweet Potato Pie

1½ CUPS SWEET POTATOES, COOKED AND
   MASHED
⅔ CUP DARK BROWN SUGAR
½ TEASPOON SALT
¼ TEASPOON GROUND ALLSPICE

2 EGGS, BEATEN
1 TABLESPOON LEMON JUICE
1 CUP MILK
1 PIE SHELL, UNBAKED
PECAN HALVES FOR DECORATION

Mix all ingredients above; spread in pie shell, and bake in a 450 degree oven for 15 minutes. Reduce heat to 325 degrees and bake 30 additional minutes. Decorate pie with pecan halves.

Mrs. Sherry Ligon Allison, *Cookeville*

Chocolate Chip Pecan Pie

3 EGGS, SLIGHTLY BEATEN
1¼ CUPS CORN SYRUP
⅛ TEASPOON SALT
1 TEASPOON VANILLA

½ CUP SUGAR
½ CUP PECANS, CHOPPED
1 6-OUNCE PACKAGE CHOCOLATE CHIPS
1 9-INCH UNBAKED PIE SHELL

Combine eggs, syrup, salt, vanilla and sugar. Mix well. Stir in pecans and chocolate chips. Pour into 9-inch unbaked pie shell and bake in a 375 degree oven for 55 minutes, or until pie is set. Serve with whipped cream if desired. *Yield:* 6 to 8 servings.

Mary Turner, *Blountville*

Sale Creek Strawberry Pie

Of all the ways to enjoy strawberries, this is the very best. It is better than shortcake, and a very beloved recipe all over the Chattanooga region.

1 QUART STRAWBERRIES
1 CUP SUGAR
1 CUP BOILING WATER
3 TABLESPOONS CORNSTARCH

ENOUGH COLD WATER TO MAKE A PASTE WITH CORNSTARCH
1 PASTRY SHELL, BAKED
1 CUP WHIPPING CREAM, WHIPPED

Bring to a boil and strain 1 cup of the smaller berries, sugar and boiling water. Now add cornstarch mixture. Cook over the fire for a couple of minutes, stirring constantly. Remove from fire and beat. Return to a slow fire and cook slowly until thick. Have ready a baked pie shell. Arrange the rest of the berries, which have been washed and picked over, in the shell. Pour the hot sauce over them. When cool, spread whipped cream that has been sweetened with powdered sugar over the top.

Mrs. W. H. List, *Sale Creek*

Perfect Cream Cheese Pastry

1 CUP BUTTER, ROOM TEMPERATURE
1 8-OUNCE PACKAGE CREAM CHEESE, SOFTENED

¼ CUP WHIPPING CREAM
2½ CUPS ALL-PURPOSE FLOUR

Cream butter and cream cheese together until well-blended, add cream, beat until smooth. Add flour in 3 batches, blending well after each addition. Shape into a ball, wrap in waxed paper and refrigerate at least 1 hour before using.

Note: This is a perfect pastry for any pie pastry and so easy to handle. Will keep several days in the refrigerator and freezes well. *Yield:* 2 9-inch pastries.

Mrs. Carrie Bartlett, *Gallatin*

Grandmother's Raisin Custard Pie

1 CUP RAISINS	2 TABLESPOONS ALL-PURPOSE FLOUR
1 CUP WATER	2 EGG YOLKS, BEATEN
2 TABLESPOONS BUTTER	3 TABLESPOONS LEMON JUICE
2/3 CUP BROWN SUGAR	PIE CRUST, BAKED

Cook the raisins, water and butter to a boiling point. Mix together in a small bowl the sugar and flour. Add to the raisin mixture and gently add the 2 beaten egg yolks. Stir over low heat until thickened. Add the lemon juice. Cool. Pour into baked pie crust.

Meringue:

2 EGG WHITES	2 TABLESPOONS SUGAR
1/4 TEASPOON CREAM OF TARTAR	

Beat egg whites well. Add cream of tartar and sugar; beat until dissolved. Cover raisin mixture and bake in a 350 degree oven for 12 minutes. *Yield:* 6 to 8 servings.

Mrs. Ernest D. Weaver, *Blountville*

Good Luck Pie Crust

Homecoming always brings extra guests which means extra cooking. For all the pies cooked for a Homecoming, the following recipe will certainly come in handy.

No matter how much you handle this dough (and you may beat it with your rolling pins if you like) it will always be flaky, tender and delicious. There'll be no more patchwork with pieces falling apart at the last minute, and when you roll it out it will do exactly what you want it to do.

Follow this recipe and remember: you don't have to attack it as though it were bigger than you. You can make a good pie crust, every time! Try your luck.

4 CUPS ALL-PURPOSE FLOUR	2 TEASPOONS SALT
1 3/4 CUPS VEGETABLE SHORTENING	1 TABLESPOON VINEGAR
1 TABLESPOON SUGAR	1 EGG
1/2 CUP WATER	

With a fork, mix together first 4 ingredients. In a separate dish, beat remaining ingredients. Combine the 2 mixtures, stirring with a fork until all ingredients are moistened. Then with hands mold dough in a ball. Chill at least 15 minutes before rolling it into desired shape. Or it can be frozen. *Yield:* Two 9-inch double crust pies or three 9-inch shells.

Mrs. Annette Fisher, *Jackson*
Mrs. Calvin (Ruth) Borden, *Fairfield Glade*
Lena Jane Dillon, *Murfreesboro*

Desserts

Tennessee Truffles

CHOCOLATE CAKE BATTER
BUTTERCREAM FROSTING

12 OUNCES COATING CHOCOLATE

Bake miniature cupcakes using bitecake pans. Remove from pans and cool. With an apple corer tool or paring knife, cut a plug out of each small cake and fill the cavity with buttercream frosting; then replace the plug.

Melt chocolate in top of double boiler and hold at 90 degrees. Dip each cake in the melted chocolate, turning to coat well. Dry on waxed paper. Each truffle may be garnished while still soft with a candy flower or a pecan half.

Sour Cream Chocolate Cake:

2 CUPS ALL-PURPOSE FLOUR	3/4 CUP DAIRY SOUR CREAM
1 TEASPOON SALT	1/4 CUP SHORTENING
1¼ TEASPOON SODA	2 EGGS
1 TEASPOON VANILLA	4 OUNCES UNSWEETENED CHOCOLATE, MELTED AND COOLED
1/2 TEASPOON BAKING POWDER	1 CUP WATER

Mix dry ingredients thoroughly. In mixing bowl, cream sour cream and shortening; add eggs and mix well. Then add melted chocolate, followed by dry ingredients alternately with water. Beat until smooth. Pour into cupcake pans and bake in a 350 degree oven for 10 to 25 minutes, depending on size of cupcakes.

Buttercream Frosting:

1/2 CUP BUTTER	2 TEASPOONS VANILLA OR 1 TEASPOON ORANGE EXTRACT
1/4 CUP VEGETABLE SHORTENING	2 TO 4 TABLESPOONS WATER
1 POUND CONFECTIONERS' SUGAR	

Cream butter and shortening; add sugar and flavoring and cream again; then add water slowly until desired (spreadable) consistency is obtained. Beat 3 to 5 minutes.

Judy Mayo Murphy, *Selmer*

Deluxe Apple Crunch

6 LARGE APPLES, SLICED	1/2 CUP ALL-PURPOSE FLOUR
1/2 CUP SUGAR	1/2 CUP OATMEAL
NUTMEG OR CINNAMON	1/2 CUP RAISINS
1/2 CUP BUTTER	1 SMALL PACKAGE NUTS, CHOPPED
1 CUP BROWN SUGAR	

Spread apples in buttered 9-inch baking dish; cover with white sugar and sprinkle with nutmeg or cinnamon. Blend remaining ingredients until mixture resembles coarse meal. Spread over apples. Bake in a 325 degree oven for 1 hour. Serve with whipped cream or ice cream or top each serving with a slice of cheddar cheese.

Susan Lee Wilson, *Johnson City*

Blueberry Buckle

1/2 CUP SHORTENING	1/2 CUP MILK
1/2 CUP SUGAR	2 CUPS FRESH BLUEBERRIES
1 EGG, WELL BEATEN	1/2 CUP SUGAR
2 CUPS ENRICHED FLOUR, SIFTED	1/2 CUP ENRICHED FLOUR, SIFTED
21/2 TEASPOONS SODA	1/2 TEASPOON CINNAMON
1/4 TEASPOON SALT	1/4 CUP BUTTER OR MARGARINE

Thoroughly cream shortening and 1/2 cup sugar, add egg and mix well. Sift 2 cups flour, soda and salt, add to creamed mixture alternately with milk. Pour into wax paper lined 8 x 8 x 2 inch pan, sprinkle blueberries over batter. Combine 1/2 cup sugar, 1/2 cup flour, cinnamon and butter until crumbly, sprinkle over blueberries. Bake in a 375 degree oven for 75 minutes. Cut in wedges.

Mrs. Jean Boiko, *Lavergne*

Creme de Menthe Brownies

Bottom Layer:

4 EGGS	1 16-OUNCE CAN CHOCOLATE SYRUP
1 CUP SELF-RISING FLOUR	1/2 TEASPOON SALT
1/2 CUP BUTTER	1 TEASPOON VANILLA

Mix well; pour into 9-inch pan sprayed with Pam. Bake in a 350 degree oven for 25 to 30 minutes. Cool completely.

Middle Layer:

1/2 CUP BUTTER	2 TABLESPOONS GREEN CREME DE MENTHE
2 CUPS CONFECTIONERS' SUGAR	

Blend well. Beat until fluffy. Ice the cooled brownies. Refrigerate until firm.

Top Layer:

1 CUP CHOCOLATE CHIPS	6 TABLESPOONS BUTTER

Melt chocolate chips and butter in double boiler or heavy saucepan. Cool slightly. Spread over creme de menthe frosting. Spread completely to edge of pan to seal cake. Cool entire cake. Slice with very sharp knife. *Yield:* 24 to 30 servings.

Jean Burns, *Paris*
Mrs. Wayne Gilchrist, *Martin*

Apple Dumplings

I have traced this recipe to the early 1800's in my family here in Middle Tennessee. It still tastes just like the ones my grandmother used to make.

Pastry:

2 CUPS ALL-PURPOSE FLOUR	1 TEASPOON SALT
2 TEASPOONS BAKING POWDER	3/4 CUP SHORTENING
1/2 CUP MILK	6 TART APPLES

Prepare pastry by mixing dry ingredients, then cutting in shortening until the mixture is the texture of coarse meal. Add the milk all at once and stir only until mixture is moistened. Roll pastry thin and cut into 6 circles the size of a salad plate.

Peel apples and core and slice them. Place a handful of apple slices in the center of each pastry circle and sprinkle with a small amount of sugar and spices. Make a pouch of the circle and pinch the edges together at the top. Place each pouch as formed into a deep baking dish. A cast-iron Dutch oven is ideal.

Sauce:

2 CUPS WATER	1/4 TEASPOON NUTMEG
2 CUPS SUGAR	1/4 CUP BUTTER OR MARGARINE
1/4 TEASPOON CINNAMON	ADDITIONAL SUGAR, CINNAMON AND NUTMEG FOR SPRINKLING

Make the sauce by combining all ingredients except the butter and bring to a boil. Allow to simmer for 5 minutes. Add the butter, then pour the sauce over the dumplings. Bake in a 375 degree oven for 35 minutes. Serve warm with cream.

Note: Depending upon your oven, the dumplings may need to be cooked a little longer. They should be brown on top and a little crusty.

Dr. Doris W. Bush, *Baxter*

Billie's Apple Fritters

1 1/3 CUPS ALL-PURPOSE FLOUR	1 TABLESPOON MARGARINE, MELTED
1/3 CUP SUGAR	1 EGG, BEATEN
1/4 TEASPOON SALT	1/4 CUP MILK
2 TEASPOONS BAKING POWDER	1 CUP DICED APPLES WITH SKIN
3/4 TEASPOON NUTMEG	

Sift together dry ingredients. Combine with liquids and apples. Drop by large spoonfuls into hot fat. I set my deep fryer between 375 and 400 degrees and cook 5 to 7 minutes. This will make 7 large fritters. This is a very thick batter. Try not to drop smooth spoonfuls as the roughness makes nice uneven crust. Lift out of grease and roll in sugar-cinnamon mixture.

Mrs. Lee Vance, *Erwin*

Chocolate Chip Bars

2 EGGS, WELL BEATEN
1½ CUP BROWN SUGAR
½ TEASPOON VANILLA
¾ CUP VEGETABLE OIL
1½ CUPS SELF-RISING FLOUR

½ CUP NUTS
1 CUP OATS
1 CUP CHOCOLATE CHIPS
DASH SALT

Mix thoroughly and bake in a 350 degree oven for 25 minutes on an ungreased cookie sheet.

Mrs. Jimmy Freeman, *Cookeville*

Rosy Rhubarb Cobbler

Submitted in memory of my grandfather, Luther Andrew Mayo of the Cades/Union Central community in Gibson County. Although he died before my birth, I remember hearing my grandmother talk about his fondness for rhubarb.

4 CUPS RHUBARB, DICED
1 CUP SUGAR
3 TABLESPOONS BUTTER
1½ CUPS ALL-PURPOSE FLOUR
¼ TEASPOON SALT

3 TEASPOONS BAKING POWDER
1 CUP SUGAR
¼ CUP SHORTENING
1 EGG, BEATEN
½ CUP MILK

Place rhubarb in greased 8 x 12 inch baking dish. Sprinkle with the 1 cup sugar and dot with butter. Heat in a 350 degree oven while mixing batter.

Sift remaining dry ingredients and cut in shortening until mixture resembles coarse crumbs. Add beaten egg which has been mixed with the milk. Pour batter over hot rhubarb. Bake in a 350 degree oven for 35 minutes, until browned. Serve warm. *Yield:* 6 servings.

Corinna Mayo Goehring, *Jackson*

Apple Crisp

4 CUPS TART APPLES, SLICED
½ CUP WATER
¾ CUP ALL-PURPOSE FLOUR
1 CUP WHITE OR BROWN SUGAR

1 TEASPOON CINNAMON
½ CUP BUTTER
2 TABLESPOONS LEMON JUICE
½ CUP GRATED CHEESE

Arrange apples in a buttered baking dish. Pour over water. Blend flour, sugar, cinnamon, and butter with pastry blender or fork. Place this mixture on top of apples. Bake in a 350 degree oven until apples are tender and crust brown, about 30 minutes. Just before removing from oven sprinkle grated cheese over crust and let melt slightly. Delicious.

Note: May also serve warm with thin cream or whipped cream. It's also extra delicious with ice cream.

Agnes G. Ford, *Hendersonville*

Strawberry Crunch

This is my original recipe.

Crust:

1 CUP MARGARINE, MELTED	2 CUPS SELF-RISING FLOUR
1 CUP NUTS, CHOPPED	

Mix the above ingredients and press into a 9 x 13 inch pan. Bake in a 350 degree oven for approximately 8 to 10 minutes.

Filling:

2 CUPS SUGAR	1 TABLESPOON LEMON JUICE
2 CUPS WATER	RED FOOD COLORING (OPTIONAL)
5 TABLESPOONS CORNSTARCH	STRAWBERRIES, SLICED
DASH SALT	COOL WHIP OR WHIPPED TOPPING
1 SMALL BOX STRAWBERRY JELLO	

Cook sugar, water, cornstarch and salt until clear and thick. Add Jello and lemon juice. Cool filling and crust. Cover crust with sliced or small whole strawberries. Pour filling over berries. Refrigerate 3 to 4 hours. Top with Cool Whip or other topping when ready to serve.

Note: You may substitute fresh peaches or blackberries with same flavor of Jello.

Wanda Richardson, *Gadsden*

Mama's Rice Pudding

This recipe is special to me because it was used by my mother and evokes memories of my childhood. And it's simple and delicious!

3/4 CUP RICE, UNCOOKED	1 CUP SUGAR
1 1/2 CUPS WATER	1 CUP MILK
DASH SALT	1/4 CUP BUTTER OR MARGARINE, MELTED
2 TABLESPOONS BUTTER OR MARGARINE	1 TABLESPOON VANILLA
2 EGGS	

Place rice in a saucepan with water, 2 tablespoons butter and a dash of salt. Bring to a quick boil, cover saucepan, and allow rice to simmer 15 minutes or until rice has absorbed all the moisture.

In a mixing bowl, lightly beat 2 eggs. Add sugar, milk, butter and vanilla. Stir well. Add this mixture to the rice. Stir well. Bake in an 8 x 8 inch baking dish in a 350 degree oven for 15 minutes. *Yield:* 6 servings.

Nancy Collins Staggs, *Jackson*

Blueberry Delight

1¾ PACKAGES GRAHAM CRACKERS
1 CUP PECANS, CHOPPED
2 TABLESPOONS SUGAR
½ CUP BUTTER (OR MORE IF NEEDED)
1 8-OUNCE PACKAGE CREAM CHEESE

2 ENVELOPES DREAM WHIP, WHIPPED
2 TABLESPOONS LEMON JUICE
1 BOX CONFECTIONERS' SUGAR
1 CAN BLUEBERRY PIE FILLING (OR ANY FLAVOR)

Make graham cracker crumbs, add chopped pecans, sugar and enough melted butter to moisten. Press into a long cake pan and cool.

Cream the cheese, add sugar, whipped cream and lemon juice. Pour in graham cracker crust and chill. Top with pie filling.

Betty Edwards, *White Bluff*

Cherry Delight

1 8-OUNCE PACKAGE CREAM CHEESE
2 TABLESPOONS SWEET MILK
1 SMALL BOX DREAM WHIP

¾ CUP SUGAR
1 PACKAGE LADY FINGERS
1 CAN CHERRY PIE FILLING

Have cream cheese at room temperature. Mix milk with cream cheese. Beat Dream Whip; combine with cream cheese and sugar. Beat well. Line bottom of a 9-inch square pan with open lady fingers to line the dish. Spread cream cheese mixture over lady fingers. Top with cherry pie filling. Chill completely before serving.

Eula Catlett, *Sevierville*

Heavenly Peach Delight

3 CUPS SWEETENED FRESH PEACHES (OR 1 LARGE CAN SLICED PEACHES IN SYRUP)
½ CUP WATER
⅓ CUP SUGAR
½ CUP MARGARINE, MELTED

1 CUP SUGAR
2 EGGS
½ CUP ALL-PURPOSE FLOUR
½ CUP WESSON OIL
DASH SALT

Pour fresh peaches, water and ⅓ cup sugar in large saucepan, let come to boil. If using canned peaches in syrup, omit water. Boil slowly, while mixing batter. Cream margarine, 1 cup sugar and eggs; add flour and mix well. Add Wesson oil and salt; beat 1 minute at medium speed. Pour hot peaches mixture in baking dish, drizzle batter over hot peaches mixture. Bake in a 325 degree oven about 30 minutes until golden brown.

Mrs. Tom Bullifin, *Brownsville*

Banana Pudding

1¾ CUPS SWEET MILK	1 TABLESPOON BUTTER
3 EGG YOLKS	1 TEASPOON VANILLA
1½ CUPS SUGAR	6 OR 8 BANANAS
2 TABLESPOONS ALL-PURPOSE FLOUR	VANILLA WAFERS

Scald milk in top of double boiler. Beat egg yolks, add sugar and flour. Mix well, add a small amount of milk to egg mixture. Stir together, slowly add to milk in double boiler, stirring until it thickens. Remove from stove, stir in butter, add vanilla. Let cool, stirring occasionally. Peel and slice bananas, place vanilla wafers in bottom of bowl to cover. Add small amount of custard. Continue to do so alternating wafers and bananas. Top with meringue, place in a 325 degree oven and bake until brown.

Meringue:

3 EGG WHITES	¼ CUP SUGAR

Beat egg whites until stiff, but not dry. Gradually add sugar, a small amount at a time. Beat well after each addition. When it peaks, spread on top of pudding and brown.

Mrs. Mariel Thompson, *Clarksville*

Ginger Pudding with Wine Sauce

½ CUP SHORTENING	1 TEASPOON BAKING POWDER
½ CUP BUTTER	1 TEASPOON CINNAMON
1 CUP SUGAR	2 EGGS, BEATEN
2 CUPS ALL-PURPOSE FLOUR, SIFTED	1 CUP MOLASSES
1 TEASPOON SODA	1 CUP BOILING WATER
1 TEASPOON GINGER	

Cream shortening and butter; add sugar gradually while creaming. Sift dry ingredients. Add eggs, then dry ingredients, then molasses and water to butter mixture. Mix well. Pour into 2 well-greased and floured 8-inch square pans and bake in a 350 degree oven for 30 to 40 minutes. Serve hot with warm wine sauce.

Wine Sauce:

1 CUP BUTTER	2 EGGS, WELL-BEATEN
2 CUPS SUGAR	1 CUP SHERRY WINE

Cream butter and sugar together. Add eggs and wine. Cook until slightly thickened in pan over double boiler.

Mrs. Sam J. Denney, *Milan*

Grandma's Bread Pudding

4 EGGS
2 CUPS MILK
1/3 CUP SUGAR
1/2 TEASPOON GROUND CINNAMON

1/2 TEASPOON VANILLA
1/4 TEASPOON SALT
3 1/2 SLICES BREAD, CRUMBLED
1/3 CUP RAISINS

Beat together eggs, milk, sugar, cinnamon, vanilla and salt. Place crumbled bread in baking dish. Sprinkle raisins over bread. Pour egg mixture over this. Bake in a 325 degree oven for 40 to 45 minutes or until a knife inserted near center comes out clean. Cool slightly.

Becky Makamson, *Lebanon*

Blackberry Roll

This is my husband's grandmother's recipe.

1 PINT BLACKBERRIES
3/4 CUP SUGAR
2 CUPS ALL-PURPOSE FLOUR, SIFTED
1 TEASPOON SALT

2 TEASPOONS SUGAR
1/3 CUP PLUS 6 TABLESPOONS BUTTER
1 EGG
1/3 CUP MILK

Sweeten blackberries with sugar. Sift together dry ingredients. Cut in 1/3 cup butter. Beat egg and add with sufficient milk to make soft dough. Mix lightly and turn out on floured board and knead enough to bring dough together. Roll out 1/4 inch thick. Spread with remaining butter. Cover with sweetened blackberries. Roll up, as for jelly roll. Bake in a 400 degree oven for 25 minutes until browned. Cut slices and serve with cream.

Mrs. Sam Durbin, *Jackson*

Congo Squares

1/2 CUP PLUS 2 2/3 TABLESPOONS BUTTER
1 PACKAGE LIGHT BROWN SUGAR
2 2/3 CUPS ALL-PURPOSE FLOUR
2 1/2 TEASPOONS BAKING POWDER
1 TEASPOON SALT

3 EGGS
1 TEASPOON VANILLA
1 6-OUNCE PACKAGE CHOCOLATE CHIPS
NUTS, CHOPPED (AS DESIRED)

Melt butter with brown sugar, let stand 10 minutes. Sift together flour, baking powder and salt; set aside. After butter-sugar mixture has set 10 minutes, add eggs, one at a time, stirring after each addition. Stir in flour mixture and vanilla. Mix in chocolate chips and nuts, being careful not to overmix so chocolate won't melt into mixture. Pour into 2 greased and floured 8-inch square pans and bake in a 350 degree oven for 25 to 30 minutes. Cool and cut into squares. *Yield:* 32 squares.

Rachel Ann Neal, *Smyrna*

Woodford Pudding

3 EGGS, BEATEN	1 TEASPOON CINNAMON
1 CUP GRANULATED SUGAR	1 TEASPOON VANILLA
½ CUP BUTTER, SOFTENED	1 TEASPOON SODA
1 CUP ALL-PURPOSE FLOUR, SIFTED	3 TABLESPOONS BUTTERMILK
1 CUP BLACKBERRY JAM	

Combine ingredients in order given and pour into a buttered baking dish (approximately 8 x 11 inches). Bake in a 350 degree oven for 30 minutes or until center springs back when lightly touched. Serve warm with Lemon Sauce.

Lemon Sauce:

½ CUP GRANULATED SUGAR	½ CUP BUTTER
2 TABLESPOONS CORNSTARCH	1 TABLESPOON GRATED LEMON PEEL
¼ TEASPOON SALT	3 TABLESPOONS LEMON JUICE
2 CUPS WATER	

Mix sugar, cornstarch and salt in a saucepan. Gradually stir in water. Cook, stirring constantly until mixture boils. Boil and stir 1 minute. Remove from heat; stir in butter, lemon peel and juice.

Note: Some prefer whiskey to taste added to the sauce.

Derita Coleman Williams, *Memphis*

Evelyn's Cherry Surprise

This is an original recipe. It is not borrowed or adapted from anyone.

Crust:

1 CUP BUTTER	2 CUPS ALL-PURPOSE FLOUR, SIFTED
½ CUP CONFECTIONERS' SUGAR, SIFTED	

Melt butter. Pour over sugar and flour. Stir well until ball of dough is formed. Pat and form to bottom and sides of a 9 x 14 inch Pyrex baking dish. Stick holes in crust with fork. Bake in a 350 degree oven for 15 to 20 minutes. Let cool before adding filling.

Filling:

1 12-OUNCE PACKAGE SEMISWEET CHOCOLATE MORSELS	1 TEASPOON VANILLA
¼ CUP MILK	½ TEASPOON ALMOND FLAVORING
1 EGG YOLK	1 CUP COOL WHIP
2 SMALL PACKAGES VANILLA INSTANT PUDDING	2 25-OUNCE GLASS JARS MUSSELMAN'S CHERRY PIE FILLING
2 CUPS MILK	COOL WHIP
	A FEW CHOCOLATE MORSELS, GRATED

Melt chocolate morsels and ½ cup milk in double boiler. Cool slightly. Add egg yolks one at a time and beat well. Spread over baked pastry crust.

Mix vanilla instant pudding and 2 cups milk. Let cool in refrigerator. Fold in vanilla and almond flavoring, and 1 cup Cool Whip. Spread over chocolate layer.

Spread cherry pie filling over pudding; spread layer of Cool Whip over cherries. Grate a few chocolate morsels and sprinkle over top of Cool Whip for garnish.

Mrs. L. Douglas Haury, *Nashville*

Amaretto Freeze

⅓ CUP AMARETTO
1 TABLESPOON BROWN SUGAR
1 QUART VANILLA ICE CREAM

WHIPPED CREAM (OPTIONAL)
MARASCHINO CHERRIES (OPTIONAL)

Combine amaretto and brown sugar; stir until sugar dissolves. Combine ice cream and amaretto mixture in blender; process until smooth. Pour into 6 individual freezer-proof serving dishes and freeze. Garnish with whipped cream and cherries just before serving, if desired.

Mrs. Michael (Susan) Renshaw, *Old Hickory*

Frozen Chocolate

This recipe is from Mrs Black's Choice Recipes, *published in 1907. The inside page says, 'Mrs. Tennessee W. Black, 51 Polk Flats, Nashville, Tennessee.' I am her granddaughter.*

5 OUNCES BUTTER
½ CUP CONFECTIONERS' SUGAR, SIFTED
5 OUNCES GERMAN SWEET CHOCOLATE
½ TEASPOON VANILLA
PINCH SALT

2 EGGS, SEPARATED
1 CUP WHIPPING CREAM
¼ CUP CREME DE COCOA
2 TABLESPOONS INSTANT COFFEE

Cream butter and sugar. Melt chocolate over hot water until smooth; add to butter and sugar a little at a time. Add vanilla, beaten egg yolks and firmly beaten egg whites. Spoon into baking (paper) cups sitting in muffin tins. Refrigerate and then freeze. Take out 1 hour before serving; serve with whipped cream flavored with cream de cocoa and instant coffee. *Yield:* 8 servings.

Note: When serving as pick-up use small paper cups and no topping. When using small paper cups it will make more than 8.

Mrs. Einer Nielsen, *Nashville*

No-Bake Squares

1 6-OUNCE PACKAGE SEMISWEET CHOCOLATE MORSELS

1 6-OUNCE PACKAGE BUTTERSCOTCH MORSELS

3/4 CUP SIFTED CONFECTIONERS' SUGAR

1/2 CUP SOUR CREAM

1 TEASPOON VANILLA

1/4 TEASPOON SALT

2 CUPS GIRL SCOUT CHOCOLATE CHUNKS COOKIES, FINELY CRUSHED

1/2 CUP ALMONDS, CHOPPED

Combine the chocolate and butterscotch morsels in top of a double boiler and melt over hot, not boiling, water. Remove from water. Add the sugar, sour cream, vanilla and salt and mix well. Blend in the crushed chocolate chunks and press into waxed paper lined 8-inch square pan. Sprinkle with almonds and press in gently. Chill until firm. Let stand for several minutes at room temperature for easier cutting, then cut into 36 squares.

Daisy Troop 30, *Sweetwater*

Apricot Coconut Balls

2 6-OUNCE PACKAGES DRIED APRICOTS, GROUND

2 CUPS SHREDDED COCONUT

2/3 CUP SWEETENED CONDENSED MILK

CONFECTIONERS' SUGAR

Combine and mix together apricots and coconut. Add condensed milk and mix well. Shape into 1-inch balls and coat with confectioners' sugar. *Yield:* 5 dozen apricot balls.

Elizabeth Weaver Winstead, *Nashville*

Peppermint Eggnog Punch Bowl

This is beautiful and most delicious!

1 PINT SOFT PINK PEPPERMINT STICK ICE CREAM

2 CUPS DAIRY EGGNOG

FEW DROPS RED FOOD COLORING

1 (1-PINT 12-OUNCE) BOTTLE CLUB SODA, CHILLED

1 CUP HEAVY CREAM, WHIPPED

16 RED PEPPERMINT STICKS (SMALL CANDY CANES)

1/3 CUP CRUSHED PEPPERMINT STICKS

Spoon ice cream into punch bowl. Add eggnog and club soda, mixing well. Stir in food coloring to tint slightly pink.

Spoon whipped cream over surface. Put peppermint candy cane stirrer in each punch cup. Top each serving with a little crushed peppermint candy. *Yield:* 16 servings.

Robbie Lee Goolsby, *Clinton*

Peach Torte

1 CUP ALL-PURPOSE FLOUR	2 CUPS PEACHES
1 CUP SUGAR	4 TABLESPOONS BROWN SUGAR
1 TEASPOON SODA	½ CUP NUTS
1 EGG, BEATEN	WHIPPED CREAM

Mix dry ingredients and add the beaten egg. Fold in peaches. Put in greased pie pan and sprinkle with brown sugar and nuts. Bake in a 325 degree oven for 35 to 40 minutes. Top with whipped cream.

Peggy Hailey, *Nashville*

Lemon Sherbet

1 CUP LEMON JUICE	1 CUP WHIPPING CREAM
2 CUPS SUGAR	1 QUART MILK OR LESS

Beat lemon juice and sugar. Add milk. Beat whipping cream and add to milk mixture. Pour into a chilled loaf pan and put in the freezer compartment. Stir when firm and finish freezing.

Mary Crowell Walker, *Maryville*

Homemade Ice Cream

2 CUPS SUGAR	1 TEASPOON VANILLA
4 EGGS	3 LARGE CANS PET MILK
DASH SALT	

Cream sugar and eggs until fluffy; add salt, vanilla and milk, mixing well. Pour into ice cream freezer and finish filling to fill line with whole milk. Add your favorite fruit, crushed bananas, strawberries, peaches, etc. and churn.

Kathy Goostree, *Portland*

Homemade Banana Ice Cream

½ GALLON SWEET MILK	3 MEDIUM BANANAS, MASHED
1½ CUPS SUGAR	1 TABLESPOON VANILLA
1 CUP SWEETENED MILK	4 JUNKETS, DISSOLVED IN WARM WATER

Mix all ingredients except junkets and heat to lukewarm. Remove from heat and stir in junkets. Pour in freezer can and put paddle in. Let stand 10 minutes. Freeze using layers of ice and rock salt. *Yield:* 1 gallon.

Mrs. Frances Grimes, *Crockett Mills*

Butterfinger Ice Cream

5 EGGS	1/2 CUP SMOOTH PEANUT BUTTER
2 CUPS SUGAR	6 CRUSHED BUTTERFINGER CANDY BARS
2 13-OUNCE CANS PET MILK	WHOLE MILK TO FILL CAN
2 TABLESPOONS PLUS 1 TEASPOON VANILLA	

Mix all the above ingredients together and pour into ice cream freezer can. Finish filling can with whole milk. Put ice cream salt and ice around can and freeze. Delicious.

Gayle Bowling, *Somerville*

Tennessee Boiled Custard

1 CUP SUGAR, DIVIDED	2 1/2 TABLESPOONS ALL-PURPOSE FLOUR
4 CUPS MILK, DIVIDED	1/8 TEASPOON SODA
3 EGGS, WELL BEATEN	1 TEASPOON VANILLA

Combine 1/2 cup sugar and 3 cups milk in top of a double boiler. Heat over boiling water; combine eggs, remaining sugar, flour, soda and remaining milk in a medium mixing bowl. Blend well; pour through a strainer into hot milk mixture; stirring constantly. Cook over boiling water, stirring frequently for 10 to 15 minutes or until mixture will coat a metal spoon. Stir in vanilla. Cool. *Yield:* 4 1/2 cups.

Louise E. Ellis, *Talbott*

Pecan Tassies

1 3-OUNCE PACKAGE CREAM CHEESE	3/4 CUP LIGHT BROWN SUGAR, FIRMLY PACKED
1/2 CUP BUTTER, SOFTENED	1 TABLESPOON BUTTER, SOFTENED
1 CUP ALL-PURPOSE FLOUR, SIFTED	1 TEASPOON VANILLA
2/3 CUP PECAN PIECES, DIVIDED	1/2 TEASPOON SALT
1 EGG	

Prepare tart shells by combining cream cheese and 1/2 cup butter; add flour and mix well. Chill 1 hour. Shape dough into 24 one-inch balls. Place in ungreased miniature 1 3/4-inch muffin tins. Press bottom and sides to form tart shells. Divide 1/3 cup pecan pieces among pastry-lined cups. Prepare filling by beating together egg, sugar, butter, vanilla and salt until smooth. Pour egg mixture into shells and top with remaining pecans. Bake in a 325 degree oven for 25 minutes. Cool and remove from pans. These can be frozen after baking. *Yield:* 24 servings.

Daisy King, *Nashville*

Chapter Eleven

Relishes and Garnishes

Ripe Tomato Catsup

2 GALLONS RIPE TOMATOES

2 TABLESPOONS SALT

1 QUART VINEGAR

4 CUPS SUGAR

2 TEASPOONS ALLSPICE

2 LARGE GREEN SWEET PEPPERS

2 TEASPOONS BLACK PEPPER

2 CUPS GROUND ONIONS

HOT PEPPER TO TASTE

1 TABLESPOON PICKLING SPICE, TIED IN CHEESECLOTH

Mix and cook until you have the desired thickness. Fill sterile jars and seal.

Eleanor M. Fleenor, *Lenoir City*

Apple Pickles

18 LARGE APPLES, PEELED

12 LARGE ONIONS

1 STRONG PEPPER

10 SWEET PEPPERS (5 RED, 5 GREEN)

3 PINTS VINEGAR

3 CUPS SUGAR

Chop all in small pieces and mix all together. Boil 10 minutes and place into jars and seal. *Yield:* 5 quarts or 10 pints.

Blonnie Sloan, *Madisonville*

Beet Pickles

Real good beet pickle, from my Grandmother, Mrs. Vallie Bennett.

1 GALLON BEETS

2 CUPS SUGAR

3½ CUPS VINEGAR

DASH CINNAMON

1 TABLESPOON ALLSPICE

1½ CUPS WATER

Peel beets by heating and slipping off skin. Add remaining ingredients and simmer all together 15 minutes, put in jars and seal.

Carolyn Seavers, *McKenzie*

Crisp Sweet Bread and Butter Pickles

4 QUARTS MEDIUM CUCUMBERS, SLICED	⅓ CUP COARSE SALT
6 MEDIUM WHITE ONIONS, SLICED	1½ TEASPOON TURMERIC
2 GREEN PEPPERS, CHOPPED	3 CUPS CIDER VINEGAR
3 CLOVES GARLIC	1½ TEASPOON MUSTARD SEED
5 CUPS SUGAR	

Make a hot brine out of the vinegar and spices and pour over vegetables. Let cool. Drain and put vegetables into sterile jars. Boil vinegar and spices once again and pour over vegetables in jars. Seal and let stand a few days. These are the best crisp pickles, so sweet and good.

Note: Can use Sugar Twin sugar substitute in place of the sugar. If so, use slightly less than called for in ingredients.

Ms. Pat Bonney Hartman, *Oak Ridge*

German Chunk Pickles

AS MANY CUCUMBERS AS DESIRED	1 STICK CINNAMON
1½ GALLONS WATER	2 TABLESPOONS MIXED PICKLING SPICES (TIED IN CLOTH)
3 CUPS SALT	4 CUPS SUGAR
1½ GALLON WATER	1 STICK CLOVES
2 TABLESPOONS POWDERED ALUM	
2 QUARTS VINEGAR	

Prepare as many cucumbers as you wish with a brine made of the water and salt. Leave in brine 3 days. Drain and put in clear water for 3 days, changing water each day. Cover with water, alum and 1 quart vinegar and let stand 2 days. Drain and throw away liquid. Mix together remaining vinegar, cinnamon, pickling spices, sugar and cloves; boil together 15 minutes and pour over cucumbers. Heat slowly to boiling point, but do not boil. Do this for 3 days. Then let all come to a good boil, put in jars and seal. Do not fill jars too full. Put in refrigerator before serving; they are better cold.

Beatrice Hughes, *Milan*

Sweet Crisp Green Tomato Pickles

8 POUNDS GREEN TOMATOES	5 TO 8 CUPS APPLE CIDER VINEGAR
2 CUPS LIME (FROM BUILDERS SUPPLY)	1 TABLESPOON SALT
2 GALLONS WATER	10 DROPS GREEN FOOD COLOR (OPTIONAL)
9 CUPS SUGAR	

Cut tomatoes into ½-inch slices. Mix lime and water; pour over tomatoes. Let stand for 24 hours. Rinse well and soak in cold water for 2 hours. Mix sugar, vinegar, salt and food coloring. Drain tomatoes and add to the sugar/vinegar mix. Soak tomatoes in mixture overnight. Bring to boil and boil for 40 minutes. Pack in clean hot jar and seal. *Yield:* 8 pints.

Mrs. Josephine Harris, *Lenoir City*

Lib's Chow Chow

1 GALLON SMALL GREEN TOMATOES	6 CUCUMBERS
14 LARGE ONIONS	SALT AND PEPPER TO TASTE
6 HOT PEPPERS	9 CUPS APPLE CIDER VINEGAR
12 SWEET PEPPERS	7½ CUPS SUGAR
2 MEDIUM CABBAGE	½ BOX PICKLING SPICE, TIED IN BAG

Grind tomatoes, onions, hot and sweet peppers, cabbage and cucumbers in food chopper. Add salt and sugar to taste (about ¼ cup each). Let drain well, then squeeze out as much liquid as possible with hands. Combine vinegar, sugar and spice and bring to a boil. Add vegetable mixture and simmer for 30 minutes. Place in hot jars and seal. *Yield:* 13 pints.

Elizabeth Hamm, *Ramer*

Pepper Relish

I remember helping my Great-grandmother make this in the summer. I turned the hand grinder while she filled it with the garden vegetables. It is so delicious with Tennessee cooked vegetables of any kind.

2 CUPS RED BELL PEPPERS, CHOPPED	2¼ TABLESPOONS SALT
2 CUPS GREEN BELL PEPPERS, CHOPPED	1⅓ CUPS SUGAR
2 CUPS ONIONS, CHOPPED	2⅓ CUPS VINEGAR
2 CUPS CELERY, CHOPPED	

Cover vegetables with boiling water and simmer 10 or 15 minutes. Drain well. Add remaining ingredients; boil 15 to 30 minutes. Pour into jars, seal while hot.

Note: Tough, shriveled pickles are the result of too much salt or sugar, or too strong a vinegar. Soft pickles are the result of too strong a vinegar or too weak a brine. Use high grade cider vinegar or pure grain vinegar, 40 to 60 percent strength.

Mrs. Karen H. Barger, *Jackson*

Yellow Squash Relish

8 CUPS YELLOW SQUASH, THINLY SLICED	3 CUPS SUGAR
2 CUPS ONIONS, THINLY SLICED	2 CUPS WHITE VINEGAR
2 RED BELL PEPPERS	2 TEASPOONS MUSTARD SEED
2 GREEN BELL PEPPERS	2 TEASPOONS CELERY SEED

Prepare vegetables and salt to taste. Let stand 2 hours and drain. In a large pot combine sugar, vinegar, and spices and bring to a boil. Add vegetables, bring to a boil and boil 5 minutes. Pour into hot jars and seal.

Linda Arant, *Martin*

Jellied Cranberry Relish

1 POUND FRESH CRANBERRIES
1 CUP SUGAR
1 ENVELOPE UNFLAVORED GELATIN
1/2 CUP APPLE JUICE

1/4 CUP CELERY, FINELY CHOPPED
1/4 CUP APPLES, CHOPPED AND PARED
1/4 CUP NUTS, CHOPPED

Wash cranberries, drain and remove stems; chop coarsely. Add sugar and let mixture stand for 15 minutes, stirring occasionally. Sprinkle gelatin over apple juice in small saucepan to soften for 5 minutes. Place over low heat, stirring until gelatin is dissolved. Add gelatin mixture, celery, apples and nuts to berries. Mix well. Turn into a 3½-quart mold or glass dish and refrigerate until firm, 6 to 8 hours. Invert on serving plate. Place a hot damp cloth on botton of mold, shake to release.

Mary Alice Cox, *Clinton*

Cranberry Orange Relish

1 BAG FROZEN CRANBERRIES
2 ORANGES, QUARTERED

1 SMALL CAN CRUSHED PINEAPPLE, DRAINED
1 CUP SUGAR (OR MORE TO TASTE)

Grind frozen cranberries and quartered oranges with peel. Add drained pineapple and sugar. Stir until well mixed. Serve as a side dish or relish.

William A. Dupuy, *Clarksville*

Sour Krout (Kraut)

This recipe is 75 years old.

CABBAGE
PLAIN SALT

DILL HEADS OR CARAWAY SEED
GRAPE LEAVES

Select solid, sound cabbage; with a very sharp knife, shred or shave very finely. Clean the stalks of the cabbage and include with the cabbage. The cabbage should be packed in a crock churn or barrel (20 to 24 firm, medium-sized cabbage will fill a 5 gallon crock). Pack in layers 6-inches deep; between the layers strew a handful of plain salt (about ⅓ cup or to taste) and 3 or 4 dill heads or 1 teaspoon caraway seed. Cover with a layer of grape leaves; continue this until container is full, ending with a thick layer of grape leaves; have it pressed very hard with a weight, tie a strong cover over it, and a weight on top of the cover. Let it remain in the container for 3 to 4 weeks to ferment.

To can kraut, remove grape leaves and pack kraut in jars. Cook 30 minutes in hot water bath until kraut is hot and jars have sealed.

Mrs. Addie S. Harvey, *Jonesborough*

Robin Hood

Ervin Flakes, Jackson

Ripe Tomato Chili Sauce

This recipe is from my mother, Mrs. Annie Wilson.

2 GALLONS RIPE TOMATOES, SKINNED	1 TABLESPOON MUSTARD SEED
2 CUPS SWEET PEPPERS, CHOPPED	1 TABLESPOON CELERY SEED
2 PODS RED HOT PEPPER	3 TABLESPOONS MIXED PICKLING SPICE
2 CUPS ONIONS, CHOPPED	1 STICK CINNAMON
3 CUPS SUGAR	2½ CUPS APPLE CIDER VINEGAR
3 LEVEL TABLESPOONS CANNING SALT	

Blend tomatoes, peppers and onion; cook for 1 hour uncovered. Add sugar and canning salt. In a gauze bag tie mustard seed, celery seed, pickle spice and cinnamon, cook with tomato mixture for 30 minutes. Add vinegar; cook in an open kettle on medium heat for 1½ hours, stirring often until mixture thickens. Fill hot jars and seal immediately.

Mrs. Nick Richardson, *Clarksville*

Hot Pepper Sauce

8 TO 10 BELL PEPPERS	1 CUP WATER
8 CAYENNE PEPPERS	2 CUPS DARK VINEGAR
1 CUP SUGAR	2 PINT JARS, STERILIZED

Split lengthwise and remove all seeds and core of bell peppers. Slice about 1-inch wide. Place slices in sterile jar with 4 cayenne peppers. Set side.

In large boiler, pour sugar, water and vinegar and bring to a hard rolling boil, stirring constantly. Allow to boil 3 minutes. Pour liquid over peppers and seal. Water bath 5 minutes.

Allow 4 to 6 weeks before using. When ready to use, refrigerate and chill thoroughly. This keeps them crisp. The juice is excellent over any type of greens and the peppers are great to eat along with your greens, white beans and cornbread or pone. When cooking white beans or turnip greens, to add a little more flavor throw in 1 or 2 fresh cayenne peppers. It enhances the flavor.

John McCoy, *Ooltewah*

Frozen Tomato Sauce

10 POUNDS FRESH, RIPE TOMATOES	⅓ CUP PARSLEY, CHOPPED
3 TABLESPOONS SALAD OIL	¼ CUP SUGAR
1½ CUPS ONION, CHOPPED	3 TABLESPOONS GARLIC SALT
½ CUP GREEN PEPPER, DICED	1 TABLESPOON OREGANO
2 12-OUNCE CANS TOMATO PASTE	2 BAY LEAVES
1 POUND MUSHROOMS	

Blanch tomatoes; peel and quarter. Heat oil in a large kettle over medium-high heat. Add onion and green pepper; sauté until onions are tender. Add remaining ingredients and tomatoes. Heat to boiling. Remove bay leaves. Ladle sauce into freezer containers, leaving 1-inch head-space. Refrigerate until chilled, then freeze immediately. *Yield:* 10 pints of delicious homemade sauce.

Vi Einstein, *Morristown*

Peachy Orange Jam

Well worth the trouble to make.

3 LARGE JUICY ORANGES	1 LEMON
6 CUPS DOMINO GRANULATED SUGAR	3 POUNDS (ABOUT 12) MEDIUM FIRM PEACHES

Grate rinds of oranges and lemon. Squeeze the juices and remove seed. Do not strain. Combine rinds and juices in a large heavy kettle. Peel and chop peaches into citrus juices. Stir in sugar and bring to boil over medium heat, stirring often. Reduce heat and let simmer slowly until thickened, about 35 to 45 minutes. Stir frequently, do not cover. Pour into hot sterilized jars and seal at once. *Yield:* 5 half-pints.

Bonnie Henderson, *Clinton*

Rhubarb and Strawberry Jam

5 CUPS RHUBARB, CHOPPED	4 CUPS SUGAR
1 CUP (SMALL CAN) CRUSHED PINEAPPLE	1 SMALL PACKAGE STRAWBERRY JELLO

Mix rhubarb, pineapple and sugar thoroughly and boil for 20 minutes. Remove from heat and stir in strawberry Jello. Mix well and pour into hot jars and seal.

Ms. Lila Jean Seal, *Sneedville*

Zucchini Pineapple Marmalade

1 20-OUNCE CAN CRUSHED PINEAPPLE	1/2 CUP LEMON JUICE
6 CUPS SUGAR	1 6-OUNCE PACKAGE APRICOT JELLO
6 CUPS ZUCCHINI, PEELED AND GRATED	

Mix all ingredients except Jello, boil for 20 minutes. Remove from heat; add Jello. Cool, and freeze in freezer containers.

Cyna McCormick, *Cookeville*

Strawberry Preserves

4 CUPS SUGAR

1 CUP WATER

4 CUPS WHOLE STRAWBERRIES, CAPPED

1 TABLESPOON LEMON JUICE

Boil together 2 cups sugar and 1 cup water until syrup spins a thread. Add 2 cups whole berries, boil 10 minutes, add 2 more cups strawberries; combine lemon juice with remaining 2 cups sugar; add and boil 10 more minutes. Skim and set aside until following day, stir well and seal cold in sterile jars.

Mrs. Jessie Harris, *Clarksville*

Easy Apple Butter

5 CUPS APPLESAUCE

7 CUPS SUGAR

1/4 CUP VINEGAR

1 TEASPOON CINNAMON OR ALLSPICE

Combine ingredients in a heavy pan. Bring to a boil on high heat, turn down and let boil 15 minutes, stirring occasionally. Pour into sterilized jars; seal at once.

Mrs. Sue Gray Walker, *Knoxville*

Hot Pepper Jelly

1 LARGE BELL PEPPER

1½ CUPS CIDER VINEGAR

6½ CUPS SUGAR

1 TEASPOON SALT

½ CUP HOT PEPPER

1 BOTTLE CERTO

GREEN OR RED FOOD COLORING

Remove seeds and membrane from green peppers and grind (3/4 cup pulp and juice). Add vinegar, sugar, salt and hot peppers (ground and seeded). Bring to a rolling boil; add Certo and bring to a boil again, stirring constantly for 1 minute. Add 8 to 10 drops of food coloring. May or may not be strained. Pour into sterile jars and seal.

Margie Flynt, *Madison*

Chapter Twelve

Miss Daisy's Favorites

Appetizers

Chicken-Liver Paté

2 CUPS BUTTER

2 POUNDS CHICKEN LIVERS

2 MEDIUM ONIONS, QUARTERED

1 TEASPOON CURRY POWDER

1 TEASPOON PAPRIKA

1/4 TEASPOON SALT

1/4 TEASPOON BLACK PEPPER, FRESHLY
GROUND

2 TABLESPOONS COGNAC

Melt 1/2 cup of the butter in a saucepan. Add the chicken livers, onions, curry powder, paprika, salt and pepper. Cover and cook over low heat for 8 minutes. Blend the mixture in an electric blender until smooth. Add the cognac and remaining butter and blend in. Chill until firm. *Yield:* 5 cups.

Crab Dip Divine

1 12-OUNCE BOTTLE CATSUP

1 12-OUNCE BOTTLE CHILI SAUCE

1/4 CUP HORSERADISH

JUICE OF 1 LEMON

1/8 TEASPOON HOT SAUCE

1/8 TEASPOON WORCESTERSHIRE SAUCE

2 61/2-OUNCE CANS FLAKED CRABMEAT

Blend together all ingredients. Chill. Serve in pineapple shell with crisp crackers. *Yield:* 3 cups.

Spinach Balls

2 BOXES FROZEN, CHOPPED SPINACH

2 CUPS HERB BREAD STUFFING MIX

2 ONIONS, CHOPPED FINE

6 EGGS, BEATEN

3/4 CUP BUTTER, MELTED

1/2 CUP PARMESAN CHEESE

1 TABLESPOON GARLIC SALT

2/3 TEASPOON THYME

1/2 TABLESPOON BLACK PEPPER

Cook and drain spinach according to directions on box of spinach. Mix in remaining ingredients. Make into marble size balls. Bake in a 350 degree oven for 20 minutes. *Yield:* 6 dozen

Note: Can be frozen and thawed about 1 hour before baking.

Soups

Broccoli Cheese Soup

This recipe was given to me by my friend Ann Cox, of Murfreesboro, to use at Miss Daisy's Restaurant in Nashville. It is a regular on the menu.

1 CUP WATER
1 CHICKEN BOUILLON CUBE
1 10-OUNCE PACKAGE FROZEN BROCCOLI
1 MEDIUM CARROT, GRATED
2 TABLESPOONS BUTTER
3 TABLESPOONS ALL-PURPOSE FLOUR
2 CUPS MILK

1 POUND PROCESSED AMERICAN CHEESE, CUBED
1 CAN CREAM OF CHICKEN SOUP
1 TABLESPOON MINCED ONION FLAKES
1 TABLESPOON WORCESTERSHIRE SAUCE
SALT AND PEPPER TO TASTE

Heat water and bouillon cube to a boil. Add broccoli and carrot. Cook according to package directions and remove from heat. Do not drain. In separate saucepan make a white sauce by melting butter and slowly stirring in flour. Continue stirring while gradually adding milk. Stir in cheese, onion, Worcestershire sauce, salt and pepper. Add broccoli/carrot mixture to white sauce mixture and cook over medium to low heat until desired degree of thickness. *Yield:* 6 to 8 servings.

Ann Cox, *Murfreesboro*

Gazpacho

1 CUP TOMATO, PEELED AND CHOPPED
1 CUP GREEN PEPPER, FINELY CHOPPED
1 CUP CELERY, DICED
1 CUP CUCUMBER, DICED
1/4 CUP GREEN ONION, MINCED
2 TABLESPOONS PARSLEY FLAKES
1 TEASPOON CHIVES
1 TEASPOON FRESH BASIL, CHOPPED

1 SMALL CLOVE GARLIC, MINCED
1/4 CUP RED WINE VINEGAR
1/4 CUP BERTOLLI OLIVE OIL
1 TEASPOON SALT
1 TEASPOON WORCESTERSHIRE SAUCE
2 CUPS TOMATO JUICE
SOUR CREAM

Mix all ingredients together and chill. Top with sour cream. *Yield:* 6 servings.

Salads and Dressings

Cranberry Chutney

2 PACKAGES CRANBERRIES
1 1/2 CUPS LIGHT BROWN SUGAR

1/2 CUP PECANS, CHOPPED
4 TABLESPOONS GINGER, FINELY CHOPPED

1 CUP RAISINS
1 CUP CELERY, CHOPPED
1 CUP APPLES, CHOPPED
1 CUP WATER

4 TABLESPOONS LEMON JUICE
2 TEASPOONS ONION SALT
1/2 TEASPOON GROUND CLOVES

In a large pan bring all ingredients to a boil, stirring constantly. Allow to simmer 45 minutes or until cooked. This is a delightful relish to serve during the Christmas Holiday Season.

Chive Potato Salad

This potato salad is delightful to serve on a picnic. My dear friend, Linda Fuson, shared this recipe with me years ago.

2 POUNDS NEW POTATOES, COOKED, PEELED AND SLICED
1/2 CUP MAYONNAISE
1 TEASPOON SALT

1/2 TEASPOON PEPPER
2 TEASPOONS DIJON MUSTARD
1/4 CUP CHIVES, CHOPPED

Cook, peel and slice or chop potatoes. Mix remaining ingredients and toss with potatoes. *Yield:* 4 servings.

Linda Fuson, *Nashville*

Frozen Strawberry Salad

1 8-OUNCE PACKAGE CREAM CHEESE
3/4 CUP SUGAR
1 10-OUNCE CONTAINER FROZEN WHIPPED TOPPING, THAWED

1 10-OUNCE PACKAGE FROZEN STRAWBERRIES, THAWED
1 CUP CRUSHED PINEAPPLE, DRAINED
2 BANANAS, DICED

Cream together cream cheese, sugar and whipped topping. Fold all ingredients together. Place in a 9 x 13 x 2 inch pan and freeze. *Yield:* 9 to 10 servings.

Poppy Seed Salad Dressing

1/2 CUP SUGAR
1 TEASPOON DRY MUSTARD
1 TEASPOON SALT
3 TABLESPOONS VINEGAR

2 TEASPOONS POPPY SEEDS
1 TABLESPOON LEMON JUICE
1 TEASPOON PAPRIKA
1 CUP SALAD OIL

Combine all ingredients but oil. Add oil a little at a time mixing with a wire whisk. *Yield:* 1 1/2 cups.

Dewey Lemon Salad

1 6-OUNCE PACKAGE LEMON JELLO	2 BANANAS, SLICED
2 CUPS HOT WATER	2 CUPS MINIATURE MARSHMALLOWS
2 CUPS PINEAPPLE JUICE	1 SMALL CARTON WHIPPING CREAM
1 LARGE CAN CRUSHED PINEAPPLE	1 CAN LEMON PIE FILLING

Mix together Jello, hot water and pineapple juice just until it begins to set. Add crushed pineapple, bananas, and marshmallows and allow to set. Whip cream, add pie filling and mix well; spread over top of the Jello. *Yield:* 9 to 12 servings.

Mrs. Reuben Pruitt, *College Grove*

Vegetables

Artichoke and Spinach Casserole

2 10-OUNCE PACKAGES FROZEN CHOPPED SPINACH	1/2 TEASPOON SALT
1/2 POUND FRESH MUSHROOMS	1/8 TEASPOON GARLIC POWDER
6 TABLESPOONS BUTTER, DIVIDED	2 14-OUNCE CANS ARTICHOKE BOTTOMS
1 TABLESPOON ALL-PURPOSE FLOUR	1 CUP SOUR CREAM
1/2 CUP MILK	1 CUP MAYONNAISE
	1/4 CUP LEMON JUICE

Cook spinach in saucepan and drain. Sauté mushrooms, reserving several to use as garnish, in 2 tablespoons butter. Sauté reserved mushrooms separately in 2 tablespoons butter. Make cream sauce using remaining 2 tablespoons butter, flour and 1/2 cup milk. Add salt, garlic powder, spinach and mushrooms. Place artichoke bottoms in 9 x 13 inch pan and fill with spinach mixture. Combine sour cream, mayonnaise and lemon juice; spoon over artichoke and spinach mixture. Top with reserved mushrooms. Bake in a 350 degree oven for 20 to 30 minutes. *Yield:* 10 to 12 servings.

Party Squash

1 POUND YELLOW SQUASH, SLICED	1 EGG, SLIGHTLY BEATEN
1 TEASPOON SUGAR	1/2 CUP CHEDDAR CHEESE, GRATED
1/2 CUP MAYONNAISE	SALT AND PEPPER TO TASTE
1/2 CUP ONION, MINCED	BREAD OR CRACKER CRUMBS
1/4 CUP GREEN PEPPER, FINELY CHOPPED	1/4 CUP BUTTER
1/2 CUP PECANS, CHOPPED	

Cook squash, drain and mash. Add other ingredients except butter and crumbs. Place in 2-quart casserole, top with crumbs, dot with butter. Bake in a 350 degree oven for 35 to 40 minutes. *Yield:* 6 servings.

Sweet Potatoes in Orange Cups

3 CUPS SWEET POTATOES, COOKED AND MASHED
1 CUP SUGAR
½ TEASPOON SALT
2 EGGS
¼ CUP BUTTER
½ CUP MILK
1 TEASPOON VANILLA
ORANGE HALF SHELLS

Mix all ingredients together and pour into orange halves which have the pulp removed. Cover with topping.

Topping:

1 CUP BROWN SUGAR
⅓ CUP ALL-PURPOSE FLOUR
1 CUP NUTS, CHOPPED
¼ CUP BUTTER

Mix thoroughly and sprinkle over potato mixture in orange cups. Bake in a 350 degree oven for 35 minutes. *Yield:* 6 servings.

Mrs. Herman King, *Nashville*

Entrees

Swiss and Onion Quiche

This is great for a Sunday night supper served with a green salad and a fruit pie.

3 EGGS, BEATEN
1 10¾-OUNCE CAN MUSHROOM SOUP
RED PEPPER TO TASTE
3 SLICES SWISS CHEESE, DICED
1 SMALL CAN FRENCH FRIED ONION RINGS
1 9-INCH DEEP DISH PIE SHELL, UNCOOKED

Mix together; put in uncooked pie shell. Bake in a 350 degree oven for 25 to 30 minutes.

Miss Daisy's Fried Chicken

4 TO 6 CHICKEN BREASTS
SALT AND PEPPER
2 CUPS ALL-PURPOSE FLOUR
1 TEASPOON RED PEPPER
1 EGG, SLIGHTLY BEATEN
½ CUP MILK
HOT OIL

Season chicken with salt and pepper. Combine flour and red pepper; set aside. Combine egg and milk. Dip chicken in egg mixture; dredge in flour mixture, coating well.

Heat 1 inch of oil in a skillet; place chicken in skillet. Cover and cook over medium heat about 30 minutes or until golden brown. Turn occasionally. Drain on paper towels. *Yield:* 4 servings.

Crunchy Chicken Casserole

5 WHOLE CHICKEN BREASTS
1 SMALL CAN WATER CHESTNUTS
2 10¾-OUNCE CANS CREAM OF CHICKEN
  SOUP

1 CUP MAYONNAISE
2 EGGS, HARD BOILED AND CHOPPED
1 CUP PEPPERIDGE FARMS HERB DRESSING
¼ CUP BUTTER, SLICED

Cook chicken breasts and cut up. Mix soup with mayonnaise. Add all ingredients except dressing mix. Top with the dressing and butter slices. Bake in a 350 degree oven for 20 to 30 minutes. *Yield:* 6 to 8 servings.

Cindy Burch, Manager at Miss Daisy's, *Nashville*

Turkey Salad Almondine

2 CUPS ALMONDS, SLIVERED OR SLICED
¾ CUP BUTTER
4 CUPS TURKEY, CUBED
1 15¼-OUNCE CAN CRUSHED PINEAPPLE,
  DRAINED

1 CUP CELERY, CHOPPED
½ CUP MAYONNAISE
1 TEASPOON SALT

Sauté almonds in butter until golden brown, stirring occasionally. Use ½ of this mixture to combine with the remaining ingredients. Refrigerate until ready to serve. Serve with Amaretto Dressing and remaining sautéed almonds.

Amaretto Dressing:

1 CUP MAYONNAISE

¼ CUP AMARETTO

Mix until smooth and refrigerate.

My Favorite Pot Roast

1 POUND BEEF ROAST, SIRLOIN OR RUMP
1 CLOVE GARLIC
¼ TEASPOON PEPPER
1 TEASPOON SALT
2 ONIONS, SLICED
3 TABLESPOONS BACON DRIPPINGS
2 CARROTS, SLICED

1 STALK CELERY, DICED
1 SPRIG PARSLEY
1 BAY LEAF
1 SPRIG THYME
2 CUPS DRY RED WINE
1 CUP TOMATO PUREE

Rub roast with garlic, pepper and salt. Brown onions in bacon drippings. Remove and brown roast on all sides. Add vegetables and brown. Add parsley, bay leaf, thyme, wine and tomato puree. Cover and bake in a 350 degree oven for 3½ hours. Add small amount of hot water during baking if needed. *Yield:* 6 servings.

Salmon Loaf

1 16-OUNCE CAN PINK SALMON, DRAINED	2 EGGS, BEATEN
1 10¾-OUNCE CAN CHEDDAR CHEESE SOUP, UNDILUTED	½ CUP CHOPPED ONION
1 CUP BREAD CRUMBS	1 TABLESPOON LEMON JUICE

Mix salmon, cheddar cheese soup, bread crumbs, eggs, onion and lemon juice. Place in a greased loaf pan and bake in a 375 degree oven for 1 hour.

Sauce for Salmon Loaf:

1 10¾-OUNCE CAN CELERY SOUP, UNDILUTED	1 TABLESPOON PARSLEY, MINCED
½ CUP MILK	

Heat celery soup, milk and parsley to boiling. Serve with salmon loaf. *Yield:* 4 to 6 servings.

Veal Scallopini Al Marsala

1½ POUNDS VEAL CUTLETS, THINLY SLICED	2 TABLESPOONS BUTTER
SALT AND PEPPER	½ CUP MARSALA WINE OR SHERRY
1 TABLESPOON ALL-PURPOSE FLOUR	2 TABLESPOONS WATER

Pound veal cutlets thin; sprinkle lightly with salt, pepper and flour. Melt butter in large frying pan. Brown veal thoroughly on both sides in hot butter over high heat. When cutlets are well browned, add wine. Cook 1 minute longer over high heat. Place veal in a serving dish. Add water to pan, scraping sides and bottom, pour over veal cutlets. Delicious served over Fettucini. *Yield:* 4 servings.

Fettucini:

8 TABLESPOONS BUTTER, SOFTENED	1 TABLESPOON SALT
¼ CUP HEAVY CREAM	1 POUND FETTUCINI EGG NOODLES
½ TEASPOON NUTMEG	SALT AND PEPPER
½ CUP PARMESAN CHEESE, FRESHLY GRATED	PARMESAN CHEESE, FRESHLY GRATED
6 QUARTS WATER	

Cream butter and sugar. Beat in the cream a small amount at a time. Add the nutmeg and beat in cheese. Cover and set aside. Bring water and salt to a boil in a large soup pot. Drop in the fettucini and stir gently with a wooden spoon to prevent strands from sticking to one another. Boil over high heat, stirring occasionally for 5 to 8 minutes or until pasta is tender. Drain immediately into a colander and lift strands gently to make sure it is thoroughly drained. Transfer at once to a hot serving bowl. Add the warmed creamed butter and cheese mixture and toss until each strand is well coated. Taste and season generously with salt and pepper. Sprinkle Parmesan cheese over top.

John Egerton

Ham Loaf with Horseradish Sauce

3/4 POUND LEAN PORK, GROUND
1 POUND SMOKED HAM, GROUND
1/2 CUP MILK

1/2 CUP DRY BREAD CRUMBS
1 EGG, SLIGHTLY BEATEN

Combine all ingredients. Shape into loaf and place in a shallow baking pan. Bake in a 350 degree oven for 45 to 60 minutes. Baste occasionally with Brown Sugar Glaze. Serve with Horseradish Sauce. *Yield:* 6 to 8 servings.

Brown Sugar Glaze:

6 TABLESPOONS BROWN SUGAR
2 TABLESPOONS WATER

2 TABLESPOONS VINEGAR
1 TEASPOON DRY MUSTARD

Combine all ingredients and mix well.

Horseradish Sauce:

2 TABLESPOONS HORSERADISH
2 TEASPOONS VINEGAR
1 1/2 TEASPOONS PREPARED MUSTARD
1/4 TEASPOON SALT

1/8 TEASPOON WORCESTERSHIRE SAUCE
DASH CAYENNE PEPPER
DASH PAPRIKA
1/4 CUP HEAVY CREAM, WHIPPED

Combine the first 7 ingredients and fold in whipped cream. Chill. *Yield:* 2 cups.

Dale Shearin, *Dinner Manager at Miss Daisy's*

Italian Spaghetti Sauce

MEDIUM ONION, CHOPPED
1/2 LARGE BELL PEPPER, CHOPPED
2 LARGE CLOVES GARLIC, MINCED
2 TABLESPOONS OLIVE OIL
1 POUND GROUND ROUND
1 14½-OUNCE CAN STEWED TOMATOES
1 6-OUNCE CAN TOMATO PASTE
2 TEASPOONS OREGANO
1½ TEASPOONS BASIL

1 TEASPOON CHILI POWDER
2 BAY LEAVES
1 TABLESPOON SUGAR
SALT AND PEPPER TO TASTE
½ PACKAGE SPAGHETTI SAUCE MIX
2 TO 3 CUPS WATER
1 4-OUNCE CAN MUSHROOMS
2 TABLESPOONS BURGUNDY WINE

Cook onion, bell pepper and garlic in olive oil until tender. Add meat and cook until browned. Add remaining ingredients except mushrooms and wine. Add water to thin. As sauce cooks, if it becomes too thick, add more water. Cook slowly for 2 hours or until sauce is desired thickness, stirring occasionally. Add mushrooms and wine. Remove bay leaves. Serve over hot buttered spaghetti with Parmesan cheese.

Breads

Honey Banana Bread

1 CUP BUTTER
3/4 CUP HONEY
2 EGGS
1 CUP OVERRIPE BANANAS, MASHED
2 CUPS ALL-PURPOSE FLOUR

1 TEASPOON SODA
1/4 TEASPOON SALT
1 CUP PECANS, CHOPPED
1 8-OUNCE PACKAGE DATES, CHOPPED

Cream butter and honey. Add eggs, then mashed bananas. Blend well. Add flour, soda, and salt; mix well. Add pecans and dates and stir. Pour mixture into greased and floured 9 x 5 x 3 inch loaf pan. Bake in a 350 degree oven for 30 minutes or until done.

Note: This makes an exceptionally light and moist banana bread.

Corn Light Bread

2 CUPS PLAIN MEAL
¾ CUP SUGAR
½ CUP ALL-PURPOSE FLOUR
¼ TEASPOON SODA

3 TABLESPOONS SHORTENING, MELTED
2 CUPS BUTTERMILK
1 TEASPOON SALT

Mix dry ingredients with buttermilk and melted shortening. Bake in a greased loaf pan until golden brown in a 350 degree oven for 1 hour. Turn on rack and cool.

Lemon Pecan Bread

¾ CUP BUTTER, SOFTENED
1½ CUPS SUGAR
3 EGGS
2¼ CUPS ALL-PURPOSE FLOUR
¼ TEASPOON SODA

¼ SALT
¾ CUP BUTTERMILK
¾ CUP PECANS, CHOPPED
1 TEASPOON GRATED LEMON RIND

Cream butter, gradually add sugar. Add eggs, beating well after each addition. Combine flour, soda, salt; add to cream mixture alternating with buttermilk. Stir in pecans and lemon rind. Pour into greased and floured pans. Bake in a 350 degree oven for 1 hour and 15 to 20 minutes.

Desserts

Tennessee Pudding Cake

2 CUPS SUGAR
1 CUP BUTTER
1 TEASPOON SODA
½ CUP BUTTERMILK
4 EGGS
2 TEASPOONS VANILLA

3½ CUPS ALL-PURPOSE FLOUR, SIFTED
¼ TEASPOON SALT
1 CUP PECANS, CHOPPED
1 CUP DATES, DICED
1 CUP COCONUT

Grease and flour a tube cake pan. Cream the sugar and butter until smooth. Add soda to the buttermilk and let it rise to double its size. Add eggs to the sugar mixture and beat until it is creamed well. Add flour, buttermilk mixture, salt and beat well. Add pecans, dates and coconut. Bake in a 300 degree oven for 1½ hours. Ice while cake is hot.

Icing:

1½ CUPS ORANGE JUICE

2½ CUPS SUGAR

Mix the orange juice and sugar together. Beat the mixture until the sugar is dissolved. Make small slits all over the top of the cake with a knife and pour the icing all over the top of the cake. Let the cake sit until it is cold.

Chocolate Chip Oatmeal Cookies

1 CUP LIGHT BROWN SUGAR

3/4 CUP SHORTENING

2 EGGS, WELL BEATEN

1½ CUPS ALL-PURPOSE FLOUR

1 TEASPOON SALT

1 TEASPOON SODA

2 TABLESPOONS WATER

3 CUPS OATMEAL

1 6-OUNCE PACKAGE CHOCOLATE CHIPS

Cream together the sugars and shortening. Add the beaten eggs. Sift together the dry ingredients and add to the creamed mixture alternately with the water. Mix in the oatmeal and chocolate chips. Drop by spoonsful onto ungreased cookie sheets and bake in a 375 degree oven for 13 to 15 minutes.

Bourbon and Chocolate Pecan Pie

This pie is labeled Jackson Pie *on Miss Daisy's Menu. Pierre Franney, food critic for the* New York Times, *described this as one of the best pecan pies he had eaten, while at a luncheon I served that he attended.*

1 CUP SUGAR

1/4 CUP BUTTER, MELTED

3 EGGS, SLIGHTLY BEATEN

3/4 CUP LIGHT CORN SYRUP

1/4 TEASPOON SALT

2 TABLESPOONS BOURBON

1 TEASPOON VANILLA

1/2 CUP PECANS, CHOPPED

1/2 CUP CHOCOLATE CHIPS

1 9-INCH PIE SHELL

Cream sugar and butter. Add eggs, syrup, salt, bourbon and vanilla. Mix until blended. Spread pecans and chocolate chips in bottom of pie shell. Pour filling into shell. Bake in a 375 degree oven for 40 to 50 minutes. *Yield:* 6 to 8 servings.

English Trifle

1½ QUARTS MILK

1½ CUPS SUGAR

2 TABLESPOONS CORNSTARCH

6 EGGS

1/2 CUP SHERRY

2 CUPS CREAM

1½ POUNDS POUND CAKE, SLICED

RASPBERRY OR STRAWBERRY PRESERVES

Pour the milk into the top of a double boiler. In a mixing bowl, beat together the sugar, cornstarch and eggs until smooth. Add to the milk and heat until the mixture is thickened, stirring constantly. Set aside to cool. Add sherry to the cooled custard. Whip the cream and set aside. Arrange the cake slices in a 3-quart or large baking pan. Spread with preserves, then top with a layer of custard and a layer of whipped cream. Repeat until all of the ingredients are used. Chill. *Yield:* 6 to 8 servings.

Sour Cream Chocolate Cake

2 CUPS ALL-PURPOSE FLOUR	2 WHOLE EGGS
2 CUPS SUGAR	1 TEASPOON SODA
1 CUP BUTTER	1/2 TEASPOON BAKING POWDER
1/4 CUP COCOA	1/2 TEASPOON SALT
1 CUP WATER	2 TEASPOONS VANILLA
1/2 CUP BUTTERMILK	3/4 CUP SOUR CREAM

Put flour and sugar in large mixing bowl and set aside. Cook butter, cocoa and water just until mixture comes to a boil. Cool 1 minute. Pour mixture over flour and sugar while beating with electric mixter. Add buttermilk, eggs, soda, baking powder, salt and vanilla. Beat 1 minute more. Stir and mix in sour cream. Pour batter into lightly greased and floured 10 x 15 inch pan and bake in a 400 degree oven for 25 to 30 minutes. Frost while hot with Chocolate Icing.

Chocolate Icing:

1/2 CUP BUTTER	1 16-OUNCE BOX CONFECTIONERS' SUGAR
1/4 CUP COCOA	1 TEASPOON VANILLA
3 TO 4 TABLESPOONS MILK	

Bring butter, cocoa and milk to a boil. Add confectioners' sugar and vanilla while beating mixture with electric mixer. Beat until smooth and spread on cake.

Orange Date Cakes

This is one of my mother-in-law's favorite recipes.

1/2 CUP MARGARINE	3/4 CUP BUTTERMILK
1 CUP SUGAR	1 8-OUNCE PACKAGE DATES, CUT IN SMALL PIECES
2 EGGS	
2 CUPS ALL-PURPOSE FLOUR	1 CUP NUTS
1 TEASPOON SODA	

Cream margarine and sugar. Add eggs and beat thoroughly. Add alternately flour (to which the soda has been added) with buttermilk. Add dates and nuts. Fill muffin tins 3/4 full. Bake in a 350 degree oven for 15 to 20 minutes. While cake bakes, make topping.

Topping:

GRATED RIND AND JUICE OF 2 LEMONS	1 CUP SUGAR
GRATED RIND AND JUICE OF 2 ORANGES	

Mix and pour over cake while hot.

Mrs. Herman King, *Nashville*

Honorable Mention

Rutledge Hill Press is grateful to all who submitted their favorite recipes for THE ORIGINAL TENNESSEE HOMECOMING COOKBOOK. The response to the contest was tremendous and the earliest postmark decided the winner when similar recipes were received. A special word of thanks to all who participated and especially the following:

Mrs. Sandra (William Tray) Adkerson, Nashville
Mrs. Evelyn Allison, Atwood
Cathy Amonette, College Grove
Elizabeth F. Arnett, Nashville

Helen L. Bache, Morristown
Pattie Banister, Clarksville
Carolyn Barnett, Humbolt
Reba Bellar, Lafayette
Mrs. Bill W. Benson, Henderson
Mildred C. Bird, Walland
Lela Blane, Clarksville
Mrs. Roy (Florence) Booher, Johnson City
Erma Booker, Bristol
Donna Borris, Clarksville
Pam Bradley, Portland
Evelyn Bryan, Calhoun
Mrs. Dorthy Burnett, Toone
Mrs. Leon Burnett, Jackson
Mrs. JoAn Burnett, Knoxville
Mrs. Katherine Burris, Calhoun
Mrs. Thomas Byrd, Nashville

Mary Carnell, Newbern
Mrs. T. L. Cely, Jr., Knoxville
Mrs. Frankie Chambers, Knoxville
Mrs. Tressie Hunt Clift, Bolivar
Mrs. Raymond E. Cobble, Knoxville
Jamie-Darlene Cochran, Indian Mound
Carol Coleman, Livingston
Ernest R. Collins, Knoxville
Emma Dee Craddock, Humbolt
Sara Lee Croft, Madisonville
Mona Commings, Lebanon

Mrs. Marceil Darden, Nashville
Mrs. Robert M. (Janet) Darden, Bartlett
Doris Davis, Rickman
Edith Robinson Davis, Loudon
Mrs. Irene Davis, Clarksville
Mrs. Wanda N. Davis, Sevierville
Mrs. Eva Deckard, Lafayette
Martha Dickson, Lebanon
Mrs. G. S. Dismukes, Mt. Juliet
Mrs. Buena M. Dobbs, Nashville
Laura Dodd, Ridgetop
Barbara Dodson, Livingston
Pat Drinnon, Morristown
Kitty Dutton, Nashville

Linda Earp, Clarksville
Mrs. Anita Easley, Murfreesboro
Rosemary S. Eby, Oak Ridge

Sophia B. Eddina, Old Hickory
Mrs. Hugh Evans, Lebanon

Kay S. Fendley, Clarksville
Mrs. Loyd Fields, Lebanon
Dorthy C. Fort, Clarksville
Mrs. J. D. Franklin, Oak Ridge
Mrs. Jodie Furguson, Johnson City

Brenda Gardner, Santa Fe
Mrs. Allen Gooch, Nolensville
Bettye Goodson, Jackson
Mrs. Judy L. Greer, Hermitage
Carolyn T. Grigg, Maryville
Mrs. Homer Grimes, Philadelphia
Sue W. Grizzard, Clarksville
Alma de La Guardia, Franklin

Calista Haglage, Donelson
Mrs. Charles Hailey, Nashville
Mrs. John C. Hailey, Nashville
Ruby H. Hamilton, Bumpus Mills
Mac Harvey, Lebanon
Aileen Hatcher, Bristol
Mary B. Hatcher, Clarksville
Sherree Hawkins, Cookeville
Mrs. S. V. Hensley, Erwin
Doris Hinson, Jackson
Wanda Holloway, Columbia
Mrs. Ted Horner, Centerville
Mrs. Hubert Houser, Bristol
Mrs. Fleta B. Howard, Knoxville
Ila Huff, Sevierville
Mrs. Casey (Jo Ann) Hughes, Alamo

Mrs. Sylvia Jetton, Trenton
Mrs. Ada Lee Johnson, Sneedville
Mrs. Jaque Johnson, Madison
Mrs. Harold Jones, Oneida

Beatrice Kelley, Tellico Plains
Sheila Kelley, Lexington
Mrs. Edward Lee (Pamela) King, Old Hickory
Mrs. Lloyd H. King, Henderson
Norma Kitchen, Henderson
Mrs. Winston T. Knowles, Chattanooga

Sheila Lawson, Brentwood
Lucille Lee, Old Hickory
Mrs. Joe Lee, Gallatin
Doreen E. Lewis, Erwin
Mrs. James Lewis, Erwin
Pauline Lineck, Talbott

Christine Littleton, Newbern
Mrs. Wanda Looney, Spring City
Jane Bice Lovelace, Chattanooga
Sara Stegall Lowe, Rockvale

Val Manley, Kingsport
Estelle Marcus, Sharon
Kathleen Martin, Talbott
Maudra Massengill, Celina
Mrs. Gertie Matthews, South Fulton
Carrie Maynard, Joelton
Genelle McDaniel, Madisonville
LeAnne McDaniel, Madisonville
Judy Meals, Jackson
Bobbye Moore, Livingston
Rachel Moore, Joelton
Johnnie Ruth Morris, Somerville
Cindy S. Morrison, Clarksville
Ruth Anne Myers, Calhoun

Debra Ann Neal, Smyrna

Elsie Parker, Big Rock
Lucille Parmenter, Newbern
Jane Patterson, Morristown
Gerline Patton, Murfreesboro
Merle Pearson, Madisonville
Mrs. John Pechonick, Jackson
Dana Peck, Clinton
Willie Pearle Pittman, Calhoun
Jo Ann Phillips, Bluff City
Mrs. Martha L. Phillips, Knoxville
Peggy Phillips, Bolivar
Mrs. Garland (Lorene) Porter, Evensville
Aileen L. Portwood, Clinton
Rebecca Collins Powers, College Grove
Marcia Price, Blush Creek
Linda Puett, Memphis

Faye Qualls, Bristol
Loretta Qualls, Livingston

Mrs. Reannza Ramsey, Elizabethton
Mrs. Theresa Ramsey, Powell
Louise Reed, Big Rock
Ella Robinette, Nashville
Alice Rogers, South Pittsburg
Louise McClellan (Mrs. Vernon) Rowland, Blountville
Sheila Runyon, Clarksville
Mrs. Faye Russell, Caryville
Rosanna Ryals, Talbott

Mrs. John Salm, Nashville
Hilda Sanders, Humboldt
Cheryl Savage, Alpine
Mrs. Edward M. (Effie) Shumacher, Nashville
Mrs. Roy Seaton, Soddy Daisy

Joyce Sells, Monroe
Cleo Sensing, Cumberland Furnace
Hubert P. Sexton, Seymour
Mrs. H. H. (Numa S.) Sharber, Rockvale
Leslie Ann Sharpe, Luttrell
Patricia Shults, Newport
Judy Sigmon, Morriston
Mrs. Edna Simmons, Nashville
Elizabeth O. Sites, Clarksville
Sue T. Slate, Clarksville
Gena Smith, Cookeville
Vondie Smith, Lebanon
Elinor Overton Sollman, Bolivar
Tana Sowell, Old Hickory
Mrs. Vickie N. Spain, Nashville
Pauline Law Walters Spencer, Pigeon Forge
Mrs. Ruth Stafford, Limestone
Rosa Lee Stephens, Donelson
Mrs. W. E. Stephens, Madisonville
Mrs. J. P. Steward, Maryville
Rosella Stooksbury, Andersonville
Imogene Suttles, Knoxville
Ruth (Mrs. James) Sutton, Dandridge
Margaret Swaw, White Bluff

Jennifer H. Taylor, Columbia
Mrs. John R. Taylor, Jr., Jonesborough
Sandra L. Taylor, Elizabethton
Betty Thomas, Bluff City
Mrs. Bessie C. Toombs, Old Hickory
Mrs. Louis Treece, Sharon
Mrs. Ward Turner, Bruceton
Mrs. John D. (Eleanora) Tyler, Nashville

Juanita F. Vaughn, McEwen
Sara (Mrs. Carson) Vaughn, Nashville
Mrs. Sue Vaughn, Lebanon

Linda Waggoner, Estill Springs
Alice Walker, Portland
Audrey Walker, Sweetwater
Cherrie Walker, Dyersburg
Onelda Walters, Clinton
Virginia Weston, Mt. Juliet
Mrs. Judy Wheeley, Watertown
Mrs. Betty Whiteside, Riceville
Mrs. Lou Lavonne Whitney, Nashville
Edna W. Wilhite, Knoxville
Betty B. Williams, Rutledge
Mrs. Johnnie Williams, Sevierville
Mrs. Debra Wilson, Spring City
Mrs. Doris B. Wilson, Knoxville
Mrs. Garland W. Wood, Harriman
Mrs. Joe P. Wright, Clinton
Mrs. Warren Wright, Humbolt

Mrs. T. J. (Genrose) Yarbrough, Dyersburg
Mrs. Carl R. Young, Johnson City

Index

Order Additional Copies

Buy additional copies of *The Original Tennessee Homecoming Cookbook* for your-self and your friends from your local book store or gift shop. If you are not near a store, you may order copies from Rutledge Hill Press for $14.95 each plus $1.16 tax for each book shipped in Tennessee plus $1.75 postage and handling for each shipment (even if more than one book is mailed). If you want to send copies as gifts, Rutledge Hill Press will enclose a gift card signed with your name at no additional charge.

- -

To: Rutledge Hill Press
    P.O. Box 140483
    Nashville, TN 37214

Please send me _____ copies of *The Original Tennessee Homecoming Cookbook* at $14.95 each plus $1.16 tax per book and $1.75 postage and handling per order. Enclosed is my check or money order for $ _____ . (Make check payable to Rutledge Hill Press and mail to the above address.)

Name _____

Address _____

City _____ State _____ Zip _____

- -

Please send me _____ copies of *The Original Tennessee Homecoming Cookbook* at $14.95 each plus $1.16 tax per book shipped inside Tennessee and $1.75 postage and handling per address to friends whose names and addresses are listed below. Enclosed is my check or money order for $ _____ . (Make check payable to Rutledge Hill Press and mail to the above address.) Sign my name on the cards as follows (Please print):

_____

My name _____

Address _____

City _____ State _____ Zip _____

Send copies of the Cookbook to:

Name _____	Name _____
Address _____	Address _____
City _____ State ___ Zip _____	City _____ State ___ Zip _____
Name _____	Name _____
Address _____	Address _____
City _____ State ___ Zip _____	City _____ State ___ Zip _____

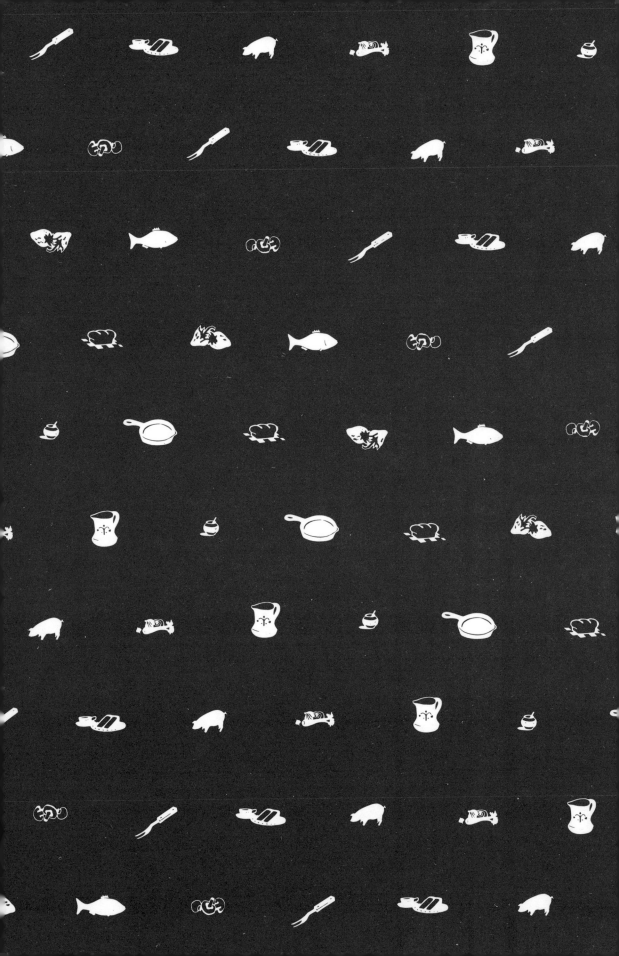